embodying
gender

embodying gender

gender

Alexandra Howson

SAGE Publications

London • Thousand Oaks • New Delhi

First published 2005

SAGE Publications Ltd
1 Oliver's Yard
55 City Road
London EC1Y 1SP

SAGE Publications Inc
2455 Teller Road
Thousand Oaks, California 91320

SAGE Publications India Pvt Ltd
B-42 Panchsheel Enclave
Post Box 4109
New Delhi 100 017

British Library Cataloguing in Publication data

A catalogue record for this book is available from the British Library

ISBN 0-7619-5994-7
ISBN 0-7619-5995-5 (pbk)

Library of Congress Control Number: 2004099438

Printed on paper from sustainable resources
Printed and bound in Great Britain by Athenaeum Press, Gateshead

In memory of John A. Howson

Contents

Preface

A recent newspaper article (that I can remember reading but cannot remember where) told a story about some feminist academics in Italy organizing a conference on certain aspects of feminist theory and textual politics. The veteran American feminist activist and writer, Gloria Steinem, was invited as a speaker to the conference, whereupon she suggested that local feminist activists and representatives from women's groups also be invited to participate. The organizers apparently objected on the grounds that the women would not be familiar with the texts under consideration at the conference, to which Gloria Steinem replied: 'But they are the texts.' In my memory of the text (the newspaper article) I may have omitted key points or taken from it something that was not necessarily intended by the writer (who was, I think, a member of Southall Black Sisters). But what struck me was the counter-posing between materiality and text (as I saw it), between real women and the refusal to efface experience as a starting point for feminist politics, on the one hand, and, on the other, the way in which representations and representational practice have become the starting point for academic feminism; between the legacy of feminist activism embodied by Gloria Steinem and the centrality of the text to contemporary academic feminism, a centrality that may have the effect of distancing those who do not possess, or are not seen to possess, the cultural capital necessary to participate in textual politics and practice.

This counter-posing is nowhere more explicit, in my view, than in new feminist theories of the body that are fuelled by post-structuralist impulses and invest in deconstructive and psychoanalytic frameworks in order to 'think through the body' and develop accounts of sexual difference. Such theories, while ostensibly focused on the female body, are resolutely committed to Derridan and Lacanian notions of the centrality of the text in their epistemological assumptions and methodological practices. While new feminist theories of the body are increasingly taught across undergraduate courses in sociology, women's and cultural studies, these texts make for heavy reading and students typically seek to go beyond the text – often by returning to their own experience – in order to assess their value. What is lost or gained by either commitment to or repudiation of the text? What is lost or gained by suggesting that academic feminism needs to go beyond the text in order to re-establish a politics that includes attention to materiality without reducing female subjectivity to the body? Materiality is precisely the dilemma for academic feminism as it moves towards strategies for embodying gender and accounting for sexual difference. The dilemma is mirrored by disciplines, such as sociology, that seek to gender the body, to explain not only the social significance of the human body in social life but also to account for the establishment and significance of difference in the social. *Embodying Gender* attempts to work through the dilemma of materiality in ways that neither privilege text nor repudiate experience as the basis of a pragmatic sociology and as a necessary struggle concept for academic feminism.

Acknowledgements

This book has taken too long to write, partly because during its period of gestation I combined part-time employment with raising daughters and partly because its aim and focus emerged more organically than perhaps I would have liked. I am, therefore, in the first instance, indebted to Karen Phillips at Sage who patiently insisted that I continue. There are also many other people without whom the manuscript would not have been completed. The idea for the book came from a seminar that Anne Witz and I organized at the University of Edinburgh in 1997 and both Anne's published work and her careful listening to early ideas about the book enabled me to think that it might be possible. Colleagues and friends assisted in this project by listening, feeding me, cheering me up and offering companionship, wine and humour. I am especially grateful to Marion and Mike Hepworth, Julie Brownlie, Pauline Padfield, Jan Webb, Alex Law, Gillian Rose and Carol Targett. David Inglis and Mary Holmes read and commented conscientiously on an early draft.

My family remain my principal source of delight and joy and have helped in myriad practical and emotionally supportive ways. I am grateful to the unstinting faith of Nancy and Will Howson, Ginny and Deb McWhorter, Maureen and Jim Watt and Jackie and Robert Fitzpatrick. My greatest gratitude goes to my husband Richard and daughters, Holly and Jodie, for putting up with a great deal of preoccupation on my part, providing software solutions and reminding me constantly of what really matters.

Introduction

It is claimed that the discipline of sociology has led the way in 'bringing the body (back) in' (Frank, 1990) to social and political analysis. John O'Neill's *Five Bodies* and Bryan S. Turner's *The Body and Society* offered distinct explanations for the body's neglect within sociological (and other social scientific) scholarship and social theory and presented sustained analyses of perspectives and approaches that could serve the aim of developing a sociological understanding of the human body. The body is now a central and distinct arena of theoretical debate and empirical research within sociology and is increasingly the focus of interdisciplinary scholarship across cultural studies and feminist theory. However, while cultural studies are more likely to engage with sociology, feminist theory has been more disinclined to do so. Moreover, feminists and non-feminists conducting empirical research on the human body within disciplinary boundaries (for instance, within sociology) and working across such boundaries habitually cite the work of feminists who are *known as* theorists, such as Judith Butler, Elizabeth Grosz, Moira Gatens and Luce Irigaray.

The theoretical insights produced by a relatively small group of women located within elite cultural Anglophone institutions has had immense impact on the direction and form of empirical research and more general scholarship concerning the body. Indeed, while there is now a considerable number of edited volumes that seek to bring together empirical feminist research on the body, e.g. judging by citation records, it would appear that feminist theories of the body are more likely to be accorded privilege within academic feminist communities. Yet empirical scholarship appears to have had little impact on the direction and form of feminist theories of the body, which *begin* from particular texts (Derrida's *On Grammatology*, Lacan's *Écrits*), interrogate and discuss those texts in meticulous and stylish detail and sustain a view of the body *as* text, despite claims to the contrary.

Embodying Gender thus explores a curious paradox. On the one hand, the development of the sociology of the body is informed by a commitment, however distinctly and variably interpreted, to the identification of the contexts, relations, practices and structures that shape human embodiment. While this scholarship has been variously accused of over- tending to the abstract, it no longer remains the case that sociological treatments of the body are overly theoretical. There are now a number of studies from a range of perspectives available to the discipline that offer theoretically informed empirical investigations of various issues concerning the body, for instance in relation to disability (Dyck, 1996), reproduction (Martin, 1984), consumer culture (Featherstone, 1982), masculinity and femininity (Mansfield and McGinn, 1993), and health (Howson, 1999). These studies, many of which are engendered from within a feminist ethos, reflexively draw on theory and work through the implications of particular frameworks for making sense of the observations and data they generate. In particular, feminist empirical research typically has the challenge of engaging not only with the implications of social theory for addressing the body, but also with what Witz (2000) has termed new feminist theories of the body.

In contrast, new feminist theories of the body rarely engage with either feminist-inspired empirical scholarship or with sociological scholarship concerning the body. Hence, while sociologists routinely read and reflect on what feminist theorists have to say about the body, particularly feminists defined as theorists and who make a virtue of interdisciplinarity, feminist theorists seldom reflect on what sociologists have to say. This one-sided discourse has the effect of not only refusing the entry of empirical observations to the development of feminist theories, but also refuses the entry of feminist *sociological* theory to treatments of the body within both social and feminist theory. This state of affairs is not new, however, as social/sociological theory infrequently responds to feminist analyses.

This book begins from a conviction that embodiment lies at the heart of human experience and that both feminism and sociology have an interest in the integration of insights about feelings, emotion, sensations with insights about the impact and significance of rational thought, action and social structure on our lives. We all have bodies, but the trick that Western thought has played has been to allow men to think and live as though they did not have to attend to or labour over their bodies, to forget the body. Academic feminism, as an interdisciplinary endeavour, has tried to grapple with and explain this trick in ways that the social sciences and humanities have found useful, and in ways that increasingly seek to place the body at the centre of theory.

However, academic feminism's contribution to this endeavour has occurred in ways that also forget the body as an experienced material and sensible medium. To some extent, this trick is a corollary of the way in which those who do theory, do so in contexts that foster a sense of isolation, individualism and disembodiment from social relationships and the physical environment. The modern Western university can be a soulless institution that places emphasis on autonomous output rather than on collectively produced scholarship. Consequently, not only can the process and experience of producing theory be characterized by bleakness and a sense of separation from others, but also theory itself, in ways that forget that the body is the basis and medium through which we forge personal and social relationships and experience the physical world. *Embodying Gender* is an attempt to work through that bleakness and contribute to academic feminism and to sociology by trying to keep the body in mind as the basis of living and active relations with others.

Though feminism has historically been exercised by the significance and importance of the particular – of women's unvoiced, invisible experiences – feminist theories of the body look increasingly to post-structuralist and psychoanalytic frameworks to establish a more generalized theory and politics of the particular. This produces a curious phenomenon: pursuit of the particular in feminism occurs via consideration of the abstract, for no conceptual framework can be more abstract than that informed by contemporary theoretical psychoanalysis. Indeed, I would argue that the body appears in much feminist theory as an ethereal presence, a fetishized concept that has become detached and totalizing for the interpretive communities it serves.

Thus, the book is concerned with the relation of body concepts to concepts of gender within sociology and feminism, and its aim is to trace the development, uses and articulation of such concepts. As some sociologists of the body have become increasingly exercised about addressing gender in their work, so feminists have considered the significance of the body for debates about gender and sexual difference. Yet sociologists and feminist theorists of the body rarely consult each other's work or address their concerns to each other. Instead, sociologists have attempted to gender the body and feminists have attempted to embody gender in relative isolation from each other. More recently, however, in considering ways to gender the body, male sociologists have turned to the work of feminist philosophers such as Elizabeth Grosz and Moira Gatens. Yet, feminist considerations of ways to embody gender largely look to continental philosophy and psychoanalysis rather than to feminist sociology. While there is sterling and erudite work here, the double marginalization of feminist sociology by sociologists and feminist theorists of the body needs some exploration. *Embodying Gender* traces the convergence of body concepts in feminism and at times in sociology on psychoanalytic concepts and deconstructive practices that have the potential to write the body out of the text. Writing the body back in points to the retrieval of feminist concepts informed by a sociological imagination that have the potential to contribute to both the process of embodying gender and gendering the body.

Localities, particularities and audiences

Following a tradition of reflexivity in sociology (Gouldner, 1970), recent work by key body sociologists (Williams and Bendelow, 1998) has explicitly identified the necessity of an 'embodied sociology'. This concept not only insists on incorporating the lived body into substantive sociology but also invites the sociologist to write her own embodiment into that work in an effort to establish her relationship to the researched (which in this case is a body of theory). I have some reservations about how that might actually proceed and am aware of the difficulties of engaging in such a task (difficulties that are well documented in feminist geography, see Rose, 1997). Nonetheless, I share with these sociologists and with many feminists, the aspiration to situate my own practices of knowledge production and to situate that knowledge in ways that 'reanimate matter' (Gordon, 1994).

The book has been influenced by a number of things. Its starting point is not really an interest in the theoretical debates that have developed within both sociology and in feminism, although those debates necessarily frame my intellectual orientation to 'the body'. Rather, my starting point has been an abiding interest in the activities, practices and experiences of what some have come to term 'lived female embodiment', that is, the embodied experiences associated with, though not reduced to, being (a white, educated middle-class) female, and the labour required to maintain one's own and other bodies. Moreover, my experience attending to the bodies of others, as a nurse and as a mother of small children, offers a particular perspective on these labours. Such experiences necessarily involve close physical and sensuous proximity to the bodies of others in ways that cut against the particular challenges of the civilizing process (Elias, 1994) and the intriguing cerebral-ness that characterizes much academic life. The work of the nurse is at times intensely physical and material, involving acute sensory work (Lawler, 1991), and the proximity to and responsibility for the bodies of children typically push against the individualized detachment that informs a Westernized sensibility.

Therefore, the tactility of the bodies of others (albeit assigned meaning via disparate cultural, social and political frameworks) is something that is deeply implicated in my own position as both a sociologist and as a feminist. It is always already present in relations and contexts of care in ways that academic disciplines have been unable and/or reluctant to acknowledge until quite recently, no doubt because of its constitution as the focus for 'dirty work' (Lawton, 1998). That is, the body is ever present for me as the focus of self-discipline, management and care of both self and others. This orientation to the body has been reflected in my research on the body, gender and health (1999, 2001a, b, 2003; Howson and Inglis, 2001) which is informed both by C. Wright Mills' concept of the sociological imagination and Michel Foucault's insistence on seeing discourse as the conditions of existence that allow things to be said and done in any particular epoch. However, my readings of body theory have often made me pause to think about the ways in which bodies (my own and those of others) are objectified not only through embodied social practices but also through the conceptual frameworks – also social practices – that seek to elucidate them.

A second influence on this book is inevitably my academic training in the discipline of sociology, which I view as a critical discipline (Mills, 1959) that grants epistemological privilege to the social in understanding and explaining the range of phenomena experienced by human beings. Mills has been an especially apposite influence because of his own philosophical commitment to a pragmatic approach that allows for the significance of personal experience in the sociological analysis of phenomena, personal involvement in the production of such analysis and a focus on practical possibilities in the present. Mills was interested in how social forces – the social origins of the thinker, the structure of the academic community and the requirements of a given social context – give rise to different intellectual styles. Though this book is neither a social analysis of the proponents and schools of body concepts nor a genealogical account of such concepts, nonetheless, my examination of body concepts and particularly their investment in text have pulled me in this direction. Pragmatism, while latterly damned by its critics as acquiescence to the prevailing social order, offers, according to Mills, a critical view of modern social life that begins from experience, rejects the idea of an overarching politics or theory and focuses on the 'practical, immediate and reformable'.

Dorothy Smith qualifies the power of the sociological imagination in her critique of the way the practice of sociology has disembodied its practitioners. Her work has attracted less attention from feminists than it ought, given her contribution to epistemological debates within Anglo-American feminism in the 1970s and 1980s. The importance of her thinking lies in her attempt to develop a specifically feminist sociology, which begins from the material experiences and locations of women, including those of the sociologist and offers a productive means of embodying gender and gendering the body. One suspects that for Smith, as for Mills, sociology loses its 'promise' and 'hope' as a critical discipline when it loses sight of the immediate experiences and issues concerning those on whom its gaze is turned and produces instead overarching programmatic statements. In this respect, Mills' – and Smith's – sociology resonates with a Foucauldian methodology that urges a detailed focus on practices and their location within the discourses that form 'a central axis of social formation and domination'. Consequently, the exploration of body concepts offered here can be seen as an account of concepts that are themselves the effects of particular kinds of academic practices and discourses.

The third main set of influences on this book is feminism. My sociological interests have been shaped by an interest in gender: in the range of differences and inequalities between men and women and among women (for critical reviews of the multifaceted meanings of gender, see Morgan, 1986; Hawkesworth, 1997), and I have pursued research and teaching projects that seek to understand the relations and practices that give shape to women's lives and define, regulate and mediate bodily experiences. However, I see myself as a sociologist who is also a feminist rather than as an 'academic feminist'. By this I mean that while my political commitments might be broadly termed 'feminist' in ways that inform my research and teaching, my academic location is within the discipline of sociology. This location has two implications. The first is that while I have contributed to interdisciplinary projects, particularly in teaching, the contribution I bring is a sociologically inflected consideration of social phenomena. Second, my primary identification with an academic discipline rather than with feminism more broadly places me 'outside' the practices associated with the forms of textual politics on which new feminist theories of the body are based. This means that the critical approach to body concepts offered here is one developed from both the inside out and from the outside in.

This brings me to my final remark about my location and its bearing on the genesis and development of the book. Publishers like to know precisely how to pitch the books they commission and writers need to attend carefully to the issue of audience. It is commonplace to see written on book jackets the identities of those proposed audiences: students of sociology, women's studies, and so on. I hope this book will offer something of value for these communities of readers. However, academic books are also written to address scholars in a specified field or series of fields as a means of establishing the place of the writer in that field. I will later take up this issue as it applies to the current shape of the field of the body in feminism. My point for the moment is that the field I seek to address is less the field of feminist theory *per se*, which I view as synonymous with feminist philosophy and literary theory, than that of a feminism seeking to operate within the field of sociology as well as a sociology sensitive to corporeally inclined feminist issues.

The human body in the sociological field

The human body has emerged as an object of substantial cross-disciplinary scrutiny in the past two decades and has achieved sub-disciplinary status in many social science disciplines, including sociology, anthropology and cultural studies, but both the sociology of the body and feminist considerations of the body have shifted from their initial focus. Early sociological approaches to the body relied on both sociological and non-sociological theory because of a limited range of concepts available for specifically sociological explanations about the social significance of the human body. As Blaikie et al. (2003) argue, the sociology of the body was initially inspired by philosophical, historical and anthropological treatments of the body which have been subsequently developed in sociologically relevant ways. Many introductory sociology texts now include a cursory section on the body in relation to issues of gender and sexuality; social theorists have addressed the implicit and explicit presence of the body in classical theory (Turner, 1996 [1984]; Shilling, 1993); phenomenologists and philosophers have examined the extent to which the body grounds experience (Merleau-Ponty, 1962); and the legacy of Foucault continues to stimulate the scrutiny of practices of power that contribute to understandings of what the body is and how it is lived.

To some extent, the body represents a conceptual space through which to redefine the sociological project in ways that attempt to transcend natural/social paradigms (Shilling, 1993, 2003; Burkitt, 1999) and address recurring binaries of structure/agency, material/discourse, and object/subject. A key characteristic of this developing field has been a debate about whether the sociology of the body should be regarded as a sub-discipline or, more radically, whether interest in body matters offers a means of (re-)embodying the sociological project (Scott and Morgan, 1993; Bury, 1995). One might, if one were so post-structurally inclined, characterize the field of the body as a 'field of discursivity' in which there is no fixed centre and a range of competing meanings and signs.

In a spirit of contextualization and reflection, many authors have sought to explain the emergence of a sociological gaze upon the human body with reference to the social context in which sociology operates. It has become commonplace to argue that demographic change, feminism, and technological progress have fuelled sociological interest in the body and forced the discipline to consider the body as both object and subject (for instance, Turner, 1996 [1984]; Shilling, 2003; Lupton, 1994; Williams and Bendelow, 1998). The emergence then of 'somatic society' is one in which the major social and political problems of the time are expressed via the human body. These explanations for sociological interest in the body look outside the discipline and reinforce a view of sociology as responsive and reactive to social change, in keeping with its development as a revisionist discipline of inquiry which achieves its present by an ongoing assessment of the past (McCarthy, 1996: 106). Indeed, sociology is defined as a discipline by its ability to situate the ideas that it generates in a specific, living context and to develop a sure-footed reflexivity that enables its practitioners to draw attention to the part they play in their own process of inquiry. While the term reflexivity may generate multiple meanings (e.g. a feminist standpoint within sociology may define the idea of reflexivity rather more differently from sociologists of scientific knowledge), the point stands that a fundamental aspect of the disciplinary evolution of sociology has been a concern to reflect upon its means of knowledge making and its relation to the 'spirit of the times'.

However, perhaps too much emphasis is placed on explaining sociology's focus on the body by reference to external changes and developments. Part of the explanation for sociology's expanding interest in the human body lies within the development of sociology itself and its relation to other forms of disciplinary inquiry. Sociology has at times been accused of seeking out and colonizing new areas of inquiry in ways that may contribute to 'second-birthings' (Haraway, 1991) of the discipline. However, in doing so, new areas of inquiry may be unsatisfactorily homogenized and transformed into objects of analysis that are reified and stripped of their 'magic'. In the case of the human body, many sociologists have struggled to develop perspectives that do not objectify the body and this issue has shaped much of the field's development, in particular, concerns for the significance of bodily experience and lived embodiment.

Part of this concern has been prompted by sensitivity to feminism, queer and disability studies, yet the feminism to which social/sociological theories of the body appeal is typically associated with the textual practices of literary theory and philosophy rather than feminist sociologies of the body. Nonetheless, concerns about the female body within feminism have helped to shape the development of the sociology of the body at least to the extent that most social/sociological theories of the body acknowledge the significance of feminism as a social movement in making the body visible as a substantive issue for academic scrutiny. Moreover, sociologists who have been instrumental in developing body concepts have increasingly looked to feminism for solutions to conceptual problems associated with Cartesian dichotomies between mind/body, culture/nature, subject/object, self/other, and male/female. Yet, while many current sociological projects address themselves to the 'problem' of the body, in fact, their substantive focus is on the body in social theory.

The female body in the field of feminism

In contrast, feminism has long addressed issues concerning the female body via issues such as medicalization, reproduction, pornography and violence, though the female body has occupied an awkward presence within feminism. While feminist activism in the 1960s and 1970s more willingly engaged with the body at the level of experience and body politics (for instance, in relation to women's health politics, pornography, or sexual violence), Anglo-American academic feminism, until the 1980s, did not generally theorize the subordination of women through attention to the body. While certain dimensions of female embodiment were central to radical feminist debates about women's subordination, female embodiment as a whole was marginal (though often implicit) to academic feminism.

Though the literature generated by feminist activism concerned itself primarily with explaining and challenging the daily oppressions and injustices directed towards the female body, the body has only recently emerged in the past decade as a *theoretical* focus for feminism in ways that have profound implications for the feminist project. Since the 1980s ushered in a new focus on sex and sexuality through deconstruction and psychoanalytic practices, feminist *theory* has reinstated the body as part of a wider project to bridge certain tensions and dualisms between the material and the discursive, the actual and the virtual. The availability of Foucault's work on the historical construction of sexed bodies fuelled scrutiny of the reproduction of femininity which was accompanied by an expanding interest in the significance of the body in social and political theory and, perhaps most prominently, in philosophy and literary theory through the work of Butler, Grosz and Gatens. Concepts have been developed with the specific aim of challenging malestream, abstract accounts of the body that have the effect of devaluing and subordinating women within both theory and academic disciplines. While some of the concepts developed within feminism in the late 1980s point to the significance of the specificity of lived bodily experience and are informed by scholarship that draws on experiential and phenomenological concerns, others are inspired largely by post-structuralist perspectives that pay particular attention to language, discourse and text. It is, therefore, somewhat paradoxical that as non-feminist social theorists have recuperated experience as a focus for theory, feminists have installed the body as a concept through which to develop theory. Indeed, the 'corporeal turn' within academic feminism is principally a turn to theory, which privileges the theme of sexual difference as the centrepiece of feminist scholarship.

Contemporary feminist approaches to the body increasingly focus on the generation and reformulation of theoretical frameworks informed by continental philosophy, phenomenology and psychoanalysis, though few feminists have been sympathetic to or fully taken up sociologically inflected claims associated with the sociological work of Norbert Elias or Pierre Bourdieu. Hence, the starting point for much sociological and feminist commentary about the human body is text rather than matter and accordingly, feminist solutions to problems of the body incorporated by sociology, are not sociologically inflected. In fact, they are premised on feminist reworkings of continental philosophy and in particular, psychoanalysis, that have the potential to evacuate concepts of a concern with the social that sociologists might consider valuable.

The starting point matters. The data that form the focus for theorizing the contemporary body are primarily other texts that are used to reformulate, reconsider and revise prior claims about the body. Consequently, the body within both sociology and within feminism has become subject to more abstraction, not less. One effect of this trend is that the body increasingly becomes a conceptual space in which debate is undertaken, rather than a focus of substantive inquiry, in which key authors enter into a particular form of dialogue with each other. This dialogue serves a purpose. First, it enables (predominantly) male social theorists to reproduce and develop theoretical frameworks that partially acknowledge feminist voices. These voices are themselves theoretical and that may be why male theorists hear them in the first place. Second, the theoretical form this dialogue takes allocates particular positions to feminists who speak and write the language of theory. It grants a legitimate position in the academy to those feminists who are able to deploy and develop the insights and practices of philosophy, psychoanalysis and deconstruction.

The move to a theoretical mode of production is seen most clearly in relation to the body in the field of psychoanalysis and its influence on the sociology of the body and feminist approaches to the body. I am particularly interested in the claims to truth made within these fields and, in particular, the ways in which psychoanalysis has become increasingly vital for the production of theories of the body. Although at times there has been a degree of feminist disquiet with psychoanalysis, there has also been a focused salvage of Lacan's psychoanalysis in the past 20 years. This project is particularly associated with the French school of feminism, which, although a disparate entity, is most closely identified by Anglophile readers with the work of Luce Irigaray, Hélène Cixous and Julia Kristeva. Their work has been developed in the context of a feminist project of theorizing the body (particularly by Judith Butler, Elizabeth Grosz and Moira Gatens) and in turn, this work has influenced debate within the sociology of the body.

About this book

Embodying Gender traces body concepts in sociology and in feminism, examines their convergence on psychoanalytic concepts and deconstructive practices and questions the translatability of concepts across disciplinary boundaries. Concepts themselves are discursively constituted yet are presented in the literature as authoritative statements about the body that are increasingly treated as grand theory. In order to address the implications of particular concepts, I choose to read them in terms of the claims being made, by whom they are made and for what purpose. In this way, I hope to approach the texts presented here in an open-ended sense that is sensitive to issues of interpretation and that foregrounds the relationship between the contexts in which they were produced and the contexts in which they are read.

The central claim of this book is that in writing about the body and about the significance of the 'particular', particular stories and experiences that are part of embodiment get written out. That is, the process of textual production within an academic mode has the potential to efface the body's materiality. Sociological and feminist analysis of the human body is pursued via concepts that could and perhaps should be able to help us locate the significance of embodiment in the twenty-first century. Yet, increasingly, concepts are the focus of text, rather than what the concepts tell us about the significance of the body in people's lives and how the body is lived. For philosophy, perhaps textual (re)production is sufficient unto itself, but such a strategy impoverishes the promise and hope of sociology, especially a feminist sociology of the body. An (over-)emphasis on text, either as a tactic for bringing (some)body into view or as the focus of analysis, incurs a loss for the sociological imagination and collapses a disciplinary boundary that is in some way important. In short, the book examines the difficulty of reconciling sociology's ways of seeing and remits to invoke the richness of social life with the flattened, abstract categories of philosophical analysis. While the development of theory is an important task for both sociology and feminism, an over-emphasis on explanation before the fact diverts our attention from the significance of the body in people's lives. Hence, one of the aims of this book is to re-emphasize the importance of substantive research that is both sociological and feminist: research that moves beyond social knowledge that asserts the centrality of the body to social existence but is unable to explain this centrality and which contributes to a reinvigoration of a politics of embodiment and perhaps, of experience.

My argument is that while new feminist theories of the body claim to be retrieving the body, they do so via a version of psychoanalysis heavily invested in text and are ultimately unable to specify which/whose body is being retrieved. This creates a paradox for a feminism trying to move towards specificity because the claims that are made about the body tend towards the general and create precisely the kind of master narrative that feminism has latterly sought to avoid. This paradox may be a corollary of the habitus of those making the claims – new feminist theorists of the body tend to be feminists in disciplines such as literary theory/rhetoric/philosophy in 'elite' institutions which place a premium on the production of particular kinds of text: that are stamped with 'erudition' and 'eloquence' and internal logic rather than those created from or in dialogue with substantive or pragmatic inquiry. The latter absence is important because academic feminists on the whole continue to claim to 'be about' some notion of political engagement but increasingly conduct that engagement within the narrow confines of textual production, which secures a position in the academy for feminism as a credible intellectual endeavour in an 'economy' of textual production.

Embodying Gender is structured as follows. First, Chapter 1 outlines body concepts within the sociological field and traces the development of that field. In particular, the chapter examines how sociological focus on the body has engaged with feminist debates concerning gender differentiation and the ways in which such debates have been incorporated within the sociological field. While sociology has begun to consider the social processes through which bodies are socially marked out in specific ways (in terms of gender, ethnicity, disability), it wrestles with the status of embodied experiences within these processes and continues to focus on the 'object-body'. Indeed, the development of the sociology of the body has tended to conflate the body and embodied experience, in part because of the inter-changeability and unstipulated nature of notions such as 'corporeality', 'materiality' and 'embodiment'. The chapter examines the boundaries between such concepts in order to address the distinctiveness of the insights provided by the sociology of the body and their potential for both (re)embodying the sociological project and gendering the body within sociology. The chapter suggests that a vital weakness in the development of the sociological field is the way in which, while this field has engaged with feminist theories of the body that are informed by post-structuralist perspectives, they have failed to consider feminist perspectives that are informed by sociologically materialist approaches. This has had the effect of shifting the sociological field too far in the direction of considering text without context.

In contrast, the body has been central to second-wave feminism although, as many feminists point out, it has often been approached obliquely rather than head-on (Bordo, 1993). Nevertheless, if sociological argument suffers from an over-emphasis on the general and has been unable to adequately identify the specificities of embodiment, feminist argument must be viewed as a statement of gendered embodiment. Hence, Chapter 2 examines the contributions of feminism to understandings of embodiment and its significance in the production of gender. In particular, the chapter turns to the development of feminist treatments of the body and traces the move towards the body as part of a wider project to reconsider gender across a range of disciplines. The chapter outlines feminist scholarship within sociology, history, geography and anthropology that has contributed to debates about the relation between the body and gender and which is part of a broader corporeal turn within academic feminism, in order to argue that, as with sociology, there persists an unresolved conflation between the body and embodied experience. On the one hand, the body has been viewed as a source of 'trouble' and liberal feminist perspectives in particular have implicitly effaced the significance of embodied experience (Hughes and Witz, 1997). On the other, radical feminist perspectives have foregrounded embodied experience as a source of knowledge and as a means of transcendence, but have done so in ways that have been open to criticism for their essentialist implications. In both broad trajectories, gender as bodily property rather than the social and political effect of differentiating processes is called into question.

Answers to emerging questions about the properties of gender are associated with the corporeal turn. Chapter 3 examines how the corporeal turn is associated with a shift in the body as a medium of experience to an object of theory through the influence of Foucault's scholarship and the work of key feminist philosophers who have become key referents for feminist theories of the body. In this work, the body begins to be written in a language of sexual difference informed by post-structuralist frameworks. While there is much to commend in this body of work, the chapter seeks to show the limits of these approaches for both sociology and for feminism, and, in particular, the ways in which the over-textualization of the body opens up a conceptual elusiveness and ambivalence that have implications for a feminist politics of the body and for the conceptual utility of gender.

Chapter 4 examines the implications of Lacanian psychoanalytic categories and the effects of deploying such categories across a range of feminist texts. In particular, the chapter seeks to show how the body is troped in these categories in ways that disavow material/ity. The potential for scholarship grounded on experience is taken up in Chapter 5, which places current feminist theories in the context of inter-disciplinarity and argues for an understanding of embodiment as the condition and constituent of agency (Howson, 1996; Witz, 2000). In particular, the chapter re-examines the work of Dorothy Smith and her development of a material-ist-phenomenological perspective as a necessary corrective to the over-textualization of the body.

Embodying Gender argues that in order to move beyond the prevalent ambivalence in many contemporary feminist theories of the body, to enable feminism to embody gender and sociology to gender the body, conceptual clarity is required and in particular, distinctions are made between the body as an object of theory and embodied experience derived from and contributing to difference. The conclusion revisits material/ity and experience as concepts that might be re-integrated into sociological and feminist argument in order to assess how best to move forward with the task of embodying gender and gendering the body.

one

Locating the body in sociological thought

Introduction

The body in sociology is 'a phenomenon considered worthy of detailed study in its own right' (Shilling, 2003: 29). The editorial of the first issue of the journal *Body and Society* was emphatic that sociology could no longer ignore the body (Featherstone and Turner, 1995). These claims are substantiated by the increasing number of texts that offer a sociological treatment of the body, the growth in undergraduate courses in English-speaking countries that focus on the body, the attention given to the body through dedicated conferences and the publishing sales in a global market. The British Sociological Association's conference in 1998, 'Making Sense of the Body', attracted the highest number of abstracts in comparison to previous years, illustrating the popularity of the body within the discipline. While the body was a fairly minor topic for sociological inquiry when Turner's (1984) *Body and Society* was published, within a relatively short period of time, the body has acquired the status of a substantial field of scholarship. This chapter traces the key concepts that currently define the field. It draws particular attention to a distinction between, on the one hand, the development of social/sociological theories of the body, and on the other, attempts to redefine sociology as a corporeal discipline, as one in which the body is not only the object of investigation but also the medium through which investigation is undertaken. The chapter also appraises how the field has taken up feminist body concepts.

Social theory and the silent body

Though the body was implicitly central to the analysis of many areas of social experience, such as health and disease (Zola, 1982), self-presentation (e.g. Goffman, [1959] 1971) and sexuality (Gagnon and Simon, 1973), little reference was made to the body within sociology either in taught undergraduate courses or their supporting materials beyond acknowledging the body as a taken-for-granted background to social agency and action. There were exceptions to this, within medical sociology and the social history of medicine and specific courses dedicated to the body, such as that taught at the University of Aberdeen by Mike Hepworth and Bryan Turner. Moreover, though the influence of Foucault on the undergraduate curriculum was beginning to develop, few courses explicitly addressed the body as a topic for sociological treatment. As Turner noted in the introduction to the first edition of *Body and Society*, though the embodiment of human beings seems central to social production and reproduction, 'few social theorists have taken the embodiment of persons seriously' (1984: 37). A tension between the body as a 'necessary precondition for all possible practices' (Berthelot, 1991: 391) and its apparent absence from sociological theory have led Shilling (2003) to remark that the body is both present and absent within the disciplinary frame. Like the absent maternal body in psychoanalytic theory, which is the necessary precondition for discussion of absence and presence, the body can be understood as integral to the issues with which sociology deals, yet marginal as a legitimate focus of inquiry. Though sociology is supposed to be a discipline concerned with living, breathing human beings, sociological writing has rarely acknowledged the significance of the human body (Freund, 1988). There are a number of reasons for this omission.

First, the legacy of Plato's distinction between soul and body, Christianity's identification of the body as the repository of sin, and Cartesian dualism (Freund, 1988) have had a crucial impact on Western systems of thought. Though there have been distinct periods in Western development which have emphasized the contribution of all the senses to knowledge acquisition and meaning making, for instance, sensory experience in medieval Europe was seen as vital to the acquisition of knowledge (Classen, 1997) and mysticism in its disparate forms was open to sensory experiences of many varieties, mind and body are reified as discrete entities (Williams and Bendelow, 1998). Cartesianism in particular has instituted an ontological distinction between mind and body that privileges the former over the latter (Turner, 1984). Like other disciplines emerging in the nineteenth century, the historical and conceptual development of sociology was in large part premised on this legacy. The Cartesian view established a view of the mind as an object or essence, which is discrete from the physical body and 'its spatially and temporally located practices' (Burkitt, 1999: 12).

In the Cartesian view of the world, vision is privileged as the primary sense that connects the self to the physical and material environment in which it is located. The eye becomes the privileged medium of communication about self (Simmel, 1969) and of knowledge production through empirical observation. Though what we see needs to be codified, it is done so via rational cognition. As Classen (1997) has noted, reason and rational forms of knowledge have been gradually equated with visual perception. Hence, a philosophical dualism between mind and body, between an isolated, rational self and a world external to him or her, formed the basis of mainstream Western epistemology and has informed the development of scientific rationality. Concomitantly, the subject of sociology, the rational actor, was disembodied in the sense that rational thought was located in a mind, already conceptually disconnected from the body (Morgan, 1993) and disassociated from 'attributes of physical presence' (Burkitt, 1999). The disembodied rational subject is most clearly present in variants of Weberian sociology, in which both social and cultural worlds are products of the mind, or the mentalistic bias of Durkheim's focus on 'conscience collectif'. Though sociological theory has been categorized as tarred with the Cartesian brush, Bury (1995) provides a vigorous rebuttal of the claim that mind/body dualism was as pervasive as some commentators have implied. For instance, though Nietzsche was in a minority, Bury and other theorists (e.g. Freund, 1990; Gatens, 1996) have argued that he operated with much more blurred – though not unproblematic – notions of the relationships and boundaries between mind and body.

Second, as a social science largely preoccupied with structure and agency, sociologists have not viewed the human body as an explicit 'problem' for analysis. If anything defines sociology as a discipline distinct from other modern disciplines, it is the pervasive and persistent tensions between structure and agency. The relative weight and value accorded to *either* structure *or* agency have characterized the development of the various schools of thought and practice associated with Western sociology. Indeed, as Freund (1988) points out, the intellectual autonomy of sociology from anthropology, psychology and from the naturalistic understanding of human nature epitomized by biology, was dependent on its capacity to deny the body any determining status in considerations of agency, though Parsons acknowledged, albeit somewhat ambiguously, the need for sociology to find a way of integrating the body into formal and substantive theory. He positioned the biological organism as the lowest and most stable aspect of social relations in his hierarchy of social life, as 'an integrative sub-system of action in general' (1966: 8), significant nonetheless for considerations of action in relation to responses to disease and the implications of these responses for social roles. While this framework has been generally interpreted as subordinating the material body to the metaphysical body or the social self, a re-reading of Parsons suggests that he at least implicitly acknowledged the analytical significance of the body as more than a biological organism, rather as the condition *and* constituent of action (Howson, 1996). Indeed, Parsons states: 'we know the physical world *only* through the organism' (1966: 8; emphasis in the original).

Yet, in general, where the social sciences assented to a biological frame of reference for investigation of the physical body, they generally resisted 'biological explanations of *social* phenomena' (Benton, 1991: 12, my emphasis). Thus the distance instituted between sociology and other disciplines was to a degree effected by its assent to the Cartesian inheritance that privileged mind over body.

Third, while the Cartesian inheritance denigrated sensory and emotional experience (Bologh, 1990) and effected an epistemological and methodological distance between the sociological imagination and its objects of analysis, the Protestant ethic exiled pleasures of the flesh (Morgan and Scott, 1993; Mellor and Shilling, 1997). Concomitantly, not only was mind privileged over body but also women were relegated to the latter as part of the domain of nature. The body's association with nature and with femininity (Sydie, 1987) further distanced it from sociological analysis. This distance naturalized the female body as a basis of social difference, bracketed out sensory experience, or carnal knowing (Miles, 1992) as a basis for developing knowledge and understanding and obscured the embodiment of men (Morgan, 1993; Connell, 1995). Hence, the discipline's specific concern with sociality and with men in action within the public sphere (Sydie, 1987) not only excluded the bodies of women but also established, yet concealed, the taken-for-granted nature of the bodies of men (Witz, 2000).

The over-rationalization of social life that has characterized sociology (Mellor and Shilling, 1997) has meant that the body was neither perceived as a source of personal knowledge or understanding, nor deemed relevant to the production of sociological knowledge. This was not necessarily so of other social science disciplines emerging at a similar historical point. For instance, as Berthelot (1991) notes, psychology partially acknowledged the importance of the physical body in personality development through concepts such as body image and body schema. Though feminist philosophy has returned to these concepts as developed via phenomenological and psychoanalytical frameworks, on the whole, they remain marginal to mainstream psychology, as indeed does analysis of the body in general (though there are important exceptions, e.g. Radley, 1995). Moreover, observations and classifications of the material body played a part in the development of physical and cultural anthropology, criminology and sociobiology (Berthelot, 1991). Where cultural anthropology developed a perspective on the human body as a bearer of symbol, physical anthropology developed procedures for measuring the size and shape of the human body for purposes of cross-cultural comparison. Criminology was initiated through the system of criminal anthropometry developed by Lombroso and his colleagues and sociobiology developed a (albeit a deeply contested) way of explaining the body's role in constituting social relationships, which is currently enjoying something of a revival in the work of popular sociobiology (e.g. Steven Pinker's *The Blank Slate*).

Therefore the human body has been implicitly conceptualized in sociology as a relatively stable organic entity onto which social categories are imposed and has not been explicitly incorporated into sociological theory (Turner, 1984). The body has been viewed as an unchangeable and taken-for-granted biological condition of agency, relegated to the 'natural' and therefore beyond the legitimate reach of the sociologist. The body is implicitly defined as epiphenomenal, and as Burkitt (1999) notes, modernity has established a distance between the material body and the symbolic objects it produces. This distance has been reflected most discernibly in the development of sociological/social theory, which has concealed the relations through which the body is constituted as a focus for analysis.

Sociology and the (re)emergence of the body

In the last quarter of the twentieth century the body has acquired greater significance within sociology (Frank, 1990) and the body is more present than absent (Williams and Bendelow, 1998), though it is an illusory body hinting at a degree of concordance and unity that may be as yet somewhat remote. What has prompted this new interest in the body? Sociology is a discipline that is uniquely and reflexively responsive to social change and it is generally noted by commentators that interest in the body reflects disciplinary responses to key social and political changes (Turner, 1984; Shilling, 1993; Williams and Bendelow, 1998). First, changes in demography have raised questions about the care and management of ageing processes, as physical competencies are potentially transformed over the life course and bodily betrayals increase (e.g. Hepworth and Featherstone, 1982; Hepworth, 1995). Second, changing patterns of disease, such as the emergence of HIV/AIDS not only raise important questions about care and treatment but also about the boundaries between the physical body and the social body (e.g. Douglas and Wildavsky, 1982; Kroker and Kroker, 1988). Third, new technologies such as gene therapy or xeno-transplantation challenge key assumptions about the human body concerning what is possible and ethically justified in terms of medical and technical intervention (e.g. Hogle, 1995). Fourth, the publication in English of Michel Foucault's work directly influenced a largely Anglo-American audience and made the body more amenable to sociological analysis. Fifth, the women's movement in the twentieth century and the establishment of academic feminism highlighted the significance of the body in the oppression of women.

Finally, changes in forms of social organization have generated corresponding changes in the meaning of the body (e.g. Turner, 1984; Martin, 1992; Lowe, 1995) as well as changing relationships between the human and non-human world that have fostered a process of politicization to which embodied experience is central. For instance, drawing on the work of Harvey (1990), Burkitt argues that 'practices of flexible accumulation have broken up local communal and familial relations, and have led to the reconstitution of social relations across wider vistas of space and time, the new technologies of social saturation allowing for changed forms of relationships in a new social terrain' (1999: 144). Consequently, this has led to a heightened focus on the body and its practices. First, social processes of 'flexible accumulation' foster a requirement for people to become more aware of their bodies in all sorts of social situations (Giddens, 1991). Bodily dispositions and their reproduction across time, space and generation, become subject to modification as social relations and contexts themselves become more complex. Second, echoing feminist work (especially Martin, 1989), Burkitt observes that the pursuit of wholeness may be a critical stance against potentially damaging, fragmenting and alienating processes associated with medical, technical and political interventions. As he puts it:

> In resisting forms of domination and dividing practices, the body becomes a point of focus because it is around the body, as it is located in relational networks, that individuals can integrate the various aspects of themselves into a whole person, and can demand to be treated as such. (1999: 145)

Such an analysis resonates with recent scholarship concerning the status of bodily wholeness in the context of infant organ retention scandals in the United Kingdom in which parents' concerns focus on re-membering the dissected bodies of their children precisely in order to reconstitute a sense of social and emotional wholeness (Sheach-Leith, 2004).

However, sociological interest in the human body is also a reflection of the development of the discipline itself and its openness to the intellectual currents associated with post-structuralism, psychoanalysis, continental philosophy and contemporary feminist theory. These currents converge on the body as a site at the interface between the biological and the social, the collective and the individual, structure and agency, cause and meaning (Berthelot, 1991: 398). Sociology's response to this convergence has been twofold. First, influenced by the impulses of modern science to control and contain, the discipline has reduced the body to a knowable, anatomical object, amenable to sociological scrutiny in terms of how society acts upon the body (Morgan and Scott, 1993). This impulse has engendered an outward-facing response concerned with understanding the body's significance in processes of social production and reproduction.

Second, the emergent impulses of postmodernism and post-structuralism, in which continental philosophy and psychoanalysis have been implicated and to which sociology has been particularly sensitive, render meaning in relation to the human body unstable. Feminist philosophy's unequivocal reinstatement of the relation between mind and body, sympathetic readings of the irrationality found in Nietzschean philosophy, a (re)new(ed) interest in the Romantic (Mafesoli, 1995), medical anthropology's efforts to develop analytic holism (Strathern, 1994), and feminist psychoanalytic retrievals of the absent presence of the body have been particularly influential. These inclinations have engendered an inward-facing response from sociology fuelled by and that reproduce an uncertainty about 'what the body is' (Shilling, 2003). While some commentators (e.g. Bury, 1995) view such an inverted gaze as an index of the discipline's sensitivity to the ambivalences of modernity, uncertainty is itself derived from a Cartesian standpoint that asserts the body can be known and understood through rational inquiry. Indeed, as Davis (1997) notes, the body provides a physical and conceptual space in which the recurring issues and tensions of Enlightenment categories of thought are revisited and reworked.

These tensions take methodological and epistemological forms. First, while there have been some very explicit attempts to 'embody' sociology (Williams and Bendelow, 1998) or to establish the parameters for a 'carnal' or 'corporeal' sociology (Crossley, 1995b), there remains a strain between attempts to 'theorize the body' and to 'embody theory' (Morgan and Scott, 1993). Whereas the former is oriented towards establishing general statements concerning the relationship between the body and society, the latter is more concerned with reshaping the conceptual tools of the discipline to address the contours of what I shall call the *particular*. Prominent commentators (e.g. Turner, 1992) have thus noted there has been very little attempt to explore the relationship between the body and agency, the 'productive capabilities of the body' or the 'phenomenology of how people experience the "lived body"' (Mellor and Shilling, 1997: 5), though at the time of writing this assertion no longer seems credible.

A second tension forces epistemological choices between concepts of the body as either a pre-given material object or as a discursively produced entity. In the former, the body is addressed as a distinct object of scrutiny, as the focus of control, coercion and restraint, but its capacity for expressiveness and mutability is obscured (Radley, 1995). In the latter, an emphasis upon the body as a 'product of certain kinds of knowledge which are subject to change' (Lupton, 1994: 22) is too easily incorporated as matter subsumed by discourse. The body as a material object disappears and inquiry is largely concerned with the representations of the body. Thus, concern about the relationship between the problem of what the body is and what can be known about it (Turner, 1997) endures in a sociology of the body that has largely polarized between implicitly foundational and anti-foundational approaches.

A third source of tension is associated with the way in which the sociology of the body has persistently co-opted feminist insights into its project of 'bringing the body in' and credited feminism with generating a lexicon of the body (e.g. Frank, 1991; Shilling, 2003; Turner, 1996). Sociologists have selectively incorporated insights from the feminist literature, without confronting the tension between its own focus on the 'abstract body' and an early feminist focus on the 'concrete body', or the particular, via the concept of experience. Moreover, despite references by 'body theorists' to feminism as a model for redirecting emphasis towards the body, it has been argued (Bordo, 1993) that feminism has not, until recently, attempted to theorize the body and that the 'abstract body' has itself been absent from feminism. Indeed, feminists (e.g. Davis, 1997) have commented upon the ironies of male theorists focusing upon the body when much of their general academic practice serves to obscure particular bodies (i.e. female, differently-abled, black). However, I argue in this book that the current direction of feminist theory reinforces abstraction as the principal building blocks in academic feminist practice.

Howson and Inglis (2001) identify three moves of particular importance in the conceptual development of the body in sociology. First, there exists a move to 'bring the body in' to the sociological frame. A second move seeks to rediscover the body in classical theory. A third move attempts to establish the body as the conceptual centrepiece of sociology in an effort to achieve integration between 'troublesome' dualisms. The following explores these developments in approaches to the body.

Sociological theory, the general and the object-body

Bryan Turner's book *Body and Society* is often identified as the point of departure in sociology which moved towards 'theorizing the body', by generating a broad framework for conceptualizing the relationship between the body and society (Williams and Bendelow, 1998). Turner's analysis of the body is eclectic and stimulating. He draws on an extremely wide range of sources and perspectives to demonstrate how modern societies are oriented towards containing and managing the human body. Identifying similarities and convergences between Foucault and Weber, based on a Durkheimian concern with the problem of social order, Turner develops an argument that the body presents a problem of government for every society (1984). In essence, each society has tasks it must confront in order to ensure the government of the body – the reproduction of bodies in time, the regulation of bodies in space, the restraint of internal desire and the external representation of the body. In consequence, societies develop 'institutional subsystems' which ensure these tasks, or functional requirements, are managed. As is surely well known, the subsystems Turner identifies are patriarchy (reproduction), asceticism (restraint), panopticism (regulation) and commodification (representation) (the four Rs). The key processes associated with these systems not only work upon and within the body across time and space but also suggest a conceptual bridge across foundationalist and anti-foundationalist accounts of the body in order to accommodate the body as both a material and socially constructed object.

Though Turner's work is generally acknowledged as a core intervention in developing a sociological perspective on the body, his framework has been subject to a great deal of criticism. His typology provides a structural-functionalist device for 'ordering empirical materials about the body in society' (Frank, 1991: 44), but it has been criticized for the way in which it reinforces the body as an object (Williams and Bendelow, 1998). His typology begins with a 'top-down' approach to the body, which reifies its objective status, thus correctives advocate a 'bottom-up' approach. As Williams and Bendelow (1998) argue, Turner reinforces the body as an object of theory, through a focus on what society does *to* and *with* the body, obscuring the ways in which the body might be understood as the basis of action, agency and as the ground of experience. Indeed, Turner has acknowledged these kinds of criticisms and has been much more resolute about developing the kind of focus advocated by his critics in more recent publications. Accordingly, the second edition of *Body and Society* (1996) develops the concept of embodiment as a multi-dimensional approach to the body. Turner's revised concept of embodiment acknowledges the body as matter (corporeality) and as sensibility subject to change across historical and biographical time. Nonetheless, his refinement of concepts continues to occur within the expansive approach that typifies his work.

Turner is not alone in developing a general framework in which to explain the relation between body and society. For instance, Frank (1991) turns Turner's framework on its head to create a 'bottom-up' analysis of the body which might grasp not only the various ways in which society works upon the body, but also how society is built up from and created through bodies in action. For Frank, societies have no functional requirements concerning the body, therefore analysis must address the 'body's *own* problems of its embodiment within a social context' (ibid.: 48). Bodies need to reproduce themselves and bodies engage in tasks that produce society, which in turn come to be experienced as social impositions. The conceptual centrepiece of Frank's approach is that of the socially given character of body techniques (Mauss, 1974 [1934]) as the process through which bodies act and are in turn, acted upon: the body and its socially given techniques offer resources and constraints for action.

Frank's action framework is fairly explicit in its mobilization of structuration theory (Giddens, 1979, 1984). He eschews the implicit linearity of Turner's 'four Rs' for the geometric elegance of a triangular model that emphasizes the relative roles of institutions, discourses and corporeality in the construction of relations between body, self and society. In short, discourses establish the normative frameworks (mappings or ideal types) through which the body is understood; institutions represent the contexts in which discursive practices occur; while corporeality refers to the body as lived matter. Frank seems to ask, if we reject a foundational view of the human body (fixed and static across time, space and place), then which body provides the starting point? Perhaps, there is no 'body' from which to begin, merely 'bodies in a social landscape' (Scott and Morgan, 1993) which need to be specified and located. Frank edges towards such specification in his evocation of *corporeality*, which partially recognizes the maternal body as the origins of the subject in his acknowledgement of the bodies of women as the source of reproduction; emphasizes scienticized understandings of the body's anatomy and physiological processes; and acknowledges the irrefutable *matter* (limits?) of bodies in any given context.

While these two models can be contrasted with each other in terms of beginning from different points in a spatial hierarchy (Turner's 'top-down' to Frank's 'bottom-up'), their similarity lies in their attempt to transcend particular dualisms. Turner, for instance, tries to accommodate an understanding of the body as both an appreciable material object that exists prior to reflection and as a variable entity subject to change across time, according to social and political contingencies. Frank attempts to develop a schema that will allow the sociological analysis of the self situated in a material body (corporeality); shaped and understood through normative discourses; located, in turn, within institutions (structures). Though Turner's view of 'bodily order' can seen as moving 'society too far into the body' – i.e., too much structure – Frank's theory of 'body use' makes 'society too much of a corporeal product' (Shilling and Mellor, 1996) – or too much agency. In some contrast, then, the Foucauldian optic has been developed to address the relation between the body as an object of regulation and as a constituent of agency.

The regulated body

Sociologists have used Foucault's framework to explore the embodiment of agency through the concept of power/knowledge. A particularly robust example is found in treatments of governmentality in relation to public health and disease prevention,[1] which examines the power of discourse to produce the body (Foucault, 1972), through, for example, social practices associated with surveillance (Armstrong, 1983, 1995). Broadly, this corpus of work has argued that new techniques and practices, critical to medical epistemology, have historically established controls over the social body through two kinds of power: regulatory and disciplinary (e.g. Lupton, 1995). The first is often associated with institutions and populations while the second refers to practices, or disciplinary mechanisms, in which individuals themselves engage, such as teeth-brushing (Nettleton, 1992), antenatal screening (Arney, 1982) or excretion (Inglis, 2000). In turn, these reinforce regulatory power and establish a form of 'liberal governance' (Rose, 1990) in which surveillance is shored up by self-surveillance.

Hence, while the 'object' body is the focus of control within this framework, controls themselves become embodied. Individuals are not coerced into the practices identified but rather, they internalize disciplinary mechanisms or 'practices of self' (Foucault, 1988). The process of being drawn into such practices as active, willing participants, in turn has the potential to transform subjectivity (Armstrong, 1984, 1993; Ogden, 1995), in ways that imply and indeed require a degree of reflexivity. For example, in the context of prevention, patients are acted upon (e.g. through the 'well-woman' check-up) and consequently internalize 'health' as a desirable value, which is incorporated in ways that inform practices (which become habituated, such as teeth-brushing, for instance). Individuals draw upon medical discourse (language and practices) to articulate and frame their experience (Lupton, 1994) and in turn are able to engage in a dialogue with medicine as knowledgeable practitioners of 'health'. Hence, power/knowledge creates a conceptual link between general body practices and the internalization of discipline in ways that potentially create new subjectivities (Arney, 1982; Arney and Bergen, 1984).

The significance of this framework is that it represents an attempt to locate subjects as agentic and knowledgeable, or as embodied agents whose bodies are acted upon and who in turn act upon others (Crossley, 1995a, 1996). However, there are two current problems with this corpus of work. The first concerns the implicit and equivocal shift in Foucault's work from surveillance to self-surveillance, or from regulatory to disciplinary power, and the implications of this when considering the particularities of embodiment. Osborne (1992) argues that the identification of such a shift is dependent on the way in which both the 'clinical gaze' and panopticism have been conceptually merged to produce a unified analytical framework. Such a framework has a tendency to perpetuate a docile, almost wholly discursively shaped body (Deveux, 1994) and, despite claims to the contrary, the lived body, consciousness of it and its capacities as a space of transformation are obscured.

The second problem concerns the basis on which observations concerning self-surveillance have been made, which have a tendency to focus on body practices (or practices directed towards bodies in general) rather than on how practices themselves become embodied and are potentially transformed (though see Nettleton, 1992). Though there are some key exceptions that I will discuss in Chapter 3, analysis of power in the Foucauldian optic is typically viewed from the perspective of how it is installed rather than from the standpoint of those subject to power and who may subject power to transformation (Howson, 1996). This may be the consequence of tendencies to treat the body as a cultural object rather than as the grounding of experience, which the Foucauldian model denies (McNay, 1992). Ultimately, though arguments about surveillance and its relation to subjectivity imply a concern with embodied agency, the latter continues to be inadequately specified.

In summary, the Foucauldian optic has been deployed in sociology in ways that offer potential for addressing the relationship between agency and the particularities of embodiment, but in practice have been unable to adequately specify the relationship between the body as *condition* and *constituent* of action (Howson, 1996; Witz, 2000). Indeed, the inherited equivocation from Foucault's own analysis contributes to a conflation between the general and the particular within sociological treatments of the body. Despite claims to the contrary, the possibility of identifying the transformation of knowledge and practices in the space of particular bodies, or indeed, the possibility of identifying 'multiple resistances', is effectively obscured. Hence, while the Foucauldian frame is able to address the social body as a target for power, it is unable to identify the body as a local, particular space in which practices and knowledges could be subject to transformation.

Revealing the body's 'absent presence'

While Foucault's legacy has been an influential analytic within the sociology of the body, health and disease, sociology's classical heritage has been increasingly examined for tools with which to analyze the social significance of the human body. A re-reading of classical sociological theory in a 'new, corporeal light' (Williams and Bendelow, 1998) challenges the view that sociology has 'neglected' the body. In particular, Marx's analysis in the *1844 Manuscripts* of alienated labour is derived from a Hegelian rejection of Cartesianism that 'forces philosophy into contact with the "other" that precedes it: human-practico activity' (McNally, 2001: 75). In this analysis, the embodied subject is transformed through practical interaction with objects of the natural world. Similarly, analysis of the influence of capitalism upon the bodies of labourers is especially evident in Frederick Engel's work in relation to disease and deformities (Freund, 1982). This kind of corporeal re-reading has made it possible to discern the embeddedness of the body within social theory, via both retrieval of Freud's materialism and analysis of nineteenth-century socio-biological terms such as 'drive' or 'instinct', 'need', 'nature' and 'desire'. As Turner notes (1992), concepts such as 'action' and the social 'agent' function as euphemisms for human embodiment in which the body is present though submerged.

Though recuperation moves remain relatively under-developed, distinct themes can be discerned concerning the sensuous and emotional aspects of human embodiment and the corporeality of human interaction. First, several authors (Bologh, 1990; Mellor and Shilling, 1997; Williams and Bendelow, 1998) stress that Weber's analysis of the rise of capitalism acknowledges that the 'Protestant ethic' was crucial to subjugating the pleasures of the flesh in order to pursue godliness. As Mellor and Shilling observe, Protestantism played a key role in distancing people from sensory experience because of a perceived relationship between carnal knowledge and a Catholic definition of the sacred (1997: 9). In contrast,

Protestantism was concerned with the establishment of the 'disciplined individual' in the pursuit of 'autonomous self-interest' (ibid.: 41). Consequently, flesh had to be subordinated and words became an increasingly central means of knowledge accumulation and understanding underpinning the rise of individualism. The corporeality of human interaction is the second theme evident in the retrieval of the body from within classical social theory. For instance, Shilling (2001) has argued that Simmel's work contains what Witz (2000: 17) refers to as a nascent 'embodied concept of agency' and recognizes the significance of the eye and visual exchange as a key medium of communication and social reciprocity. However, Witz and Marshall (2003) caution against an uncritical retrieval of the sociological classics on the grounds that not only is the social invoked overwhelmingly masculine in character but also the social is constituted via the suppression of difference in which male embodiment is normalized though visible while female embodiment is a visible 'matter-out-of-place'.

Within micro-sociological theory the work of Goffman has been retrieved as a key proponent of the corporeality of social interaction and order, and of the fundamental importance of the body in establishing social relations. Crossley (1995a), in particular, contends that a re-examination of Goffman's main texts integrates intersubjectivity with intercorporeality, a viewed shared by others (e.g. Williams and Bendelow, 1998). Though Goffman positions the physical body as a surface or filter through which expression of self is performed via the 'carnal interchanges' of everyday life, Shilling (2003) has argued that his work reproduces a dualism between body and self. His central focus was on how social order is preserved, how self-identity is sustained and how self is performed. The body is implicit but peripheral to these concerns (ibid.). Moreover, though the interaction order links structure and agency and 'shapes, but does not determine people's bodily dispositions' (Mellor and Shilling, 1997: 749), Goffman's own account of how the interaction order is related to social structure was vague. Nonetheless, his work offers the possibility of conceptualizing the body as an instrument over which we have some control in order to establish and repair self-identity (Williams and Bendelow, 1998). Indeed, though the corporeal foundation on which the interaction order is based is unclear (Mellor and Shilling, 1997), for some commentators the buried interactive body in Goffman's work provides a bedrock for the analysis of habitual, routinized social interaction and social reproduction.

Embodied agency/embodiment

Retrievals of agency combine established sociological accounts of the relation between structure and agency with a concept of embodiment to

emphasize the interplay between embodied experience and social structures. To a degree, Frank's action framework also attempts such a bridge
via structuration theory (Giddens, 1979, 1984), which defines structure as
both medium and outcome of interaction, and highlights the importance
of language in the creation of the social. Agency depends on 'practical
awareness' and what people do with this knowledge (which is not necessarily amenable to articulation). Hence, the agent of structuration theory is
not reducible to the system and can be differentiated from it through the
stocks of knowledge that guide them in everyday life and which are subject to modification and change (Shilling, 1997). However, critics of structuration theory (e.g. Archer, 1982) argue that concepts of embodiment
derived from it conflate structure and agency and fail to identify their distinctive properties. Though early versions of structuration theory
acknowledge the significance of the body as a source of practical awareness, this concession disappears in later work on identity and modernity
(Giddens, 1991), which places much greater emphasis on a form of reflexivity, grounded in consciousness.

In contrast, Archer's bridge across structure and agency is attentive
to the body and emphasizes the need to grasp the 'lived experience' of
social reality and people's understanding of this experience. Archer's view
of the agent is threefold: (1) the social agent (members of collectivities such
as class, gender); (2) social actor (incumbents of roles which predate the
occupants); and (3) embodied matter and potential. This latter alludes to
'a "non-social" experience of non-social reality' (Shilling, 1997) and rejects
notions of the self that emphasize its contingent nature. Archer's bridging
apparatus emphasizes that reflection occurs in categories that are not fully
derived from the social and cultural world, that the body exists and is
experienced beyond the social. Nonetheless, Archer's conception of
embodied agency is insufficiently specified and her framework fails to
account for the ways in which forms of embodiment *are* socially shaped
(Shilling, 1997).

In contrast, Shilling has developed embodiment as a bridging concept across structure and agency in an attempt to avoid conceding analytical dominance or to privilege reflection and thought. His concern is with
the 'somatic mediation' of agency and structure. Shilling stresses that
'human agents possess senses, sensualities and physical habits that have
been *partially* socialized, but that *continue to shape* as well as be shaped by
social structures' (ibid.: 738). As he puts it: 'embodied actors are partially
socialized through a variety of relationships and media, yet possess *an
active existence apart from the extant social factors*' (ibid.: 747, my emphasis).

His framework stresses a dialectic between socially shaped embodiment and embodiment beyond the social. While reflection and cognition
have been privileged as important components of agency within the sociological rubric, new models of embodiment seek to develop an embodied

concept of agency that also retains an emphasis on the significance of practice and material context. Shilling's bridge across structure and agency works by building in an anthropological concept of embodiment that stresses the importance and influence of forms of knowledge and consciousness that cannot be reduced to language and/or rationality. Shilling (2001) has also more recently elaborated the directions the sociological imagination might take in appealing to the work of both Durkheim and Simmel as a means of constructing 'an embodied sociology' that takes account of the 'corporeal character of social life' (ibid.: 341). According to Shilling, Durkheim's sociology of collective effervescence (see Mellor and Shilling, 1997) and Simmel's sociology of forms of social life provide a framework through which to develop such an account.

In brief, Shilling argues that in the scholarship of Durkheim and Simmel we find a nascent emphasis on embodied experience as the medium for the constitution of social life. First, the body is the source of social life as a generator of symbol (Durkheim) and through bodily dispositions that enable social contact (Simmel). Second, the body is the location for social life via its symbolic representation of social value (Durkheim) and is the means through which social and emotional attachment occurs via interaction (Simmel) via its capacity for mimesis, motor skills and consciousness of distinction between self and other. Third, however, while the body operates as the medium through which forms of social life are constituted, and though embodied experience is shaped by social contexts and structures, it is not reducible or identical to those structures. There are, for both Durkheim and Simmel, dimensions of experience that are undetermined by society (hinted at by Simmel in his discussion of cognitive and evolutionary forms of creativity). This view of undetermined dimensions of experience is reflected in Durkheim's model of 'doubled' human nature (*homo duplex*) and Simmel's 'body double'. The similarities of these models lie in their emphasis on a distinction between an instinctual, sensory basis for experience and a cognitively ordered basis for experience that reflects a particular social and moral order. Hence, though Shilling pushes the sociological imagination towards a corporeally inflected notion of agency that takes account of the body's social and material context, it also preserves a domain *beyond* the social, in a way that is influenced by and reproduces arguments about the status of the social in the sociological imagination (see Wrong, 1961; MacInnes, 1998).

The social body

Similarly Crossley seeks to produce a synthesis of the body as object (passive, acted on by society) and as subject (active, constituting and reconstituting the social) by integrating 'what is done to the body' with 'what the body does', in addition to 'what the body experiences' (Crossley, 1995b), keeping in mind that we are not always already conscious of ourselves as selves since we are, literally, our own 'blind spot' (2001). Crossley's solution to the problem of, on the one hand, reifying the body as an object upon which society acts and, on the other, reifying the body as a transcendent force or truth which arbitrates meaning, is to use Merleau-Ponty's philosophy of embodiment, and in particular, the way in which his analysis of perception critiques philosophical privilege to the idea of experience (or embodiment) as prior to consciousness.

In Merleau-Ponty's philosophy, mind is not separate from body but located within and of it, hence, mind/body are relational and intertwined rather than distinct entities. Perception is *a priori* an embodied experience. Perception is not an 'inner representation of an outer world of given objects' but is an 'opening onto the world' or an 'opening with Being'. Hence, the body cannot be conceived of merely as an object. Sharing an affinity with Frank's 'body-selves', Crossley's phenomenologically derived body-subject's 'being-in-the-world is at once mediated through physical presence and perceptual meaning' (2001: 47) – it is a *body-subject*. Moreover, as O'Neill (1972) so carefully outlined, perception is based in conduct and practice, in acts of looking, listening, writing, which are influenced by 'acquired perceptual schemas' that make the world meaningful to us. Sense data are not individually discrete, but active participation in and perception of the world provide the basis through which such data are organized and made coherent, a set of corporeal representations that inform our activity in the world (McNally, 2001: 97). Thus, language acquisition and use are patterned by bodily practice, experience and mimesis and in this way can be said to have a material base.

Accordingly, there is no independent and prior object/subject relationship, but a situation in which 'people and things only have an existence and an identity in relation to one another'. Thought is not abstract cognition, but habituated active engagement with the world, or bodily knowledge (Bourdieu, 2000): perception is not simply impulsive but nor is it fully self-reflexive or articulated. Perception *is* practical knowledge and is 'constituted through an active relation of the body to its world' and 'the active body embodies meanings and ideas' (Crossley, 1995b: 48). The degree of action here is relative as Young's (1990) critique of Merleau-Ponty suggests, nonetheless the presupposed articulation of mind and body is cardinal as a state of being that precedes objectivity. 'Intersubjectivity' is forged only through 'intercorporeality', since we cannot know of other minds without also, simultaneously intersecting with other bodies. Therefore, action in the world is prior to cognitive thought and is, in this view, the foundation of cognition and self-consciousness. Apprehension of the world can only be constituted through a particular active engagement with the world and we are not therefore, spectators in/of the world (as in a Cartesian model of perception that privileges vision) but engage with the world through our bodies and all its senses. Schilder's (1950) concept of 'body image' has been deployed to elaborate this phenomenological concept of perception in relation to self-construction. Body image is shaped in and through social relations (Williams and Bendelow, 1998) and mediates between *Körper* and *Leib* (objective and subjective body). When we use our bodies for a particular purpose (voluntary action) we have a view of it moving towards its object of action (self or others) which is in turn, shaped by our relation to social space, time and other bodies.

In order to answer questions of difference, Crossley (2001) draws on Iris Young's account of comportment and the potential for not only physical but also social disempowerment in the limited agency associated with female modalities. In particular, self-objectification arises from a culture in which women in particular are made aware of themselves as objects in ways that have the potential to develop a persistent self-consciousness and contribute to a sense of alienation from self. For Crossley, in Young's analysis the body is gendered through classificatory processes that render particular bodily parts as symbolic markers of social difference. The body is lived as gendered via processes that limit the physical capacities of women in ways that in turn have consequences for their capacity as agents to act upon the world. Finally, the body is reified as gendered via processes of self-reflection (taking on the gaze of the other) through which women become objects not only for others but also for themselves.

Crossley thus locates gender in a discussion of the embodiment of difference more generally, rather than sexual difference *per se*. He argues against the notion of essential differences between bodies, at least in terms of bodily experience, and argues that difference is only 'felt' as such in comparison or in relation to the existence of other bodies which are subject to historically and culturally specific forms of classification as part of a more general process of social grading (Goffman, 1968). Drawing here on Bourdieu, Crossley comments that the various ways in which bodies are classified assume 'specific "value" within any given social formation or social field' (2001: 151). For instance, anatomy is used to differentiate between male and female bodies in ways that are meaningful and produce not only differences but also inequalities between men and women. Hence, all aspects of the body are open to being developed as signs and symbols that carry particular meanings according to place and time (Douglas, 1970). However, the consequences of such categorization/symbolization include the way in which people come to *inhabit* or embody the categorizations – or differences – into which they are placed. That is, social meanings become attached to bodies in ways that constitute social differences, which effectively become embodied (Crossley, 2001: 153).

This argument reflects a more general chicken and egg argument about what comes 'first' – social/cultural categorization or bodily differences. Put another way, while it is not necessarily clear that are there inherent bodily differences that are taken up as symbolic markers of social difference, or that significant social differences contribute to the interpretation of particular bodily parts as different, Crossley seems firmly located in the latter camp, such that bodily variations (for instance, in comportment, conduct, idiom and anatomy) are used as markers of *social* difference. Moreover, bodily hexis (dispositional properties and features) is a critical way in which social groups establish distinction, of which gender could be seen as part, and in turn, social distinction literally becomes embodied through bodily hexis (Bourdieu, 1992). The body, then, is symbolic in the way it is used to communicate relative social positions, and analysis here focuses on the phenomenological implications of bodily hexis and what it might mean to live difference.

Concepts of lived experience and action refer not only to a sense of intellectual being grounded in the material body, but also a sense of the material body as the grounding of emotional, social and linguistic being. However, while the phenomenology of embodment provides a basis for challenging Cartesian dualism through its analysis of perception, the philosophical framework of phenomenology taken on its own is an insufficient base for a sociological analysis of 'action' and 'control' (Williams and Bendelow, 1998; Howson and Inglis, 2001), though it may be necessary to effect analytical distinctions between the representational and the lived, there may be no ontological distinction. Furthermore, the phenomenology of embodment fails to incorporate both power relations (Young, 1990), their impact on embodment and transformations to and within the body across historical time (Burkitt, 1999). Nor can it account for the potential for changes to social relations and the material contexts in which humans exist. These sociological criticisms of phenomenology are not new but serve as a reminder that a dominant version of sociology is oriented towards synthesis between structure and agency as its primary dualism, rather than between subject and object. Nonetheless, phenomenology has provided a resource with which to bridge structure and agency through the development of a concept of embodiment that seeks to capture the materiality of experience and develop a means of explicitly gendering the body within the sociological field.

The thinking body

Ian Burkitt (1999) similarly emphasizes that an account of the body needs to attend to both experience (as it is lived and interpreted) and practical engagement with the world (action and intention). He offers a synthesis of the scholarship of both Norbert Elias and Pierre Bourdieu in a framework that conceptualizes mind/body as ontologically indivisible and relational. Burkitt's version of embodiment emphasizes the inseparability of physical being from mental and emotional life and elaborates Elias's five dimensions of experience and location: breadth, depth, height, time, and symbol. The intimate articulation of these dimensions with each other makes it infeasible to identify where one dimension begins or ends. While they *may* be experienced as distinct, they are inextricably linked. That is not to say that all experience blends unmarked and unnoticeably together. Indeed, in conceptual terms, it is important to acknowledge and specify their relation to one another. Like Crossley, Burkitt argues that the body is not in space in time, nor are space and time objects of consciousness, rather the body belongs to space–time: it 'combines with them and includes them' (Burkitt, 1999: 74), and like other writers, he emphasizes how the material and active relationship between the body and its environment exists prior to thought and representation. Hence, there is no view from nowhere: knowledge of the world is developed through our own embodied subjective positions, and perception of the world is specifically situated in relation to the 'agent's field of action' (ibid.: 74). For Burkitt, this is 'being-in-the-world' and represents not only the body's 'mindful' relation to the world but also alludes to a pre-linguistic sense of intentionality.

However, Burkitt differs from, for instance, Frank's action framework in his emphasis on the significance of material objects rather than language. Elias demonstrates how the 'civilizing process' develops language through not only organic evolution but also as a key mechanism of expression in modernity such that subjectivity and discursivity submerge the body (Burkitt, 1999). As the proliferation of diaries and biographies as the focus of bourgeois self-conscious thought and reflection in the eighteenth and nineteenth centuries suggests, the bourgeois self was increasingly created through language and in text. Indeed, the 'narrated self becomes the ground for all truths' (1999: 56). In contrast, Burkitt develops – a by now familiar – phenomenological account of language as shaped by human activity that also grounds the concept of human embodiment in material objects.

To support his analysis, Burkitt develops Bourdieu's (1992) concept of habitus as a notion of bodily knowledge that is pre-linguistic and irreducible to language. The concept of habitus, which represents the internalization of social structures, is developed through readings of Merleau-Ponty's phenomenology of embodiment and Mauss's 'techniques of the body', which are understood as a 'set of learned dispositions which a body may reproduce within an appropriate social context or field' (Burkitt, 1999: 76). The 'socially instilled bodily dispositions' of the habitus are developed through childhood training and are therefore 'durable' and difficult to change even if we become conscious of them (ibid.: 87). Dispositions are structured because they reflect the relations and material contexts in/through which they are developed and reproduced through practice. They are not inevitable but developed in interaction/practice with contexts or fields: they can, therefore, change. Moreover, the internalization of social structures is made active and agentic through the articulation and performance of such internalization as choice. Therefore, Burkitt's concept of embodiment instates the body as a 'thinking body' and action as embodied action, rather than thought as an abstract process, which occurs beyond/outside, the physical body. In this sense, Burkitt's 'thinking body' can potentially exist in the absence of language which itself is tied to human activity and praxis, and embodied knowledge – psychoanalytical-ly derived or evolutionarily formed capacities – can be seen as perceiving patterns or schemas that enable the coordination of human activity in the world (McNally, 2001).

In contrast to other concepts of embodiment, artefacts have an essen-tial bearing on embodied action in the way they alter perception and knowledge (Burkitt, 1999). Artefacts and material objects 'invite and enable practice' (ibid.: 83) by being functional and by the functions they are given which enable transformation of the social and material world and by being bearers of symbolic meaning (which give shape to culture). This returns the body to a materialist analysis of the social as active engagement in 'relations of transformation with material circumstances' (ibid.: 82). In this view ontology and epistemology are intertwined, and relations in and of the world have implications for our understanding and comprehension of it. Hence, thinking is itself action. Importantly, 'mind' is not an entity distinct from the body (or opposed to it, as in Cartesian dual-ism) but is part of embodied engagement with and practices in the mate-rial world, in particular, social contexts and relations, mediated by arte-facts.

Burkitt's approach to embodiment is extensively indebted to Bourdieu's concept of habitus. However, Bourdieu is accused by his critics of being over-deterministic in the weight he accords structure (Boyne, 1998) and the marginalization of the potential for creativity (Shilling, 1997). Moreover, there are evident tensions in the passive enculturation implied by Bourdieu's emphasis on bodily dispositions (derived from Mauss, 1973) and the practical, active engagement implied through bodi-ly practice (derived from Merleau-Ponty). However, Burkitt views habitus as an orientating rather than a determining concept. It provides a 'practi-cal consciousness' and an 'inclination about how to do things as opposed to knowledge of *why* one is doing them' (1999: 87). Structure is reproduced through practices (or embodied actions) that shape thought and feeling, rather than, as for instance with Giddens, conscious knowledge of the rules (cognition and subjectivity). For Burkitt, dispositions and practical sense are also subject to power relations that not only enable but also inhibit or constrain action. These 'inscriptions of the habitus' or 'tech-niques of the body' are forms of bodily knowledge, 'extra-linguistic capac-ities and forms of understanding, activities intelligible in and of themselves' (McNally, 2001: 108) which cannot be reduced solely to cognitive skills and which provide the basis of being.

Burkitt's concept of embodiment is derived from a more general attempt to deal with an enduring epistemological issue, namely the contrast between realist models of the world as a transcendental ontological realm that exists independently of human knowledge but that can be accurately represented through increasingly rational forms of knowledge, and constructionist accounts of a world that humans can never know with certainty beyond their linguistically formulated knowledge of it. Like Williams and Bendelow, while Burkitt challenges the division between ontology and epistemology in realism and the rejection of ontology in constructionism, nonetheless he seeks to maintain a distinction between ontology and epistemology on the grounds that 'there is a realm of the objective existence of things that is independent of human knowledge and action'. However, all knowledge is 'generated in a community of speaking subjects and is an aspect of communication within relations and interdependencies' (1999: 70). Hence, there can be no appeal to facts or experiences that stand outside language because if facts and objects stand outside our knowledge and language, they cannot be understood. Burkitt's framework attempts to relocate the human body in a field or network of relations and objects. His model of materiality reinstates an early Nietzschean tradition of thought connected to everyday being-in-the-world in which thought is derived from engagement with the empirical world. He imagines a body as a *thinking* body in which thinking is understood as an embodied activity located within particular social and material contexts. Though his approach is a distinct attempt to conceptualize cognition as a materially grounded practice, it is curious that his attempt to gender the body appeals to post-structuralist feminist theories that ultimately privilege text and discursivity in ways that dematerialize the body that produces such text.

Like Williams and Bendelow, Burkitt views Cartesianism (the experience of the division between mind and body) as a consequence of particular configurations of social and historical relations, rather than as an inevitable and universal state of affairs. Consequently, he argues for a sociological approach to embodiment that is not ontological (or does not attempt to 'critique being'), but is concerned instead with identifying and explaining the contexts and relations through which the body comes to be experienced and understood in particular ways. Also, like Williams and Bendelow, Burkitt turns to feminist scholarship that attempts to develop new conceptions of materiality and corporeality that reject binary opposites. As he is especially concerned to develop a framework that deals with the constitution of human beings and things/objects in *relation* to each other in order to establish 'how we are constituted and divided relationally' (ibid.: 65), difference is clearly of concern, but constituted via social relations rather than defined through relations between signs.

Burkitt examines gendered embodiment through the work of feminist anthropologists (especially Emily Martin) and philosophers such as Elizabeth Grosz (1994), whose view of the body as both a material and symbolic construct and a corporeal/psychic entity is typical of the feminist post-structuralist canon and potentially offers a means of thinking about the body as a thinking body. However, ultimately her emphasis on inscription practices that reflect bodily or organic processes as the means through which bodily interiority is established makes a virtue out of unstable or destabilized identity because of persistent tensions between the imaginary and anatomical body. Moreover, the psychoanalytically derived textual and metaphorical privilege embedded within Grosz's approach works against a sociologically inflected understanding of corporeality as pointing to a materially constituted physical body and of difference. Corporeality, when deployed by new feminist philosophies of the body, loses the materiality of difference and of embodiment anticipated by the sociological field.

Feminist theories that foreground bodily use, action and practice have thus been more appealing to attempts to develop sociological theories of the body that incorporate difference. For Burkitt, Moira Gatens is particularly significant here, on the grounds that she partially draws on Bourdieu's concept of habitus in her explanation of gender differentiation and development of embodied ethics. Yet, as Chapter 3 suggests, Gatens does little more than point to the potential for examining bodily use in practical engagement with the world. Her real tool for explaining gender differentiation and thus for identifying the potential space for differentiated ethical embodiment is post-Lacanian psychoanalysis. As outlined in Chapter 3, Gatens draws on Bourdieu's concept of habitus and bodily dispositions to explain the constitution of difference between sexed bodies (Gatens, 1996) through a dialectical framework in which images of bodies are developed according to a sense of being embodied in a particular way, which in turn are mediated by cultural representations. This framework has not only affinities with that proposed by Martin (1984, 1989, 1990) but also establishes common ground between feminist philosophers and sociologists.

Yet there are significant differences in how each group use Bourdieu's work. For sociologists, a major contribution of his work is its success in developing social explanation grounded on extensive empirical investigation. As Rojek and Turner (2000) note, methodological questions and the practical process of undertaking research and issues concerning the researcher's location in the field are of as much importance to Bourdieu as his concern for sound theory. In contrast, Gatens's interest in Bourdieu is principally theoretical and concentrates on the extent to which his framework lends support for a theoretical case derived from analysis of philosophical categories. Hence, sociologists interested in examining bodily practice in contexts of material social relations, such as Burkitt, may be premature in their enthusiasm for Gatens' philosophically inflected discussion of Bourdieu.

Ultimately, the aims of those contributing to the development of sociological theories of the body and those contributing to the development of new feminist theories of the body differ. Sociologists have partially engaged with questions of difference and its relation to embodiment and the emerging literature on sexual difference through considerations of materiality though they are primarily engaged with a quest to establish a general framework with which to approach the relation between the body and society. Though this quest increasingly emphasizes practice, context and location (or embodied action in Turner) as a counter to the strong criticisms of abstraction that have followed the development of sociological theories of the body, concerns about (sexual) difference are ultimately subsidiary. However, this subsidiarity has implications for the development of the sociological field. Women have been incorporated into sociological analysis of the body via philosophical and psychoanalytical discussions that supplant sociological concepts of gender with concepts of sexual difference that emphasize a textual/discursive body (Witz, 2000). This route of admission not only reduces the potency of gender as a sociological concept but also obscures the relation of male corporeality to the production of sociological knowledge (Smith, 1990). Sociological theories of the body acknowledge the importance of the body for understandings of subjectivity but are historically divided as to adequate frameworks that enable identification of mechanisms which link social structures to embodied subjectivity. Thus, sociological theories of the body are faced with the task of developing not only an embedded sociological sense of the body but also specifying the relation between corporeality and sociality. In doing so, such theory turns to feminist philosophies of the body, which highlight corporeality at the expense of sociality, which treat the body as an empty conceptual space, and emphasize embodiment as a conceptual tactic rather than as mediated corporeality (Witz, 2000).

Biologizing corporeality

The preservation of a domain beyond the social implicitly invoked by some sociologists could be read, first, as a tacit acknowledgement of the unconscious, though this link with (non-Lacanian) psychoanalysis has yet to be more fully explored by sociology and, second, as a critical response to the stubbornly elusive character of corporeality, which refuses to yield itself completely to discursivity. A notion of the domain beyond the social, the extra-discursive, is increasingly conceived of as the physiological and the biological, which, for the reasons outlined at the beginning of this chapter, have hitherto been exiled from considerations of corporeality. The social sciences have been unsettled by new ways of thinking about relationships between human and non-human subjects (Latour, 1993) and by what is termed the malleability of the body (Newton, 2003). Benton has explicitly raised the challenge to sociologists to develop: 'sophisticated models of the dynamic interactions between organic and psychological processes at the level of the individual person, and between persons and their socio-relational and bio-physical environments' (1991: 6). This is clearly a holistic restatement of the Parsonian approach to systems with more explicit reference to the body as an organic and cultural entity which in part is no doubt shaped by the emergence of 'life politics' and the focus of new social movements on the interdependence of the social and biological, and the tendency in folk theories as well as in the social sciences towards the pursuit of integration between the personal, the embodied, the political. There are writers working across social and biological boundaries such as Benton (1991) and Birke (1999) who argue that the dualisms inherent in many of the sociological approaches to embodiment retain a model of biology and the biological sciences as oppositional domains in ways that obscure their interrelatedness.

Contemporary social theory is generally uninformed by familiarity with the natural sciences and with major exceptions, for instance (Elias, 1991), scholarly treatment of the centrality to social life of the complex musculature that underlies the smile, a capacity that precedes the social meanings attributed to it, evades confrontation with the biological because of the way in which it is seen to stand for a reductionism to driving physiological processes or genetic codes. However, as scholarship in the field of the sociology of scientific knowledge has made plain (Latour, 1993; De Landa, 1997), and as Benton (1991) in particular points out, there are both sufficient changes and controversies within the life-sciences themselves to substantiate an anti-reductivist stance towards the knowledge they generate, and at the same time, a substantial degree of anti-reductionism within those disciplines which have generated new knowledge about biological processes which do not *reduce* all of life to 'biology' (and suggest a more holistic approach to biology).

Birke (1999) also argues that biology, both in the sense of practice and of the biological processes that underpin human life, is dynamic and responsive to the environment. For instance, contemporary biologists emphasize the interplay between genetics, biological processes and the physiological and social environments in which they operate. Moreover, contemporary biological discourse emphasizes how the body regenerates itself, self-organizes and creates order in a non-linear process of constant becoming (Hird, 2004), while there is emerging acknowledgement within the life sciences that the social environment has a bearing on the development of biological processes and patterns, including natural selection.

Hence, there is emerging within the social sciences a 'new material-ism', which draws on critical realist and critical naturalist approaches to explore relationships not only between mind and body but, more widely, between mind, body and environment. 'New materialism', refracted through Deleuze and Guattari's elaboration of relationships between liv-ing and non-living matter within the social sciences, has been influenced by a revival of interest in evolution and biology within sociology (Benton, 1991) that emphasizes interconnectedness and hybridization (Latour, 1993) and the body's location within and contribution to hetereogeneity (Burkitt, 1999; Thomas and Ahmed, 2004). Body concepts in sociology are increasingly sensitive to the idea that evolutionary adaptations produced by environmental selection occur within particular social contexts, located in space and time, supporting an understanding of natural selection or sexual reproduction as non-linear. This scrutiny is particularly evident in relation to what is argued to be an integrated and complex relationship between health, disease and illness. Freund (1982, 1988), for instance, has focused much of his scholarship on socializing biology through a psycho-somatic approach that includes attention to issues of power, emotional stress and physiology.

However, while many sociologists bid a 'cautious' welcome to the return of the biological body to the field of sociology, others offer a caution against a too enthusiastic reception. In particular, Newton (2003) has recently made the following observations. First, it may be difficult for social scientists unfamiliar with the life sciences to unequivocally make judgements about the veracity of claims about physiological and biologi-cal issues when there is a range of internal tensions within those fields. As Birke (1999) also notes, there are areas of considerable disagreement with-in the field of biology that cut against any straightforward importation of observations about the biological body. Second, incorporating the biologi-cal/physiological needs a particular and knowledgeable sensitivity to the complex ways in which physiology responds to social and environmental influences. This is not necessarily a sensitivity that is part of the know-ledge base of social scientists, who tend to be trained without exposure to life sciences. As noted by Armstrong, one of the few social scientists with medical training, it is difficult 'to reliably infer relationships between "internal states" [physiology] and experience' (1987: 1217). Finally, Newton cautions against reading the social from the biological since it can be tricky to pin down what both are (2003: 34) and the historical separa-tion of the social from life sciences makes it unlikely that they are on the same ontological/epistemological plane.

Though more general retrieval projects differ in their focus, they con-verge on a range of dualisms that the field seems unable to resolve or tran-scend. Hence recent approaches have addressed themselves to persistent dualisms such as mind/body, subject/object and structure/agency and underscore the body as the material grounding of experience. These interventions have produced a range of bridging concepts that place emphasis on different dualisms. First, body concepts such as 'lived' or 'embodied' experience are used to highlight the unity of mind/body and indivisibility of subject/object. This emphasis is most discernible in studies influenced by the phenomenology of cultural and medical anthropology (e.g. medical sociology). Second, body concepts such as 'habitus' stress the materiality of the body as socially shaped through practical enactment and active engagement with the world. Third, concepts such as embodiment are used as a bridging concept between structure and agency. Common to these body concepts – and this is by no means a complete list – is the influence of Merleau-Ponty's philosophy of embodiment. However, as the following section outlines, concepts of embodiment vary in the treatment of related concepts such as language, perception and interpretation.

The lived body, lived/embodied experience

The sociological field has admitted the *lived body*, *lived experience* or *embodied experience* in response to abstract accounts that reify the body as a pre-social object and privilege structure (e.g. Scott and Morgan, 1993; Crossley, 1995b; Frank, 1995; Nettleton and Watson, 1998; Williams and Bendelow, 1998). The concept of the lived body emphasizes embodiment as a site of knowledge and experience and redirects sociological attention away from the body as a reified object (of processes, forces, theory) towards the ways in which the body is lived (Nettleton and Watson, 1998; Watson, 2000). This shift is described as one towards an *'experientially* grounded view of human embodiment as the existential basis of our being-in-the-world' (Williams and Bendelow, 1998: 8; italics in original) and draws on feminist insights as well as aspects of Merleau-Ponty's philosophy of embodiment.

The concept of the lived body (or lived/embodied experience) avows materiality and directs analytical focus on 'tacit knowledge' or 'gut feelings' (Burkitt, 1999: 149) that stand in contrast to rational, reflective knowledge. The lived body 'tells it how it is' (Nettleton and Watson, 1998) and alludes to a form of materially-based authentic experience, on which people draw to challenge particular kinds of knowledge claims. A discernible analytic emphasis is placed on individuals themselves as the authors of valid and reliable accounts of embodied experience through the personal stories in which experience is invoked (e.g. Frank, 1995). For instance, the embodied experience of disability has been mobilized as a rebuttal (Zola, 1991) to professional (medical) knowledge claims. The concept of lived/embodied experience not only operates as a phenomenological counter to abstract theory, but also on a political level as a challenge to orthodox forms of knowledge. The concept of embodied experience privileges the idea that a 'truth' of the body exists (Game, 1991) though it has been subdued by processes of modernity (Boyne, 1998). The assumption being set in place in this work is that, despite all sociological and other kinds of attempts otherwise, the body can and will 'talk back'. How it will do so, and whether we will 'hear' it are another matter entirely, but such a view is similarly alluded to by Falk (1994) in his psychoanalytically derived discussion of the 'consuming body', and is influenced by the idea that premodern forms of knowledge and sensory experience are subdued by modernity. However, the notion of a body 'talking back' is a latent allusion to the (Freudian) unconscious as the voice of the body as shaped by the materiality of biology as by psychic processes.

However, as feminists have noted (notably Scott, 1992), appeals to 'experience' are contentious because political use of the concept has a tendency to conceal the contexts and situations through which appeals to experience are constituted. Moreover, for feminists, concepts of experience tend to carry a particular biologically-laden load. Frank (1995) acknowledges these accompanying tensions in his avowal of experience, and cautions against using concepts such as embodied/lived experience or corporeality in ways that imply a solely material (i.e. socially unmediated) arbitration of being. For Frank, bodies are more than matter and people interpret their materiality in various ways. Hence, negotiation of the tensions accompanying experience requires an epistemology that works against an appreciation of the body as the stable centre in a world of de-centred meanings (Csordas, 1994). Attempts to avoid the reification of experience accord analytical privilege to consciousness, reflexivity and language. Frank, for instance, advocates the notion of 'body-selves' to examine the 'problem' of the body as one of experience, action and meaning, as a critical intersection of history, politics, signs. He draws heavily on cultural anthropology here in his use of body-self in order to reject boundaries between experience and representation.

Like many cultural anthropologists, Frank is interested in how experience is made distinct through language, but also how experience informs language. For Frank, the core analytical problem for sociologists is that of the body's communication with other bodies and its consciousness of itself. Concomitantly, he draws on interpretative and discursive analytical methods and focuses on the stories that people tell themselves and each other about their bodies, particularly in the context of betrayal, breakdown, disease and decay. This approach is well developed within narrative analysis (e.g. Shotter and Gergen, 1989) but is also derived more generally from understandings of the materiality of language associated with Derrida's deconstructionism, Lacan's psychoanalysis, sensuous thought and aesthetic modernity's insistence on language as constitutive of experience (Ian, 1993). Though such a concept emphasizes experiential narrative as a welcome corrective to 'top-down' theory, reinstates individuals as authors of their own experience and roots that experience in the living, material body, nonetheless it has the potential to sit uneasily between materiality and representation and, ultimately, privileges representation at least in terms of methodological focus.

Yet Frank does not subscribe to the view that experience can only be understood through language, rather that 'the body is not mute, but it is inarticulate; it does not use speech but it begets it' (1995: 27). In this view, language, as part of embodied experience, provides an opening onto experience but does not fully determine it and thus the emphasis on language as mediator and constituent of experience avoids reinforcing a sense of the body as a pre-objective 'transcendent force'. A way of avoiding this analytic separation has been to insist on the materiality of language and its production through embodied engagement with the world. This tactic subtly blends the concept of *embodied experience* into *lived experience* and in doing so, elides distinctions between phenomenological considerations of experience and the animated way in which experience is shaped not only by matter but also by the contexts in which matter exists.

Conclusion

This chapter has presented an overview of body concepts in current sociology and tried to demonstrate their differences and points of similarity. The field of the body in sociology, which has been the leading discipline with such a field, is expansive and expanding, focused on the social significance of the body, the relationship between body and society and issues of power, order and resistance, addressed through substantive topics such as ageing, interaction, health and culture. These issues are approached from a diverse range of perspectives and the concepts of embodiment discussed here are welcome interventions in sociological imaginings of the body. There is a discernible orientation within the discipline towards 'embodied social theory' (Burkitt, 1999), 'carnal sociology' (Crossley, 1995b) and 'embodied sociology' (Williams and Bendelow, 1998). Moreover, body concepts within sociology have been developed in ways that seek to move beyond the troubled dualisms that have accompanied the development of Western metaphysics. Current body concepts are concerned with achieving synthesis between the body as producer and cultural product, as thinking and emotional, communicative and productive, material and symbolic. While early scholarship focused on processes and practices that implicate and enact upon the body, the current emphasis is much more on the body's significance in producing meaning and grounding experience. Moreover, current body concepts acknowledge Cartesian dualism as a consequence of particular configurations of social and historical relations, rather than an inevitable and universal state of affairs (Williams and Bendelow, 1998). The new sociology of the body seeks to avoid establishing the essence of things and instead to establish context and relations.

The scholarship associated with the new sociology of the body draws on a range of perspectives and disciplines including anthropological models of embodiment derived from phenomenology that highlight 'pre-reflexive experience' (Csordas, 1990: 6) and feminist post-structuralist theories that place emphasis on ontological and epistemological indivisibility. The field has also been moving towards a reconsideration of the relationship between the social and biological. What makes sociology distinct among the social sciences is its empirical focus on the social conditions of the present (Weber) of which changes in the relations between body and society are part (Turner, 1997), its historical and comparative reach (context) and its attention to diverse issues of power. The turn to the body in sociology has strengthened as historical materialism has been undermined and ambivalence over the 'thingness' of things has heightened. This turn has been influenced by the 'cultural turn' and an emphasis on representation, yet as Rojek and Turner (2000) note, not all problems can be addressed as problems of representation and cultural encoding. Hence, the central challenge for the sociology of the body is the reconciliation between the body as a thing (a particular kind of evolving material object in a world of material objects) and its openness to social influence and (limited?) malleability.

Yet the body also occupies a symbolic space at the heart of the discipline, emptied of its material heart since the fading of materialist analysis as both political practice and as a theory of socio-economic change (Barrett, 1992; Rojek and Turner, 2000). While the core focus of the field remains a concern with reconciling the body as materiality with the representational forms in which it is located, understood and experienced, I have tried to show in the literature surveyed here that most social/sociological theories struggle to hold onto some notion of the real: a body beyond the cultural, rooted in and part of a physical, material, social world that is known and transformed through human practice and activity. As Game puts it: 'My concern has been to argue that the body provides for a different conception of knowledge: we know with our bodies. In this regard, the authentics of experience might be reclaimed; if there is any truth, it is the truth of the body' (1991: 192). While Game's own strategic intervention is part of a more thoroughgoing postmodern epistemological break with older versions of materiality/materialism, her work exemplifies the tension for sociological scholarship that tries to square a non-foundational body of the here and now with the historical and cultural construction of experience and the wider social and political significance of the human body. Yet the current methodological strategies available to sociology that deny the possibility of ontological boundaries between the body and society or between body and self inevitably recast notions of materiality/reality as ethereal because everything that matters is not held as concrete. While most of the theories outlined here claim the value of focusing on the precarious and contingent nature of institutions and spaces (Bauman, 1994), the contingency of interdependence between time and space, interaction and process (Bourdieu, Elias), the persistent focus on secondary materials rather than substantive studies has the potential to reproduce the body as a field in which the production of convergent master narratives is predominant.

Moreover, the general problems of the human body as engendered by the field's development has not, generally speaking, entailed a sustained concern with difference, or with gendering the body. This task has been left to those working within and across feminist theory, and in general, where the body has been gendered in social/sociological theory, it has been done so through consideration of the work of feminist theorists. Valuable as this work is, its value in gendering the body may be limited. The scholarship used by sociologists to gender the body has shifted considerably from the meanings and moorings of materiality to which much sociology of the body implicitly remains attached. While second-wave feminism developed a range of ways of thinking about matter and materiality, recent feminist theories of the body have converged on the notion of materiality as text, or rather, on text as a particular form of materiality. This notion squeezes out the active, practical sense of materiality associated with much of the scholarship surveyed in this chapter. Moreover, attempts to gender the body in sociology are made through feminist scholarship that is purposefully focused on embodying gender, or to put this another way, to examine the (non-foundational) foundations of sexual difference. Strategies to embody gender have been developed primarily via feminist engagement with the deconstructive tactics associated with the work of Jacques Derrida and with textual tactics based on new renderings of the psychoanalytic framework of Jacques Lacan that seek to rewrite the body. As such, the projects of gendering the body and embodying gender, as currently formulated, may be unbridgeable.

Note

1   Conceptual distinctions have emerged between the terms governance and governmentality (see, for instance, Bunton and Petersen, 1997) but they generally refer to a framework that links 'practices of self' with societal regulation.

two

Academic feminism and the corporeal turn

Introduction

In contrast to the body's absent presence within sociological/social theory, female embodiment and the bodies of women have occupied both a more implicit and explicit presence within feminism. Indeed, for some feminists: 'all feminist thinking might be described as an engagement of one sort or another, with what it means to be, and to be perceived to be, a female body' (Brook, 1999: 2).

Given liberal feminism's dominance in the politics of early second-wave feminism and the 'somatophobia' and disavowal of the body embedded within it (Spelman, 1998), this may seem an astounding claim. Second-wave feminist engagement with the female body has undoubtedly been shaped by the legacy of Cartesian dualism in which the material (body) and immaterial (mind) are split. While Western culture has a tendency to elevate mind over body, as feminists have observed, there is no transcendence over the material for women in Western discourse. Consequently, a dominant approach to the female body within second-wave feminism has been influenced by de Beauvoir's (1972) claim concerning the limits of the body to women's freedom (Hughes and Witz, 1997) and its burdensome status (Moi, 1985). Women are correlated with the body, which in turn is viewed as nature and immanence (Kirby, 1997) and bodily function and purpose have been a predominant explanation and justification for unequal relations between men and women (Ortner, 1974).

At best, the female body has occupied an ambiguous place within second-wave feminist theory and certainly feminists have remained fairly ambivalent about the significance of the body in relation to social membership and participation. At the core of this ambivalence is the challenge of addressing gender. The materiality of gender has been denied within liberal feminism in order to liberate women from the burdens of the female body (de Beauvoir, 1972) and clear the way into the public sphere and the marketplace. There is a well-defined literature addressing the female body and social control that advocates strategies for empowerment within a liberal model of citizenship that include education and the encouragement of 'women's knowledge' as the basis from which to challenge perceived bodily restrictions.

Feminists offer critique of the various strategies through which women, by virtue of association with the body (and emotionality, sensuality and irrationality), are excluded not only from social and political participation but also from the categories of social and political theory. Feminist writing, inspired by an Enlightenment ethos, has tended to deny notions of difference based on nature or the body on the basis that areas of experience specific to women have been used as a way of preventing their full social, economic and political participation. Hence, as Bordo (1993) notes, the female body has rarely been the focus of feminist *theory* nor have feminists contributed to the wider social scientific project to *theorize* the body (Hughes and Witz, 1997).

However, in the past two decades there has been a proliferation of feminist texts that focus explicitly on and seek to theorize the female body. Though some feminists have expressed unease about the project of theorizing the body and have argued for ways of refocusing on 'lived experience', others have vigorously pursued the body as an *object* of theoretical inquiry. This latter project has been undoubtedly driven by philosophy and feminists' concerns within that discipline to establish a non-reductive concept of difference within metaphysics in order to reshape social and political theory more generally. Consequently, feminist debate has discernibly shifted from material body struggles that involved concerns about reproductive and sexual control towards efforts to ensure the body's inclusion in theory. Within academic feminism, the political stakes have shifted from concerns about actual lived relationships between men and women and the embodied experiences at their heart to concerns about talk and textual accounts of those relationships.

Chapters 2 and 3 outline the transformation within feminist writing of the body from a (burdensome) medium of experience to an object of theory within academic feminism and trace the development of body concepts from the emergence of second-wave Anglo-American feminism to the present time. The chapters examine the content and shape of the corporeal turn in academic feminism and describe the claims made by feminist theorists about the body. In doing so, the chapters identify the work such claims do for feminists in academic contexts, as well as what they do for academic understandings of the significance of the body. This involves characterizing different strands of feminist theorizing, which address the body's significance for women, as well as its significance for theory.

Feminism has approached the status of the female body in the central categories of Enlightenment thought from two main directions. The first is typical of Anglo-American academic feminisms that remain unstintingly bound to freedom projects that rely on interrogation and 'diffraction' (Haraway, 1999) (though not exclusive to Anglo-American feminism, for instance, see Thapan's (1995) overview of Indian feminist approaches to embodiment that draw on but are also critical of Western feminist notions of embodiment). Though motivated by and contributing to theory, these feminisms are concerned with situation and situated knowledge. They begin from a concern with the material conditions of living beings and advocate feminist interventions that are practical as well as textual. Hence, the chapter begins by tracing popular and academic feminist writings in their approaches to the body of the 1970s and early 1980s. These approaches were largely concerned with body politics, such as women's health projects, sexual violence and pornography and associated mainly with radical feminism in the Anglo-American world.

A second discernible approach to the body taken by contemporary academic feminist writing has been influenced by these early feminist concerns with a 'politics of the body' (Bordo, 1993) and their attempts to make visible and politicize the *problems* of embodiment that women face in conditions of patriarchy. While the materiality (or unresolved residual facticity, Witz, 2000) of the female body vexes feminism, feminism has refused to tolerate embodiment as a 'thing-in-itself' or as noumenal matter. Hence, academic feminism in the 1980s increasingly turned to deconstructive practices and discourse analysis to consider the human body as socially produced and constituted.

Drawing on a range of perspectives from the work of Mary Douglas, Michel Foucault and Donna Haraway, the approaches taken by feminists in anthropology, geography and sociology have typically focused on substantive issues concerning women and recast them as problems of bodily regulation and discipline. Michel Foucault's insights into a range of substantive areas and his insistence on the discursive production of the body have appealed to feminists with an interest in developing a non-reductive approach to the relation between the body and gender, to examine issues of power, domination and resistance. Similarly, Maurice Merleau-Ponty's philosophy of embodiment has been developed to address philosophical dualisms between subject/object.

Finally, Chapter 3 sketches the development of body concepts in feminist accounts of subjectivity that draw upon and rework the insights of established malestream theories. This work has both substantive and theoretical concerns at heart but starts from the critique of central categories of Enlightenment thought. Moreover, this work is explicitly concerned with a project of embodying gender that engages with and tries to move beyond a sex/gender distinction and advocates a non-reductive recuperation of difference as a means of developing epistemology and/or ethics based on specificity. Feminist attempts to engage with and embody subjectivity introduce concepts such as embodiment and embodied specificity. The focus of these two chapters, then, on the emergence of the 'corporeal turn' within feminism prepares the ground for extended discussion in Chapter 4 of feminist theories of the body that are particularly indebted to post-structuralist and post-Lacanian psychoanalytic perspectives, that arguably take feminism closer towards a theory of the particular, by focusing on sexual difference.

Women's body politics

It is generally accepted that Robin Morgan advocated the idea that 'the personal is political' as a radical feminist inflection on the political and public shaping of aspects of women's experience hitherto deemed 'private', including the experience of female embodiment. The development of second-wave feminism as a movement and as an intellectual project has been diverse and has become increasingly fragmented (Whelehan, 1995). Its emergence in the Anglophone world in the 1960s as a social and political movement stemmed from post-war contradictions between the expansion of education provision and new opportunities for women through education, on the one hand, and, on the other, from a reinvestment in idealized visions of femininity associated with marriage and motherhood, as exemplified by Friedan's *The Feminine Mystique* (1963). As a movement, feminism was much influenced by the Black civil rights movement in the USA (Seidman, 1994) and trade unionism in much of Europe. Popular and academic feminist writing made visible many aspects of women's lives and in general emphasized the ways in which such lives were socially shaped and potentially transformable. Popular and academic feminist texts focused on inequalities and women's oppression in general and the various ways and levels in which cultural, social, economic and political differences were created between men and women.

As commentators on second-wave feminism have noted (e.g. Seidman, 1994; Whelehan, 1995) while the emphasis on the social construction of divisions and differences was shared among feminists, there emerged considerable variation and debate as to how to address difference. Where liberal feminism emphasized the power of legislative reform which had some successes (in the UK, the 1967 Abortion Act, the 1970 Equal Pay Act and the 1975 Sex Discrimination Act), socialist and materialist feminists emphasized the radical transformation of the politico-economic order and engaged in a sustained and at times protracted analysis of the relation between gender inequalities and class-based divisions. While radical feminists also stressed comprehensive social, political, cultural and economic transformation they differed from liberal and socialist/materialist feminists inasmuch as they came to see gynocentrism as the grounding of that transformation.

While gynocentrism celebrated differences – natural and/or cultural – between women and men (Seidman, 1994), it was met with critical responses in particular from women of colour (Davis, 1981; Lorde, 1983) and the inseparability of gender subordination from the oppressions of race and class. Despite these important interventions, variants of gynocentrism influenced a sustained focus on the politics of the female body. The fiction of writers such as diverse as Marge Piercy (1979) and Margaret Atwood (1986) was an important contribution to making not only the concerns of women visible but also those aspects of embodiment that *defined* femininity for a generation. The writing engendered by radical feminist activism specifically addressed the significance of the female body to women's subordination, for instance, in relation to experiences such as sexuality (Koedt, 1970), rape (Brownmiller, 1976), representation (Greer, 1970; Millett, 1970) and reproduction (Firestone, 1971). As Birke (1999) argues, these texts were grounded in a language of activism and quite explicitly engaged with a range of women's bodily experiences, 'from foot-binding and corseting to rape and battering to compulsory heterosexuality, forced sterilization, unwanted pregnancy, and explicit commodification' (Bordo, 1993: 22).

The emergence of the women's health movement in the Anglophone world, the development of body consciousness and the publication of radical texts such as *Our Bodies Ourselves* (Phillips and Rakusen, 1971), placed particular emphasis on bodily and self-knowledge, and specifically examined the relationship between medical knowledge and experiential knowledge of the body. In particular, many feminists argued that acquiring knowledge of one's own body was vital to challenging medical orthodoxies and its problematic definitions of female embodiment (Dreifuss, 1978). For instance, the cervix was vigorously politicized by the women's health movement and self-visualization was identified as an empowerment strategy that would enable women to 'own' their cervix and dispute medical expertise (Frankfort, 1972). In particular, academic feminist writing influenced by Anglo-American health activism challenged the ways in which health was defined in the language of biomedicine and rejected expert constructions of the female body as deviant. This work addressed substantive issues concerned with fertility control (Gordon, 1978); misogyny in biomedical, scientific and technological practices (Scully and Bart, 1978; Ehrenreich and English, 1979); and the politics of childbirth and reproduction (Ehrenreich and English, 1974; Donnisson, 1977). This scholarship enabled feminists to challenge the general tendency in medical practice for women's experiences and knowledge to be disregarded by practitioners (Ruzek, 1978) and to refocus on the embodied experience of health and health care through a range of tactics. These included body consciousness groups (Dreifuss, 1978), which encouraged practices such as cervical self-examination; a return to 'traditional' female approaches to health and healing (e.g. Lewin and Olesen, 1985); and 'well-woman' clinics (Gardner, 1982).

Though radical feminist writing on the body is diverse, a common thread in the 1970s and early 1980s was the retrieval of bodily experiences hitherto concealed, thus, the emphasis placed on the potentiality of women's daily, lived (bodily) experiences. An organic model of the female body as a repressed body is emphasized within this writing (Sawicki, 1991) though there are tensions even within radical feminism in the solutions generated to address its subordinate status. On the one hand, some feminists claimed that the female body has been 'naturalized' in ways that are exploited by patriarchal power. These naturalized capacities, such as reproduction, were used against women in patriarchal societies and therefore created a problem that needed solutions such as technology as a vital means of transforming women's experience of and control over reproduction (Firestone, 1971). Yet as Currie and Raoul (1992) note, the advocacy of technology as a solution to women's reproductive subordination potentially reifies the female body as a 'natural' problem.

On the other hand, radical feminism also emphasized how particular forms of social organization and institutionalization re-order embodiment and produce cultural definitions of the female body (as naturally deviant) that are used against women. Consequently, radical feminism also sought to envisage how 'corporeal specificity' (Williams and Bendelow, 1998: 116) – the female body as a source of *actual* lived and experienced pain, distress and pleasure – could be developed as a source of empowerment and as a resource for social change (Rich, 1976; Daly, 1978). As 'maternal' and communitarian feminists (e.g. Gilligan, 1982; Elshtain, 1993) argued more generally, though women have been confined to domestic spheres and relations that emphasize attention to one's own body and caring for the bodies of others, these conditions have produced experiences and perspectives that women can value positively and celebrate. Of particular influence was the work of Adrienne Rich and her conceptual re-evaluation of the ways in which feminine subjectivity and embodiment are intertwined as a potential 'resource' for women rather than as an inevitably physiological and biological 'destiny' (1976: 21). Rich in particular is credited with consistently defining the female body as specific, subordinated matter that could be important in transforming social relations and arrangements. Hence, where liberal feminism implicitly accepted de Beauvoir's interpretation of the female body as 'troubled' (Moi, 1985), radical feminist writing argued that female embodiment could and should be viewed as the basis of female empowerment.

Materialist feminist scholarship in relation to body politics began from a different set of concerns and addressed not only the political economy of embodiment but also the social shaping of bodily experiences. For instance, feminists were concerned about the commodification of the female body through pornography (MacKinnon, 1987), prostitution (Edwards, 1993), and more recently surrogate motherhood (Singer, 1994). Moreover, women in North America and in the UK were identified as the major users of health care services (Stacey, 1977; Verbrugge, 1985), as the principal formal and informal producers of health in the public domain

(Gamarnikow, 1978), and as the foremost providers of health care in the private sphere (Finch and Groves, 1983). Within sociology and social policy in the UK, feminist scholarship was concerned with the substantive analysis of women's bodily experiences in relation to health and health care and focused on the analysis of a gendered division of labour in the production and maintenance of health (Doyal, 1983). Such scholarship sought to make gendered divisions in the production of health visible and to highlight the various ways in which women undertake paid and unpaid work in the (re)production of healthy bodies and minds (Lewin and Olesen, 1985; Stacey, 1988). Ann Oakley's work on pregnancy and childbirth (1980, 1984) exemplified this approach in British sociology in that it located women's bodily experiences within capitalist structures and patriarchal relations. Though bodily experience is in attendance in this work, as Brook (1999) notes, Oakley's aim was primarily to redress the 'sociological unimagination' by developing an analysis of the medical management of childbirth from women's accounts of their experiences. The advantage of this approach was its attempt to make visible not only experiences specific to women, beyond the scrutiny and interest of conventional sociology, but also its commitment to giving voice to *experience*. There are problems with the concept of experience that are relevant to and embedded within discussions of embodiment to which we will return. Similarly, American feminism focused on the invisibility of the pregnant body in the context of paid work and the absence of allowances for the physical and emotional changes pregnancy brings (Ehrenreich and English, 1979).

The female body provides a distinct reference point within this scholarship since the production of health requires and depends on the embodied labour of women as mothers, wives, or daughters. 'Health' is not an abstract concept in this work but refers to specific *bodily* experiences that are shaped by material circumstances. Moreover, materialist feminists in this work are clear about the ways in which relations of production in a capitalist economy structure the experience and status of female embodiment in ways that have crucial oppressive implications for women. For instance, material circumstances give rise to bodily experiences that may give cause for discomfort or disruption in ways that highlight and make it difficult for women to undertake the dual and diverse burdens associated with capitalist patriarchy. For materialist feminists in the 1970s and 1980s, the materiality of the female body, experienced as either discomforting or liberating, was understood to be produced through specific social, economic and political conditions.

A more sustained analysis of the vicissitudes of female embodiment is discernible in the 1980s as more women moved into higher education, including more mature entrants, many from a health or nursing background, and as female embodiment – experiences – became increasingly visible in consumer culture through women's magazines in particular.

Academic feminism in the 1980s, particularly in sociology, social policy and anthropology, continued to focus on the various ways in which material conditions and, in particular, paid work, obscure the specificities of female embodiment and the processes that make women sick (Doyal, 1983). This work identified the division of labour and the social location of women across and between worlds of paid and unpaid work. Particular aspects of female embodiment, such as menstruation and menopause (Lewis, 1993; Hunt, 1994), bridge these worlds and have been exposed to sustained academic scrutiny. Concepts of pollution and taboo have been especially important in the analysis of menstruation and menstrual blood as historically constructed 'matter-out-of-place' (Douglas, 1966) from biblical discourse to contemporary anxieties expressed in the sanitized language of advertising (Treneman, 1988; Laws, 1990). This scholarship examines how women's experiences of menstruation are structured by male attitudes and institutions (Laws, 1990; Thorne, 1993); how the disciplinary regimes of paid work and education in capitalist economies fail to accommodate menstruation (Martin, 1989); how young girls' experience of the onset of menstruation is effectively silenced (Brumberg, 1997; Lovering, 1997); and the ways in which women are implicitly encouraged to adopt concealment strategies in their management of menstruation (George and Murcott, 1992).

Similarly, while conditions such as premenstrual syndrome (PMS) has been understood as a hormonal category that requires special medical attention, some feminists have argued that PMS should be understood as a 'symbolic safety valve' (Johnson, 1987) through which women give expression to the social contradictions that accompany expectations about production and reproduction. PMS is a broad term developed and used within gynaecology and general practice to refer to a range of symptoms and embodied experiences (Rodin, 1992). Feminists view PMS as a medicalized category of experience that constructs the female body as a deviant body. There are historical continuities between the development of PMS as a diagnostic category and nineteenth-century ideas about hysteria (ibid.). Within the latter, legal and medical discourses were developed and deployed to highlight the irrationality and lack of control embodied by the hysterical woman. Such discourses contributed to the exclusion of women from higher education. Similarly, PMS, with its focus on hormonal imbalance and the association with 'unpredictability' this brings, is deployed to legitimize claims that women ought not to be given positions of responsibility in the public sphere (ibid.).

However, feminists have also used this line of argument about embodied difference to support claims about the need to recognize the impact of hormones on women's experience. For instance, the category of 'diminished responsibility' is deployed within legal discourse as a defence for women charged with crimes of violence (Atkins and Hoggett, 1984).

Moreover, women themselves have participated in the construction of medical categories, such as PMS, in order to find solutions to those embodied experiences that pose disruptions to their lives (Riessman, 1992). The medicalization of PMS through the construction of medical terms and the development of interventions such as surgery and hormone replacement therapies simultaneously can be understood as the construction of a deviant female body and as a means for women to authorize and authenticate their embodied experiences.

A particular thrust of feminist scholarship in the 1980s concerning female embodiment concerned the various ways in which the female body is defined and addressed as a deviant body. Such definitions preserve perspectives that originate from professional specialization in the nineteenth century and the emergence and consolidation of scientific medicine, which viewed the female body as unstable (Poovey, 1987), as a source of sexual pollution (Walkowitz, 1980) and as inferior to the male body (Gallagher, 1987). These definitions were not merely part of a cultural superstructure but had material implications for the labour of both working- and middle-class women. For instance, the Contagious Diseases Acts of 1864 and 1866 identified prostitutes as the carriers of disease and enabled the regulation and examination of the bodies of working-class women in garrison towns in England. Moreover, as women began to identify possible routes of entry into professional and political spaces, the female body was defined in medical discourse and supported in legal discourse as a pathological body in need of containment and control (Sachs and Wilson, 1978).

Much of the feminist scholarship on reproductive capacities, technologies and choices in the 1980s and 1990s focused on the experiences involved and the various ways in which such experiences are structured (by medical power, commercial interests, the legal system and emerging public debates concerning the ethics of reproductive technologies). Feminists emphasized the ways in which biomedicine objectified the body by categorizing it into parts and fragments (Oakley, 1984; Stacey, 1988; Martin, 1989) through technological interventions and the development of a range of visualizing techniques. The surveillance of the female body as part of a more general shift towards visualizing the unseen (Stafford, 1991) has been enhanced with the development of particular kinds of tools, which help to visualize parts of the body hitherto inaccessible. Techniques of visualization that have contributed to the fragmentation and objectification of the female body in pregnancy include the speculum, which made the vagina and cervix more accessible for professional scrutiny (Moscucci, 1990); ultrasound (Oakley, 1984); and fetal photography. Stabile (1994) for instance, examines how such technologies have transformed the status of the developing foetus and shifted its relation from one of dependency within the maternal body to a relationship that is apart from and autonomous to the mother. Similarly, Duden's work (1993) is concerned with the relationship between the technologies available for 'reading' the female body and the feelings/experiences shaped by these technologies. In addressing the experience of pregnancy and the physical and emotional changes that can accompany it, feminists have observed, from different perspectives, the implications that technological interventions hold for embodied experience (Howson, 2001b) and how technological forms of knowledge have the potential to displace bodily forms of knowledge (Young, 1990; Duden, 1993).

As Petchesky (1987) has noted, technological confirmations (such as chorionic villi sampling) and visual representations of pregnancy (ultrasound) redefine the terms of embodiment (Rowland, 1992) in ways that have the potential to undercut the validity of embodied experience and knowledge. This observation has contributed to broader challenges to medical knowledge that emphasized the authenticity and specificity of female embodiment. Campaigns such as the Natural Childbirth movement sought to reshape the choices and possibilities that women might experience in pregnancy and childbirth and insist on women's entitlement to be listened to and included as active participants in the birthing process (Arney, 1982). However, while the impulse to reclaim the authenticity of embodied experience may have sprung from recognition of the collectively produced nature of such experience, in relation to women's health, this impulse typically reverts towards a liberal discourse of individualized choice.

As feminism has expanded within the academy, it has also continued to provoke scholarship that addresses substantive issues concerned with body politics and their contribution to women's subordination. While this scholarship has typically developed along disciplinary lines, cultivating dominant perspectives within a particular discipline, it has also travelled across disciplines in order to establish a complex analysis of particular bodily experiences and issues. Yet, this scholarship is rarely addressed by the inter-disciplinary work undertaken by feminists to theorize the body.

Gender, the body and material/ity

The material – bodily – concerns and experiences of women are discernible elements of much feminist scholarship in the 1970s to early 1980s. Yet, second-wave feminism was also concerned with identifying gender as a social and cultural category (Witz, 2000) in ways that rejected the reduction of women to the body. As Scott and Morgan (1993) note, for many academic feminists in the 1970s, the body was synonymous with biology, and feminist sociologists avoided concepts that might reinforce a sociobiological view of gender. Furthermore, Birke (1999) argues that because biology typically operated within feminism as a concept that signals the reduction of the complexity of human beings, feminism did not generally engage with the substantive nature and content of biology. Yet, feminist sociologists, particularly within an Anglo-American context, were at the forefront of initiating research that addressed bodily experiences, though the materiality of *experience* was the focus of this work, rather than the *body's* materiality.

The deliberate and meticulous focus on experience that accompanied sociological and anthropological studies of women's health and other issues was part of and crucial to the development of a *sociological* concept of gender. Feminist sociologists sought to make women's experiences visible within sociological inquiry, without reducing women's experiences to those of the body or, more specifically, biology. Feminist sociologists focused their work on describing and explaining female sociality in terms of gendered and/or patriarchal relations, institutions and structures (Witz, 2000). They did so with a clear emphasis on the social character of gender, not only in the sense that gender is distinct from sex/biology but also in the sense of it as an empty category that is filled by social practices and cultural assumptions. This view of gender as fundamentally social and cultural not only distinguished it from psychological uses that emphasized traits, attributes and behaviours but also signalled an understanding of difference as socially rather than physiologically, biologically and psychologically produced. While the psychological analysis of gender as a set of learned roles provided a taxonomy of 'artificially rigid distinctions' between men and women and highlighted the agencies responsible for instilling them, it did not enable analysis of the forms of power that create and sustain the distinctions in the first place (Connell, 1987). Indeed, feminist sociology was highly critical of a sex-role approach as adequate on its own and did not remain attached to this view of gender.

As with other disciplines (Hawkesworth, 1997), gender was and is used in a number of ways within sociology (Morgan, 1986), yet its initial defining characteristic was linked to a sociological insistence on and location of gender within social relations, institutions, structures and practices (Finch, 1993). A feminist sociological imagining of gender insisted that it had no biological base though such an imagining certainly and variously insisted on other kinds of base (capitalist or patriarchal relations). There have been extensive debates about the social base(s) of gender and the utility and sensitivity of linked concepts such as capitalism and patriarchy. My point here is not to describe these debates and offer a better view of 'what works' but to suggest that sociological concepts of gender have been distinct from other disciplinary uses of the term. This sense of distinction arises from a tacit insistence within the discipline that its common 'object' of analysis is social life, even where there are debates about how and what constitutes the social (see Game, 1991).

The power of the sex/gender distinction as initially developed within the sociological production of knowledge was that it resolutely focused on *women's* subordination, women's *experiences* (in contrast to *men's* experiences, *experiences* in contrast to *abstractions*, experiences in contrast to experience). Though sociological explorations of gender through a feminist lens,[1] saw that gender (in the sense of roles, practices, identities and divisions) could be shaped through social scripts, reinforced by agencies (the family, the state, the media, and so on), this vision was tied to a politics of transformation that stressed the mutability of gender. Thus, gender in feminist sociological imaginings emphasized that not only are traits and characteristics at a psychological level socially shaped and produced, but the social, economic and political inequalities that can be observed between women and men are not an extension of biological differences, a superstructural elaboration of a biological base, but a product of particular social relations, contexts and epochs. Feminist insistence on gender as a *social* concept however, has been interpreted as bracketing of the body. The view of gender as a 'particular and changeable coat on the immutable rack of the body' reinforced a view of the body as a stable foundation across time and place (Nicholson, 1994). As Nicholson argued, academic feminists, in their use of the sex/gender distinction, tended to fix the body as a biological foundation and exile considerations of its relation to the social construction of gender.

However, it is not fully the case that feminist sociologists bracketed out the body as a stable foundation. Ann Oakley's (1976) book *Sex, Gender and Society* offered a key text for early feminist sociological imaginings of gender and its relation to social and cultural practices. It was inspired and framed by a focus on sex differences but sought to locate observed and observable differences within a social context, to disavow explanations about such differences through appeal to 'nature'. Nature was here conceived of as biology, but Oakley demonstrated that even what we conceive of as nature is variable. She drew on a range of materials 'scattered across disciplines' in order to show how physical characteristics (size, shape, the possession of anatomical attributes viewed as genital), are used to categorize bodies into male *or* female. That despite the considerable evidence that suggests variability within the bodies of either men or women (which calls into question the extent to which either/or can be appropriate points of categorization) and also points to overlap and similarity between the bodies of men and women, the body is used not only to categorize people into either/or social groups (male/female) that are constituted through and overlaid by social practice and cultural assumptions, but also is used against women. Though Oakley is clearly a self-identified 'daughter of de Beauvoir', it is not clear that she accepted de Beauvoir's implicit and sometimes explicit characterization of the female body as a burden or as 'trouble'. Indeed, Oakley has consistently and persistently focused on the various ways in which different kinds of relations and contexts 'make' trouble for women in relation to the body.

Oakley's analysis succeeded because of her meticulous trawl through an impressive range of materials, much of it technical and dealing with claims made within the disciplines of psychology and biology, in order to show how deeply implicated the body is in social constructions of gender *and* gender is in constructions of biology. Her analysis did not so much exile the body, as show how assumptions and claims about the body are used to create and support divisions between categories of persons. Her analysis suggested that *despite* empirical observations concerning variation in the possession of particular chromosomes, the effects of hormones or anatomical characteristics, societies group and categorize persons into either male or female. This grouping underpins a sexual division of labour, where sexual refers to the processes and practices of division between men and women, and where division refers to differences in role allocation, access to resources and learned differences in attitude and/or disposition.

Therefore, it is possible to argue that the body was implicitly present in Oakley's analysis though it was not her focal point. The body was certainly equated with biology, hormones, reproductive organs, chromosomes and moreover, categorized as sex, but it was present as a socially and biologically variable entity. Perhaps it is only possible to make such an observation because history teaches us about fundamental interpretative shifts that have framed knowledge production about the body. The body enters historical scholarship and sociological imagining through the work of historians such as Thomas Laqueur (1991), who identified and explained a shift from a one-sex to a two-sex model, characterized by what (Garfinkel, 1967) described as invariant, dimorphic and complementary. The meaning of the body, including the sex we assign to it (and its reliance on notions of distinctiveness, opposition and hierarchy), is greatly determined by the interpretative framework through which it is viewed (see Hood-Williams, 1996).

While the sex/gender distinction is now viewed as problematic and unstable, its initial value was that it denaturalized accounts of women's bodily experiences and relocated those experiences within social structures and processes. Oakley's analysis has been subject to extensive criticism not least because it implicitly reinforces a functionalist explanation of how roles are assigned to particular social groups rather than questioning why such assignation occurs (Charles, 2000). Nonetheless, it prised apart the previously accepted essential and determining connection between sex (the biological body) and gender (social and cultural artefact) and provided a means to challenge the various ways in which differences between men and women are naturalized and made immutable. Moreover, though Oakley's analysis separates gender from sex, locates the former within the social and the latter within biology, nonetheless her analysis suggests that this separation was never complete, in either an empirical or conceptual sense. Indeed, her analysis challenges claims about the determining power of biology by providing evidence of the variability of roles assigned to men and women and the variability of biology (anatomy and physiology) itself. However, it does not *exclude* the body from the sex/gender distinction, even though its exclusion is somewhat taken-for-granted in recent debates within feminist sociology about the body and its absence (see Nicholson, 1994; Delphy, 1993; Gatens, 1996).

The body has been subsequently viewed as reduced to sex, defined in turn as a neutral platform for the inscription of gender identity. Gatens, for instance, acknowledges that the sex/gender distinction was particularly important for those she defines as 'socialist-feminists' as a tactic for breaking the 'arbitrary connection between femininity and the female body' (1996: 4) and emphasized the development of gender identity via socialization processes. However, the sex/gender distinction was, in Gatens' view, a body/consciousness distinction in which the former was smothered by the latter because of the baggage notions of consciousness bring with them and the way it 'abstracts from embodied beings' (Witz, 2000). Gatens views this distinction and the tactics it generated as 'theoretically naïve' and based on assumptions about the neutrality of the body – the biological foundationalism to which Nicholson refers – and the relationship between materiality and experience. Yet her criticism also consigns gender to an analysis of identity rather than to the wider set of issues intended within feminist sociology.

Much of the emphasis within feminist theory in the past decade has been on challenging the utility of gender, recuperating the body in imaginings of gender and in doing so, arguing for the constructed nature of sex. Feminist sociology has participated in these debates and imaginings too. Christine Delphy (1993), in particular, has asserted that sex needs to be understood as both socially constructed and as a corollary of gender (in the sense that gender precedes sex). Sex, or more specifically, genital anatomy, is not outside practices of social and cultural determination that transform 'a physical fact ... into a category of thought' (Delphy, 1984) which converts sex into a marker that is in turn implicated in the division of persons into two oppositional and unequal social categories. Hence, echoing the claims of cultural historians in which meaning is sought primarily in image and language, sex in this case is not fundamental or foundational. What is understood as 'sex' (as a physical body designated either male or female with a corresponding invariant gender and complementary sexuality) has a historically acquired symbolic value. The cultural assumptions and material practices embedded within the concept of gender are those which inform the categorization of bodies as either male or female, that mark them as 'sexed'.

Though feminist sociologists have not focused explicitly on the female body in their attempts to examine women's lives and experiences and explain inequalities, feminist scholarship within sociology has examined, first, body politics and the various ways in which women's bodies are exploited and managed in conditions of patriarchy. Second, such scholarship has explored how the capacities of women's bodies to both reproduce and enter into productive labour are located and materialized within specific economic and social conditions (Witz, 2000). Third, some feminist sociologists have been more or less willing to signal the significance of the female body as a foundation of experience. A common thread running through this scholarship is the relation of women's bodily experiences to knowledge and consciousness and it is to this thread that I now turn.

Body/knowledge

Though a predominant vein in second-wave feminist writing on women's bodily experiences appeared to accept de Beauvoir's assessment of the female body as limiting, nonetheless the 1980s produced attempts to revalue the significance of the body in women's lives and its relation to identity and consciousness through the development of materialist, psychoanalytic and phenomenological methodologies. For instance, working within a socialist frame of reference, (O'Brien, 1981), midwife and academic, analyzed reproduction as a 'substructure of history', or as historically shaped ontology that enabled women to gain access to a distinct knowledge system. Female participation in conception, gestation and birth offers women a 'sensual knowledge of the body' (Miles, 1992) that is unavailable to men and that stands in opposition to male abstracted modes of being (Brook, 1999). In a move that was consonant with radical feminist strategies of the period, O'Brien maintained that the experience of female reproduction was part of a bodily continuum from conception to birth that gives rise to a 'reproductive consciousness' (Shilling, 2003) that valorizes 'knowing through being'. However, in conditions of patriarchy, the abstract is privileged over material particularity and the organization of societies appropriates and devalues women's experiential knowledge (Frank, 1991). Moreover, the social organization of reproduction in conditions of patriarchy establishes cleavages between women and creates a 'new class division ... between those who breed and those who do not' (1981: 193). Hence, O'Brien argued that the task for feminism was to move beyond the paralysis of this devaluation and division.

To some degree, Mary Daly's 'gynocentric' analysis provided a means of moving beyond the devaluation of female embodiment in her assertion that as women become more conscious of their alienation from the world, they gain access to distinct ontology. Thus, the female body in Daly's view was the 'beginning point for an epistemological revolution that will emerge when women learn to "think through their body" rather than through patriarchal values' (Daly, 1978: 6). Though Daly's position and argument have been of marginal influence to the development of feminist epistemology, it clearly foregrounded more recent claims (drawing in part on Bakhtin's retrieval of the carnivalesque) concerning the transformation of female embodiment in modernity and women's corporeal relation to the 'grotesque', to the wild zone (Showalter, 1985) and the monstrous (Shildrick, 2002). The forms of 'carnal knowledge' (Miles, 1992) displaced by the 'cognitive apprehension' of the world characteristic of modernity and effected via the processes of rationalization (Weber, 1978) and civilizing processes (Elias, 1994 [1978]) have remained modes of understanding to which women, through their relation to the grotesque, continue to have moderate access. It is this relation that O'Brien highlighted in her discussion of reproduction.

While O'Brien contributed to a sociological understanding of the relation between knowledge and consciousness, in that it foregrounded the significance of the body (Shilling, 2003), her work has been subject to criticism. First, though her analysis of reproduction insisted on its historical materiality, nonetheless her framework assumed a subject for whom the experiences and meanings of reproduction are universal (Brook, 1999). Yet, as anthropological and sociological scholarship reveals, such experience and meanings vary considerably according to class, ethnicity and context. Second, while her analysis highlights the relation of the body to knowledge and consciousness, it over-prioritizes and privileges one set of corporeal experiences over another (Shilling, 2003). Third, as current fertility and demographic data indicate, not all women in industrial capitalist societies share the experience of childbirth or do so in varied circumstances. Moreover, current fertility trends suggest a rejection of reproduction among 25–34-year-olds in higher socio-economic groups that reinforce the division between those who breed and those who do not, a division about which O'Brien was concerned.

Nancy Hartsock (1985, 1987) similarly emphasized the relation of the body to knowledge and consciousness in her merger of historical materialism and object-relations theory. While she saw the former as a method for the analysis of women's oppression, she viewed the latter as a hypothetical explanation for processes of differentiation and individuation. Hartsock was especially interested in the female body (or of women's lived experiences) because 'the lived realities of women's lives are profoundly different from those of men' (1998: 153). However, she argued that while material feminists may subscribe to this view, they had failed to examine the 'epistemological consequences' of this claim and her work developed the notion of a standpoint acquired through processes of production and the material conditions determining that production (Hartsock, 1987).

Like O'Brien, Hartsock focused on the special circumstances of reproduction but located this within a wider discussion of the dual contribution women make to subsistence and social reproduction. The latter entails nurturing the emotional and psychological well-being of others and is grounded in the development of a relational approach to human relationships. Women's relation to social reproduction is not characterized by the instrumentalism required by the rational, public sphere, but by a unity of mind and body seldom experienced by men. For Hartsock, though the experience of pregnancy and child-bearing 'changes the world and consciousness of the woman' (1998: 156), in more general terms, women's relational experience is partially dependent on female embodiment and the impact of female physiology and biology on consciousness.

The materialist psychology of object-relations theory epitomized by Nancy Chodorow's *Reproduction of Mothering* (1978) emphasized the oppositional relations between mothers and their children as central to human development. Where girls experience self-connection with mothers (or boundary confusion), boys experience separation and otherness (or boundary strengthening). Hartsock developed these oppositions into a distinction between concrete and abstract, in which the former is associated with a privatized, female material reality and the latter with the public world of masculinity. The material structuring of consciousness described by object-relations theory differentiates women from men in terms of the former's 'relationally defined existence', the 'bodily experience of boundary challenges' and the 'activity of transforming both physical objects and human beings'. Women, Hartsock argued, are less likely to view the world in dichotomous terms and more likely to value the concreteness of the everyday (see also Gilligan, 1982). In Hartsock's argument, the female body's sensory connections to the everyday, its capacity for change (through the boundary challenges associated with menstruation, pregnancy, lactation), its connection to the mother's body as the social entry point to the world are combined with an analysis of the labouring body to suggest a material foundation for unity between mental and manual labour, between natural and social worlds.

Though Hartsock's fusion of historical materialism with object-relations theory has been developed primarily within feminist epistemological debates as the basis for a feminist standpoint, the importance of bodily experience in this position is evident. She carefully avoided naturalizing bodily experiences by locating them within historical and material contexts. Though women's experiences may differ and are never self-evident, the task for feminism was to examine the 'common threads which connect the diverse experiences of women' and to search for the structural determinants of the experiences (1998: 159), or, in other words, to describe those experiences in order to explain them. What differentiates women's experiences from those of men, and here Hartsock joins company with O'Brien (and Gilligan, 1982), is that female experiences are characterized by concrete relations, while men's experiences are defined by abstraction. Thus defined, the knowledge produced through abstract relations at a particular historical juncture can be seen as partial knowledge. For Hartsock, a feminist standpoint characterized by women's 'experience of continuity and relation – with others, with the natural world, of mind and body' emerges from the contradiction between the structure of men's and women's experiences. Hence, like O'Brien, female embodiment provides a distinct ontology for Hartsock, but one that is structured by particular historical and material circumstances. She developed an account in order to transcend dualistic social relations that suggested how hierarchical dualisms shape epistemology and relegate women to lesser status. A feminist standpoint offered a means of revaluing women's experiences in terms of their connectedness and continuities with persons and with the natural world.

Hartsock successfully negotiated her way around women's bodily experiences as materially and historically contingent and developed through processes of (re)production. Moreover, her method allowed for scrutiny of the conditions that structure processes of social reproduction and privilege abstract knowledge over concrete forms of knowledge and, hence, subordinate women. Like other feminists, such as Sandra Harding, concerned with starting from the experiences of women as a way of beginning to think through and theorize subordination, Hartsock's work implicitly emphasized *embodiment* as crucial to the location of women in a specific relation to daily life that is shaped by material (embodied) knowledge and marked by connections with rather than distance from others. However, embodiment was defined through Chodorow's discussion of the relaxed ego boundaries between mothers and daughters, their capacity for connectedness and self-identification. However much imaginative appeal such a version of embodiment offers, locked into object-relations theory in this way reiterated a notion of male/female identities as core and stood for a state *prior to* alienation and thus, an embodied place from which women might re-understand community (Hartsock, 1985). Moreover, Hartsock's theory of social relations, and the historical materialism it represented, have been seen as over-privileging and universalizing (material) bodily processes unique to women in ways that view their meaning as self-evident and intelligible (Ebert, 1996).

However, while Hartsock's historical materialism may have little place in contemporary feminist theories of the body, it offers some fruitful directions for a sustained scrutiny of variation in meaning and bodily experience that has emerged from feminist anthropology, geography and sociology. While feminists have expressed concern at the biologism implied within historical materialism/object relations, Hartsock's scholarship is a reminder that that an individual's primary physical connection is with the body of a mother via the umbilical cord (Ian, 1993). Thus, the female body is undeniably the carnal entry point into the social world. However, the body of the (m)other is the absent body of current feminist theories of the body and it may be that far from dismissing object-relations theory, feminism needs to revisit the actual relationships between mothers and infants as a way of examining the links between the physical body, its social location and hierarchical divisions between women and men.

Experience

While the category of experience is evident in this work, as it is in some of the work outlined in Chapter 1, as a starting point for knowledge, feminists have been critical of the way in which it has the potential to reify individuals as prior to their production. Scott (1992), in particular, has argued that appeals to experience have the effect of obscuring the social, political and historical processes that create the effects of 'differentiation', constitute individuals and shape the ways in which they think of themselves *as* individuals (see also Ebert, 1996).

The – by now familiar – epistemological problem here concerns the way in which unmediated authenticity is attributed to the concept of experience in ways that conceal relations between the location of subjects to knowledge production (e.g. see Haraway, 1991) and preserve its contingent nature from inquiry (Scott, 1992). The problem for Scott in particular is that experience tends to be used by historical materialists as a unifying concept that valorizes one particular set of experiences (class) over another particular set (gender). Nonetheless, feminists have used the concept of experience to highlight a 'reality' distinct from that which is made visible in conventional academic accounts of, for instance, the social (Witz, 2000). Moreover, while experience cannot be presented as unproblematic, as accessible through observation and represented in the categories of mainstream academic discourse (Stanley and Wise, 1993), nonetheless for many feminists it remains a unifying term, often implicitly rooted in the 'body'.

Drawing on Foucault's invitation to the study of genealogies, Scott's analysis was a clear example of the emerging tendency within post-structuralist and postmodern feminisms to deconstruct the relationship between experience and knowledge and displace the presumption of authenticity within experience with practices that untangle how experience has come to be constituted as a foundational concept. However, as elsewhere in the feminist lexicon (namely, Butler), a genealogical approach that refuses any distinction between experience and language privileges language as the site of social and historical analysis, whereas Foucault can be sensibly read as advocating discourse as inclusive of social (as in material) practices that produce effects and constitute subjects.

Women's bodily experiences have been central to the ways in which women in sociology brought themselves into the discipline as feminists by emphasizing the significance of women's experience in relation to existing sociological problems (e.g. social production and reproduction). The incorporation of women's experience sought to highlight sociology's assumption of a universal subject and to force recognition of women's differential and subordinate position. Yet an analytic emphasis on experience need not be underpinned by a view of the body as a residual facticity and, indeed, a critical materialist analysis can demonstrate how modernity has shaped the collective experience of female embodiment and the stakes involved in such shaping. Indeed, a key contribution of the sociological optic has been to insist that the female body be acknowledged as socially mediated materiality rather than as an organic (and therefore mystified) basis for difference. Rather, the material (and implicitly, bodily) differences experienced by women are viewed as a product of social and economic process and structure. Feminist geographers have also been engaged in ways of developing the concept of experience – or embodiment – in non-reductive, contingent ways.

Bodies of geographical knowledge

The body has surfaced within feminist geography as a means of criticizing the way that the production of geographical knowledge privileges the conceptual over the corporeal (Longhurst, 1995: 97). The (female) body within geography has represented the discipline's 'other' and has been both 'denied and desired' (ibid.: 99). On the one hand, the female body has been obscured in what Rose (1993) terms 'time-geography', while, on the other, it has been developed within human geography through sustained engagement with Foucault's studies of particular social spaces (the prison, the school, the hospital), Maurice Merleau-Ponty's phenomenology of embodiment and Donna Haraway's insistence on the importance of situatedness. The predominant focus for current feminist geography is a consideration of how differently embodied subjectivities contribute to an understanding of spaces and places. The development of an embodied perspective is at the forefront of this work, which is both empirical and conceptual, and concerned with how places and spaces are experienced through the body in ways that shape and are shaped by subjectivies. In this respect, feminist geography shares much in common with materialist feminist sociologies concerned with women's experience of substantive issues and pays considerable attention to the *contexts* in which inscription practices occur and identities are formed.

Though feminist geographers have begun to develop conceptual frameworks for incorporating the body into the production of geographical knowledge, the body continues to be positioned as geography's 'other' through the reproduction of a distinction between sex and gender (Longhurst, 1995). The emphasis within feminist post-structuralist scholarship on embodiment is undoubtedly tactical, in that it explicitly challenges what is viewed as masculine knowledge production within the discipline of geography, and invites a definition of gender as a naturalized form of social difference. In this tactical move, *space* provides a means of talking about 'material contexts of oppression and resistance' and a way of establishing the 'grounds on which communities of resistance are to be constituted' (Nast and Pile, 1998: 412). This kind of work, then, not only shares a concern with correspondence between body and society (what happens to bodies cannot be separated from their material and social contexts) and with the nature of social relationships, but also explicitly retains a commitment to, if not social transformation, then at the very least, forms of resistance such as transgression and disruption. In this work, the concept of embodied subjectivity emphasizes the various processes through which bodies are discursively and materially shaped via visualizing (gazes) and inscription practices.

Historicizing the female body

> Nothing in man [*sic*] – not even his body – is sufficiently able to serve as a basis for self-recognition or for understanding other men. (Foucault, 1977: 153)

Perhaps nothing has shaped the shift away from a material conception of the body as defined through exploited and alienating biological and physiological processes more than the translation into English of the work of Michel Foucault. The body appeared as an emergent object of theoretical interest in feminist scholarship via scrutiny of biomedical discourses (Diprose, 1994), the stories biomedicine has told about the body and the gendering implicit in these stories (Birke, 1999). Historical scholarship, following Foucault, imbued the body with histories and re-instated the body into the discipline of history. Cultural historians and anthropologists in particular have focused on the various ways in which the body has been inscribed by images and metaphors and how changing representations of anatomy and biology have contributed to a differentiated and hierarchical conception of the human body. Examining the body's history became a way for feminist historians to appraise the relationship between gender and sex, by studying what have come to be seen as the various ways that biology has developed and is shaped by professional and patriarchal interests. Hence, the mutability of not only of gender but also of the human body has been the conclusion of this work, challenging any certainties about the body as a natural, stable, biological object, beyond intellectual scrutiny and the influence of the social and cultural (Schiebinger, 2000).

There is considerable convergence in feminist histories of the body on the claim that shifts in perception from the late eighteenth century (Armstrong, 1983), cultural practices and social relations were inscribed on the body and established it as the foundation of sex and gender (Laqueur,

1991). The consolidation of divisions between women and men, nature and culture occurred via the transformation in ideas about the position of women in public space. Though contemporary understandings of the human body have inherited these contrasts, feminist histories of the body invalidate absolute distinctions between male and female bodies and between sex and gender. They rebut claims about the natural inferiority of the material female body and demonstrate how practitioners located within social relations and contexts that *are already gendered* have interpreted the body. Hence, feminist historical scholarship places explanations of the sharpening of distinctions between the bodies of men and women in the context of political and social changes.

In particular, historical scholarship has demonstrated how scientific rationality and medico-legal constructs have contributed to the development of a range of dichotomies that associated the female body with nature. It has been argued by feminist scholars that the differentiation between the bodies of men and women which seemed so 'natural' to twentieth-century contemporary ways of thinking are the legacy of changes in modes of perception and thought in the period of the Enlightenment. Divisions emerged during this period between knowledge of the world based on sensory experience and knowledge derived from rational thought. The professional development of scientific medicine played a particular role in defining the body through the development of the clinical examination (Foucault, 1973), which established the body as a exclusive object which 'permits knowledge of life' (Benoist and Catheras, 1991). As Illich (1986) put it: 'We experienced a special moment of history when one agent, namely medicine, reached toward a monopoly over the social construction of bodily reality.'

Historical scholarship converges around the view that the Enlightenment produced new ways of thinking about the human body and introduced a conceptual separation between body and mind in which the latter was increasingly celebrated and knowledge associated with empirical – visual – observation. Moreover, as the mind became associated with masculinity and culture, the body became gradually associated with nature and femininity (Sydie, 1987). The period between the sixteenth and the end of the eighteenth centuries was characterized by rapid and extensive social change in relation to the nature of knowledge and the social position of women, as well as by broader shifts in the meaning of culture, nature and civil society. Jordanova (1989) argues that this period was one in which crucial dualisms were engendered which allocated women to the sphere of the natural and men to that of the cultural.

The practice of biomedicine was crucially significant in the process of establishing differences between the bodies of men and women in ways that contributed to the cultural subordination of women as a group (Jordanova, 1989). The meaning of the human body, including the sex assigned to it, was increasingly determined by the interpretations placed on it (Hood-Williams, 1996). For instance, there is some evidence that prior to the Enlightenment, practitioners and illustrators did not view the female body as radically different from the male body, nor was the female body evaluated in the negative terms associated with later nineteenth-century views (Lupton, 1994). Images and illustrations produced by anatomists during the Renaissance appear to represent the female body as a continuation or inverted homologue of the male body, rather than as completely distinct (Shildrick and Price, 1994). This seems to be clearest in early representations of reproductive anatomy, from which it is difficult for the modern, unpractised eye to distinguish male from female.

The work of Thomas Laqueur (1991) has been especially important in the development of feminist histories of the body. He notes that differentiation in the representation of the body and of reproductive anatomy in particular became especially marked after 1800, when illustrations began to emphasize anatomical and physiological differences between bodies. Furthermore, illustrations were accompanied by an increasing insistence in texts of the oppositional difference between the male and female body. The emerging practices of both pathology and anatomy helped to forge perceptual differences between the bodies of men and women. Pathology was based on the idea that the body could be made legible through clinical examination or that the truth of the body's interior could be revealed through signs evident and available to scrutiny on the surface of the body (Armstrong, 1983). Similarly, anatomy developed as a practice associated with dissecting the many surfaces and layers of the body, in order to identify and reveal nature (Stafford, 1991).

Illustrations and texts began to emphasize differences not only in anatomy but also in the shape and contours of the body. Moreover, analysis of nineteenth-century anatomy texts (Jordanova, 1989) reveals that the language used to describe the relation of science to the body is a language of exploration and colonialism. These texts depicted the female body as a territory to be mapped and as a secret to be unveiled. Thus science and sexuality have been historically linked in ways that reinforce a nature/culture dichotomy and there is evidence from contemporary sources that anatomy texts continue to represent the female body as distinctly different from the male body, as feeble, inferior and designed for the purpose of reproduction (Martin, 1989; Lawrence and Bendixen, 1992). In this way, the male body is constituted as a standard from which the female body deviates (Scully and Bart, 1978). Furthermore, the development of new technologies consolidated the female body as a body open to expert scrutiny. Such technologies included the development and widespread use of the speculum (Poovey, 1987), the expansion of women-only hospitals (Moscucci, 1990), the growth in surgical interventions which this facilitated (Daly, 1991), and the emergence of a mode of surveillance into which women were drawn as mothers and patients (Armstrong, 1983).

Feminist historical scholarship has also demonstrated how cultural ideas about gender inform the meanings attributed to anatomy and physiology and in particular, ascribe gender to anatomical parts and physiological processes (Oudshoorn, 1994). For instance, though anatomists were aware of the existence of the ovaries from the late seventeenth century, their role in hormone production was not fully understood until the twentieth century. Oudshoorn shows how ovaries were increasingly described as control centres in which hormones were isolated as especially important signallers of the essence of femininity. As she argues, the discovery of sex hormones was reworked into the 'two-sex' model described by Laqueur, which underpinned a view of men and women as not only anatomically distinct, but also morally and politically different. However, different body parts have been emphasized as symbols of femininity at different historical periods. While the uterus was a significant marker of femininity in the nineteenth century, and central to debates about women's social and political position, breasts were important in the eighteenth century as the embodiment of maternity and as symbols of nurturing (Jordanova, 1980).

Other examples from the world of anatomy reveal how social and political changes shaped the production of knowledge about the body and how the body was increasingly used as evidence to establish moral and social differences between men and women. Schiebinger's (1993) work on the skeleton, for instance, suggests that skeletal differentiation and differences in anatomical representation appeared at a historical point when women's social positions were being redefined. She notes that while illustrations of the human skull were relatively undifferentiated prior to the Enlightenment, by 1750, visual representations of the skull depicted marked differences in size between the male and female skull. Schiebinger attributes this to the responsiveness of anatomists and their illustrators to emerging anxieties about population growth in a context of demographic decline and a concern to promote reproduction as the proper role for women. As debates ensued about women's place in modernity, anatomists and other practitioners focused on body parts that differentiated the female body from the male body. In turn, these body parts came to stand for gender difference and to be used as the basis on which to make claims about female inferiority. Hence, emergent differences in the anatomical representation and skeletal modelling of the body were the product of changes in women's social and political position (Laqueur, 1991), and changing gendered assumptions that informed scientific accounts of 'nature'.

Feminists have used these histories to develop the point that a range of practices and discourses have habitually conceptualized and devalued the bodies of women as distinct and different from those of men, through normalizing and reiterating processes (e.g. Shildrick, 1997) that elevated the male body as norm. During the Enlightenment, knowledge of the world based on faith and superstition was at least partially – but crucially – replaced by knowledge based on empirical observation, especially for the newly emerging professional classes. Visual observation became the most secure means of knowing the world, replacing other ways of knowing and creating a division between a world amenable to knowing (nature) and a set of practices through which it might become known (culture). Moreover, femininity was increasingly associated with the former and with the body, men and masculinity with the latter and with the mind. Hence, historical scholarship has contributed to the claim that an interpretative shift in the perception and categorization of gender occurred, underpinned by socio-legal and political discourses. This shift framed knowledge production in relation to the female body, defining it as qualitatively distinct from the male body in terms not only of anatomy, but also of physiology and psychology, in ways that had profound implications for women's citizenship.

In summary, much of this scholarship typifies the prevailing view of the body within the social sciences and humanities. While the body is taken for granted as a universal condition, unchanging across time, the relation between the physical and social body has been historically and socially shaped in various ways. Synott (1993) uses the notion of 'somatization' to draw attention to the ways in which metaphor 'distorts our understanding of the physical body' (ibid.: 19). That is, the body's parts and functions are used to describe the world in which we live and impose a physicality upon organizations, objects, institutions that suggests a naturalness and inevitability. Other scholarship (e.g. Scheper-Hughes and Lock, 1987) provides an excellent summary of the deeply implicated relationship between body and society and the mediation of this relation via image and metaphor. Such a claim draws on Douglas's (1970) view that the body should be seen as a natural symbol, a resource common to all in which understandings of the body are dialectically shaped via social relations and cultural practices and vice versa. Hence, as the work of feminist historians insists, 'natural' categories have social histories.

As Schiebinger (2000) notes, the central issue now for feminist historians of the body is that of working through what she terms the 'difference dilemma'. This refers to the tension between emphasizing differences and thus, reinforcing them, and minimizing differences in ways that fail to challenge how they are sustained by power relations and structures. Yet feminists face other dilemmas concerned with how to balance historically changing representations of the body with contemporary experiences of embodiment. This dilemma has influenced a range of approaches to the ways that changing representations of anatomy and physiology have contributed to a differentiated and hierarchical conception of the human body and how these representations shape contemporary understandings and experiences of embodiment. In their different ways, these approaches seek to work through dualisms *between* the body (as an ontologically distinct material object) and embodiment (as a set of experiences at once shaped by though not reducible to, image, metaphor and discourse).

Changing concepts of materiality: image and metaphor

By the late 1980s, emerging postmodern social critique was beginning to make its intellectual mark on feminist scholarship. This later became most evident, as the chapter suggests, in the historical studies of sex and gender undertaken by cultural historians (outlined above) and cultural anthropology. While Foucault's work was palpably significant in unsettling the meanings and moorings of materiality/materialism for historians, the idea of the indivisibility of objects and ideas impelled by aesthetic modernity and latterly manifest in French post-structuralism has been more influential in feminist and cultural anthropology. In particular, the direction of feminist (cultural) anthropology has been influenced by considerations of the relationship between the phenomenally experienced body, the social body and the body politic (e.g. Crawford, 1984, 1994; Scheper-Hughes and Lock, 1987) derived from the semiotic and symbolic anthropology of body movements in the 1970s (Jackson, 1986). These considerations have largely played out in scholarship concerning the relationship between experience and representation that attempts to link concepts of self/body with representations of social, cultural and political contexts. Such scholarship, while privileging the relationship between the experiences associated with female embodiment and imagery through which it is shaped, foregrounds the interruption instituted by Derrida's claim that there is no-thing-in-itself that can escape representation by signs and no thing beyond the text.

As Chapter 1 noted, the human body has been a more explicit focus for anthropology than for other disciplines in both conceptual and empirical terms. While anthropological scholarship has more recently developed Merleau-Ponty's (1962) argument that consciousness is based on praxis rather than on thought and thinking (Jackson, 1986; Csordas, 1990) and generated inventories of body styles, techniques and practices, and of which the published work of Mauss (1973 [1934]) is the most frequently cited (though see also Polhemus, 1978), the work of Mary Douglas (1970) in particular has been vital in establishing the conceptual groundwork for viewing the body as a symbolic resource through which the body politic and social body are represented (Scheper-Hughes and Lock, 1987). Her work has underpinned feminist analysis of the perceived instability of the female body and its role in sustaining cosmologies through pollution taboos (e.g. Gottlieb and Buckley, 1988; Laws, 1990; Thurren, 1994). The emergence of pollution taboos, by invoking the disgust function (Elias, 1994), are themselves a consequence of and help to preserve the individualization of the body in Western culture and reinforce a sensitivity to boundaries between one's own body and the bodies of others.

Where feminist sociology has been interested in the material significance of the body in relation to knowledge, experience and agency, feminist anthropological scholarship has focused on how representations of the body are tied to material relations and forms of social organization (Harvey, 1998) through substantive studies that are concerned with a range of experiences from menstruation (Thurren, 1994) to breast feeding (Murcott, 1993). Through this work, feminist anthropology has begun to tackle issues around cross-cultural variations in sex differences and challenge the 'foundationalism of western biological categories' (Harvey, 1998: 79). This scholarship addresses both the varying meanings attached to sex and how these inform cultural understandings of gender and, similar to the feminist histories outlined above, addresses the contribution that material attributes and characteristics make to the symbolic meanings attached to gender (e.g. Moore, 1994). Emily Martin, an anthropologist whose concern with embodiment is marked by its focus on embodied experience, has made an important contribution in this regard. Her focus is resolutely on experiences unique to women by virtue of their embodiment, developed through scrutiny of cultural variations in such experiences. Her approach has been dialectical in an attempt to examine the significance of visual and literary representations to embodied experiences such as pregnancy and menstruation, the ways in which meanings are made intelligible and mediated via social arrangements and the structure of the symbolic order. Particular forms of social organization shape representations for Martin, and in this way her work attempts to retain a relation between the materiality of the body (experience) and the materially produced basis of representations about the body.

The Woman in the Body argues that biomedical discourses provide a scientized account of female embodiment that is informed by industrial capitalist modes of social organization and is expressed through an emphasis on reproduction. Drawing on existing anthropological scholarship on the significance of language – specifically metaphor – for organizing human experience (Lakoff and Johnson, 1980) and on the emergent, phenomenologically inflected concept of embodiment (Csordas, 1990), her general thesis is that as forms of social organization vary, so too do scientific images and explanations of biology. Science is responsive to changes in forms of social organization because its practitioners are part of a social and cultural elite. In other work (1990, 1992) Martin emphasizes how scientific images and depictions enter into public consciousness via a range of routes and shape embodied experience. The media is especially important in this respect, and like Susan Bordo, the data Martin analyzes are drawn from widely accessible sources such as newspapers and popular magazines.

For Martin, reproductive imagery and discourse illustrate the centrality of the Fordist production metaphor for ordering and categorizing the body, and representing a system of production that so pervades all domains of life such that it is 'internalized' as a mode not only of production but also of living. Martin (1984) illustrates how women in industrial capitalist societies routinely separate self from body in the context of the very experiences which are supposed to define them as women, for instance, their capacity for pregnancy and childbirth. On the one hand, she argues that pregnancy has been 'captured' from women by a medicalized management that serves to alienate women from their bodies. On the other, while arguing for the importance of creating experiences and contexts that help to reconnect mind and body, it becomes difficult to avoid a nostalgic gloss on pregnancy and labour as a pre-cultural form of experience which is tampered with by modern, industrial culture. The body, in anthropological conceptions, may be subject to social and cultural constitution and representation but also lies *beyond the social*. This implicit yearning for a pre-social experience of self (as an embodied self), typical of the work of other anthropologists such as Csordas (1990), may be seen by some feminists as placing limits on the value of Martin's work for addressing the significance of the body to the relationship between sex and gender.

Conclusion

This chapter has argued that while feminist interventions from the 1970s to mid-1980s admitted the body by paying attention to a range of bodily experiences, especially in relation to health and health care, this attention was masked by the intensity of debates concerning historical/feminist materialism which typically displaced bodily materiality with social materiality. The publication of Foucault's work and the influences of symbolic and semiotic anthropology (Douglas) reintroduced concerns about the body to feminism via considerations of its historically contingent and culturally variable construction. Subsequently, feminist sociology has begun to acknowledge the limits of the sex/gender distinction (Delphy, 1993; Lorber, 1994; Hood-Williams, 1996) and work towards a sociological account of gender that improves upon the dualisms inherent within this distinction and incorporates sensitivity to the body.

Yet feminist scholarship that is commendably focused on the cultural and social significance of the human body, and of female embodiment in particular, nonetheless foreshadows an overly discursive approach to analysis of the body by privileging visual and textual representations. While feminism has struggled to avoid the Hegelian impulses that institute the body as an abstract universal stripped of its concrete particularities and empirical content, as Chapter 3 observes, the increasing emphasis in feminist scholarship on imagery, representation and a linguistic notion of discourse has resulted in a process of dematerialization in which the female body has become feminist theory's 'other'.

Note

1 There were non-feminist conceptions of gender such as Parson's structural-functionalism.

three

Imag(in)ery, representation and subjectivity

Introduction

Chapter 2 began the process of tracing the development of body concepts in feminism from radical feminist politics through debates concerning the sex/gender distinction, and from historical materialism to representational analyses that foreshadowed the collapsed distinctions between matter and representation so evident in (some) Foucauldian, phenomenological and psychoanalytical feminist theories of the body. This chapter picks up on threads of feminist scholarship that unpick the sex/gender distinction in order to rethink relations between not only subject/object, but also cultural/material and in particular, between language and matter. First, the chapter examines the influence of Foucault on feminist attempts to rethink power/knowledge and body/subject. This is followed by a discussion of the influence of phenomenology in the work of Iris Young and her efforts to establish the grounds on which a specific feminine subjectivity is constructed and its consequences for women. Finally, the chapter examines attempts to construct a specifically feminist ethics via a sustained engagement with social theories that offer some potential for grounding such ethics in embodied specificities. The chapter shows how feminist interventions in ethics that begin by drawing on arguments associated with Foucault and Merleau-Ponty begin to move more explicitly towards a post-Lacanian psychoanalytic framework that privileges the imaginary over imagery, and textual tactics over social practices.

Foucault, discipline and docility: foregrounding corporeality

While notions of pre-social embodiment uncomfortably hover at the margins of some feminist scholarship concerning the embodiment of gender, Foucault developed a critique of the self-conscious subject of history through specific studies of madness, sexuality, medicine and penality, that, *inter alia*, foregrounded the body. His concern was largely with how the human body becomes subject to new forms of power that emanate not (exclusively) from the state but are embedded within the micro-practices of everyday life. While he developed an analysis of the female body that differed considerably from post-Freudian psychoanalytic theories of sexual identity, and although he identified the hysterization of the female body as a key marker of the development of modern society based on discipline and surveillance, his work has been criticized for failing to fully acknowledge gendered embodiment and difference (Bell, 1993). Nonetheless, feminists have developed many of his observations about the nature of modern power to analyse the female body and demonstrate the ways in which the human body is constituted as a gendered body (Ramazanoglu, 1993).

Foucault was critical of historical accounts that define rational knowledge as a progressive, continuous liberal force and instead, accentuated discontinuities in the development of knowledge. His methodology defined discourse as 'practices that systematically form the objects of which they speak' (1972: 48) and he challenged the empirical basis of modern knowledge, including that of the body. Both *Discipline and Punish* (1979) and *The Birth of the Clinic* (1973) emphasize the constitution of bodies via disciplinary practices that represent the 'materiality of power operating on the very bodies of individuals' (Foucault, in Gordon, 1980: 55). Feminists have used this approach to examine the creation of new knowledge and orthodoxies about the body and in particular, the female body's implication in the social constitution of femininity (Bartky, 1990; Smith, 1990).

Of particular interest to feminists is Foucault's model of power and his claim that repression acquires an exaggerated role in other models of power. Power for Foucault is not a force held by subjects that can be used to exclude, block or censor. Nor is power centrally held, co-ordinated or exercised by one group or individual over another, nor is it embodied in the rule of law (Smart, 1990). Rather, power produces effects in terms of both desire and knowledge. Moreover, power and knowledge are bound together in ways that ensure the exercise of the former produces the latter. This conceptual synthesis encourages a detailed focus on practices or, as Foucault puts it, the 'meticulous observation of detail' (1979: 141) and their location within discourse.

In addition, Foucault was highly critical of liberal, humanist models of the subject and he argued that a model of the subject as an autonomous individual has itself been discursively constituted. Feminists have taken up this view of the subject in order to criticize the persistence of Cartesian dualism in accounts of the subject, and its relegation of femininity to the body and to nature (Hekman, 1992). Moreover, feminists, joining company with others, have been interested in Foucault's critique of Althusser and the latter's account of ideology. The concept of ideology is directed primarily towards minds rather than bodies, and has been used by feminists to explain how 'power "conditions" the mind' (Gatens, 1996: 66). Foucault, in contrast, provides a way of thinking beyond a threshold of consciousness that foregrounds a body that is socially and historically constituted through the effects of power.

While Foucault himself offers a caution to those who appeal to the body as a source of authenticity and warns against viewing the body as the basis of self, the focus of his work on the body has been especially seductive for feminists who have found his emphasis on materiality and the *local* production of knowledge useful. In particular, the concept of disciplinary power has provided a means of identifying the specifically differentiated ways that female bodies are marked out and empowered to perform particular tasks (Gatens, 1992). Power produces the particular forms of embodiment that social organization requires (Lowe, 1995) and as Singer (1994) notes, the modern body is well managed and made useful in a variety of gendered ways.

Embedded within Foucault's emphasis on disciplinary technologies is a focus on agency and resistance, which has been substantively developed within feminism in relation to subjectivity and sexuality. First, feminists have developed insights into the self-regulatory forms of power that objectify the female body and have examined disciplinary mechanisms through which female subjectivity is constituted. For instance, Bartky (1988) claims that myriad forms of advice (disciplinary technologies) subjugate women by instilling competencies rather than subordinating experiences. Hence, though the female body is subject to regulatory processes, it is also, in a Foucauldian view of power/knowledge that insists on its productive character, the site of women's endeavours for empowerment. Examples concerning the control of body shape and size have been especially clear on this point.

Susan Bordo (1989, 1992, 1993) has produced a genealogy of the ways the female body is culturally constructed and how contemporary feminist notions of eating disorders uphold a view of them as deviant. Drawing on a cultural analysis of advertisements, conversations and dietary advice, she observes that while most women engage in 'body work' of one sort or another, such as exercise, or 'watching' what they eat, women are encouraged to discipline their bodies in ways that have the potential to restrict and confine their social and political participation. In *Unbearable Weight* (1993) Bordo documents a variation in ideals associated with women's size and shape and places such ideals in the context of changes in women's social, economic and political position. For instance, the nineteenth-century hourglass figure was promoted by corsets, which restricted breathing, digestion, circulation and movement. The hourglass figure lingered into the matronly curves of the 1950s but was rejected and replaced by the more androgynous figure of the late twentieth century – long-legged, small-breasted, with a slender silhouette. As women have moved into the public sphere in the context of paid work and other forms of public participation and visibility, the thin body – a body that takes up less physical space – has been internalized as the current Western ideal.

Female protest is often channelled through the body and Bordo

(1993) argues that the anorexic body can be seen both as a protesting body and as an embodiment of modern consumer culture. The pursuit of slenderness, by making the body smaller, appears to conform to idealizations of contemporary feminine appearance. The anorexic body takes up less physical space, loses the curves associated with the hourglass version of the female form, controls hunger and suppresses desire. However, the anorexic body also denies those cultural stereotypes associated with contemporary femininity, such as weakness, precisely because the pursuit of slenderness requires obedience and self-discipline. Eating and menstrual disorders among women, from hysteria to bulimia, represent embodied responses to the experience of social exclusion and the various ways modern capitalist societies encourage women to nurture others at their own expense (Radley, 1995). MacSween (1993) notes how anorexia in particular is accompanied by a sense of revulsion towards one's own body and consists of cultural contradictions about contemporary femininity. The expurgation of the body through control of food intake captures the contradictions associated with obedience to social injunctions to pursue slenderness (and the docility this produces) and the forms of protest or resistance available to women.

Though diet and exercise regimes need to be seen as practices that train the body in 'docility', they are contradictory in that they are experienced as empowering practices that enable women to feel they are in control and have control over their own bodies and lives. Management of the female body is a dominant theme in Foucauldian analysis of other practices that embody gender such as female bodybuilding, which exemplifies discipline of the body via both rigorous physical training and a regime of femininity (Mansfield and McGinn, 1993). Though female bodybuilding is perhaps a more exaggerated example of the self-discipline to which Bordo refers, it nonetheless demonstrates the fragility of the boundary between self-empowerment and containment.

Central to Bordo's approach is an awareness of agency and its relation to docility, and much of her work can be seen as a way of explaining the significance of the body to both. A similar privilege is accorded agency in Davis's study of women's use of cosmetic surgery. Both Bordo and Davis locate cosmetic surgery within a broader set of shifts in Western culture, as testimony to the body's increasing malleability (Shilling, 2003), and highlight the contradiction inherent within such practices. On the one hand, cosmetic surgery is presented to women within a discourse of neoliberal choice as a means through which to fashion their bodies in ways that will make them happier. On the other, cosmetic surgery and other modification practices mask the ongoing disciplinary regime that has power over women's bodies by normalizing an idealized, imaginary and racialized (hooks, 1992; Kaw, 2003) female body. Such scholarship highlights how body modification practices position and reaffirm women as consumers of signs and images 'written' on the body – part of a more general trend in Western culture in which all are encouraged to consume (Falk, 1994). Davis, in particular, has listened carefully to women as they articulate their experiences and the discourses that frame such experience. While the narratives told to Davis acknowledge the morally dubious status of cosmetic surgery, they also represent modern heroic tales and appeal to a 'phantom natural body' (Brush, 1998) in which embodiment and narrative are inherently connected (see Young, 1989). Yet, while women make choices about body modification, the homogenizing and disciplining discourses through which modification possibilities are constituted, constrain their choices.

Acknowledging this circularity, feminists have further developed a Foucauldian framework through which to analyze women's complicity with and resistance to the active constitution of embodied subjectivity. Through research undertaken to examine young women's negotiation of sexual encounters in the context of sex education and AIDS, Holland and her colleagues (Holland et al., 1990a; Holland et al., 1990b; Holland et al., 1992; Holland et al., 1994a; Holland et al., 1994a, 1994b) have developed a post-Foucauldian model of power, pleasure, risk and trust. This model attempts to affiliate the relations, powers and forces that shape particular heterosexual experiences with how young women negotiate and interpret their interactions and sense of self within those relations. Their analysis of interview material with young women supports the claim that the female body is constantly under male scrutiny of one sort or another (from health examinations to pornography) and that this monitoring is interiorized in ways that produce gendered subjectivities.

Their analysis supports the notion of an imaginary body that is linked to the constitution of the material body and material practices. In the context of negotiating heterosexual encounters, young women appear to experience a degree of alienation from their own bodies, while they strive to achieve and publicly present a body that meets the expectations of their peers and young men. There are evident tensions in young women's accounts between lived bodily experiences and the presentation of the body in sexual encounters in which the former is at times denied in favour of the latter. As Holland et al. observe, (1992) the imaginary body that contributes to the social constitution of embodied subjectivity and organizes women's perceptions of their own bodies is dominated by the norms of male heterosexual desire. This analysis implicitly draws on the notion of a *male gaze*, which has increasingly been invoked within feminism as a disciplinary technique shaping women's perception of self. Its original meaning is derived from post-Lacanian psychoanalytic terms and was developed in Laura Mulvey's (1975) influential contribution 'Visual pleasure and narrative cinema'. Its current use has taken on a more Foucauldian inflection and refers to a gaze as a collective endeavour that produces an imaginary body that informs the constitution of embodied subjectivity in accordance with male heterosexual norms. Consequently, the body's materiality has to be managed and contained in sexual encounters in ways that conceal its noises, discharges, and hair and presented as a civilized body. These norms effect a contradiction between images of idealized femininity and the materiality of lived embodiment such that the latter is subordinated in favour of the former in ways that compromise not only the potential for sexual pleasure but also jeopardize the potential for safer sex.

While the Foucauldian optic has been especially productive for feminism and provided a framework for addressing particular substantive areas such as sexuality, body modification and health, as Chapter 1 observed, it nonetheless offers a unsatisfactory model of power for many feminists. For instance, not only does Foucault short-circuit any consideration of ethnicity in his attention to European bourgeois discourses (Spivak, 1988) but also his emphasis on discourses of sexuality has the potential to exclude consideration of other equally powerful discourses such as class (Skeggs, 1997). In particular, the Foucauldian concept of discourse has been generally read within feminism as characterized by language and text rather than by social practices. This has led some feminists to circumscribe Foucault as a post-structuralist theorist and accuse his work of being as reductionist as the Marxist theory he criticizes (Ebert, 1996). What is seen here as reductionism in Foucault is the reduction of the social to talk and text; the reduction of matter to the biological body; and an overemphasis on the local production of knowledges (discourses). Moreover, it is seen as a reductionism that displaces the transformative politics of feminism with a focus on local resistances through the body, embodied subjectivity and ethical practice.

Feminism and phenomenology: embodied subjectivity

Feminist philosophers have begun to develop accounts of how the 'lived body' is gendered in order to initiate a phenomenologically inflected feminist concept of embodied subjectivity. Notably, Iris Young (1990) draws on Merleau-Ponty's rebuttal of a Cartesian conceptualization of the relationship between mind and body and its concomitant understanding of perception as an 'inner representation of an outer world of given objects' (Crossley, 1995b: 46). In contrast to the Cartesian view of self, Merleau-Ponty asserts that mind and body are not separate entities, and that their articulation is fundamental as a state of being that precedes objectivity (Diprose, 1994). Perception is always located in and through the space of the lived body and the material body is an integral dimension of the perceiving subject (Csordas, 1990). Following this argument, we do not reflect on our own bodies or the bodies of others as objects *a priori*, but live our bodies as our selves. However, the lived body/self can become an object for self and others (Crossley, 1995b) through various processes and events that create phenomenological disruption, such as interactional betrayals (Goffman, 1972), injury or sickness (Leder, 1990). Hence, Merleau-Ponty's philosophy of embodiment asserts that self is projected in and through action and that awareness of one's own body as an object emerges as a form of alienation.

However, Young (1990) challenges the universal account of the neutral body suggested by Merleau-Ponty, and asserts that gendered modalities are partial, inhibited and ambiguous, reactive rather than proactive, and discontinuous in their engagement with the world around them rather than continuous. The female body is not necessarily experienced as in direct communication with self, as an active expression of self, but as an object, a thing. Young notes that studies in the use of space demonstrate differences between men and women and suggest a distinctly feminine style of comportment and movement. On average, women walk with a shorter stride than men; hold their arms close to their bodies; avoid meeting the gaze of others in public spaces (particularly men); use their arms to shield themselves and protect themselves; and draw back from objects thrown to them rather than reach out to receive them. For Young, there are two possible explanations for this 'modality'.

First, drawing on de Beauvoir, women are not born but are taught to become feminine in ways that emphasize containment and control. Young theorizes that the restricted space in which women operate and the closed body characteristic of feminine comportment and movement signifies an imaginary space that confines women. She suggests that women are inhibited by lack of confidence about their bodies, which comes from under-use and differences in the relative exposure of boys and girls to physical play and activity. Second, women are encouraged to become more aware of themselves as 'objects' of others' scrutiny. In public spaces where the female body is potentially transgressive, the 'male gaze' (Mulvey, 1975) operates as a disciplining mechanism that encourages docility. Awareness of being watched and of seeing oneself as an object has the potential to shape how women move through and engage with the physical environment and reinforce an objectified consciousness. As Diprose puts it, 'consciousness is the process of making one's body an object for oneself in response to being objectified by others' (1996: 44) and is thus, rooted in corporeality. Corporeality here, for Diprose, relies on a Hegelian notion of 'sensation' formed through reciprocal interaction between the individual and the community. However, in contrast to Hegel's view that for the self and other to 'meet in unity' the body has to 'disappear', both Diprose and Young favour traditions of the self that collapse boundaries between knowledge and being (phenomenology), privilege contextual and relational models of self (discourse) and emphasize the ambiguities inherent within self-formation (psychoanalysis).

The sense of physical space and body use that accompanies feminine modalities represents a shared vocabulary of body idiom – the term 'body idiom' belongs to Goffman (1963) and though it is not used by Young, it is an apt way of referring to what she has in mind – which reinforces gender distinctions. Modalities (or body idiom) arise via objectification and are consolidated as habit. Habit here is used to refer to practices and acts that are performed repetitiously and give rise to sensations and feelings that are expressed physically (such as the smile). Though such a definition clearly resonates with Butler's notion of performativity, it also has affinities with Bourdieu's concept of habitus and shared bodily dispositions. Critically these dispositions and the self-objectification that arises from a culture in which women in particular are made aware of themselves as objects in ways that develop a persistent self-consciousness and contribute to a sense of alienation from self, hold the potential for not only physical but also social disempowerment and limited agency (Crossley, 2001). Hence, the body is reified as gendered via processes of self-reflection (taking on the gaze of the other) through which women become objects not only for others but also for themselves. Consequently, the body is lived as gendered via processes that limit the physical capacities of women in ways that have consequences for their capacity as agents to act upon the world.

Yet Young acknowledges that this line of argument presupposes femininity as 'liability' in ways that reinforce masculine modalities as the 'norm'. Furthermore, she suggests there are aspects to female embodiment that are pleasurable and premised on 'movement and energy' rather than on 'thingness'. In particular, her account of the experience of and assumptions surrounding pregnancy challenges philosophical claims concerning the way the body impinges on self only in contexts of pain and 'dysruption' (Leder, 1990). In contrast, Young argues that self-awareness of the pregnant body is not necessarily an awareness of the body as an uncomfortable object from which one is alienated but an awareness of continuity with life and change, pleasure and growth. Moreover, the disruption is not necessarily spatial rather it is temporal. Self-reflection is itself a retrospective process which 'necessarily precludes the immediate present' and involves the 'I' 'looking back' at the 'historical image' of ourselves associated with the 'me' as a 'representation of myself', as a 'mirror image' or 'kind of narrative history' (Crossley, 2001: 147–8).

In Young's view, the relocation of the body in time and space effected by pregnancy offers a distinct challenge to philosophical assumptions concerning boundaries between mind/body, transcendence/immanence and self/other (Brook, 1999) and contributes to an expansion of the borders of the self. Yet her claim need not efface the alienating capacities of technological (medical) interventions as other phenomenological treatments of pregnancy (Marshall, 1996) and health-related experiences (such as cervical screening participation (Howson, 2001b)) suggest. The distinct contribution Young's intervention and critique makes is her insistence that feminist scrutiny of female embodiment needs to begin from women's lived bodily experience in ways that treat experience as materiality and acknowledge women's own understandings of their experience.

Nevertheless, as Scarry (1985) observes in her study of pain and torture, while 'what is "remembered" in the body is well remembered', such experiences may not necessarily be amenable to translation into language in general and analytic languages in particular, therefore there may be a profound disjunction between experience and its cognitive apprehension by self and others. Western culture privileges talk and text as legitimate forms of communication, yet there may be no words or language to name and communicate certain forms of experience, particularly physical sensation and its contribution to subjectivity.

Ethical bodies: Rosalyn Diprose

The previous discussion focuses on particular kinds of practice implicated in the social constitution of subjectivity, the boundaries between docility and resistance and the potential for a phenomenologically inflected notion of embodied subjectivity in considering ways to embody gender. This section concerns feminist scholarship that is focused on a notion of ethics initially derived from Foucauldian notions of embodiment in contrast to conventional abstract notions of ethics that rely on the disembodied, rational individual. The work of Rosalyn Diprose, Margrit Shildrick and Moira Gatens has contributed to an account of the relationship between the worlds one occupies and one's embodied character or habitual way of life by developing the claim that practices and discourses socially constitute embodiment. Foucault's later work has been especially relevant here, particularly his interest in developing an account of ethics that moves beyond the disciplinary framework of earlier work.

Foucault (1988) defines ethos as a manner of being and ethics as techniques of self, where the former has four components: (1) ethical substance; (2) relation to the moral code; (3) self-forming activity; and (4) the goal of this activity. Ethical substance for Foucault is corporeal (by which he means the physical body) and techniques of self are either normalizing or aesthetic, 'depending on one's relation to the disciplinary moral code'. The relation to the moral code elaborated in *Discipline and Punish* is self-subjection via disciplinary techniques through which one comes to monitor one's own performance as though one were being watched. This is the interpretation of Foucault evident in the work outlined above by Bordo and Bartky. In later work, Foucault develops this claim with greater sensitivity to the constitutive *relation* between ethical substance (one's body), moral code (social context) and the techniques of self that mediate between them.

Despite Diprose's insistence on the power of discourse to constitute embodied ethos, she does not foreclose the *possibility* of specifically located ethical resistance. The key issue for Diprose is the development of an ethical framework that starts from and takes account of location, place and position in contrast to what she views as a model of ethics based on disembodied notions of principle and judgement. Her definition of ethics is based on a reconsideration of its roots in the Greek word *ethos*, which refers to dwelling or habitat and was used in its original sense as both a noun (the place to which one returns) and a verb (the practice of dwelling), which both contribute to character or specificity. Ethos is not given, it is 'constituted through the repetition of bodily acts the character of which are governed by the habitat I occupy' (1994: 19). Therefore, ethics is connected to 'one's embodied place in the world'.

Concepts of the body in contract law are unable adequately to address 'specific modes of embodiment' (ibid.: 3) and privilege a disembodied self that implies a degree of ownership over the body (Brown and Adams, 1979). This model of property relations to one's body underpins prevailing notions of autonomy but cannot account for changes in one's body across time such as that suggested by phenomenological accounts of the experience of pregnancy (Marshall, 1994). Drawing on Carole Pateman's work, Diprose notes how the social contract assumes a disembodied individual agent, which in practice is male. Women are assumed to be deficient in the rationality required to enter into contract, and are indeed presumed to be property. The terms of the sexual contract effectively 'gives men the right of access to women's bodies' (1994: 6). Hence the rights of access which women now have to civil, economic and political participation are based on a model of contract that denies the specificities of female embodiment. Liberal feminist notions of a 'conscious agent' have viewed access to such rights as separable and distinguishable from the body on the grounds that explicit acknowledgement of female embodiment (or specificity) may circumscribe women's participation.

Hence, the price feminists have paid for upholding the notion of contract as a model of social relations has been the way it obscures the specificities of female embodiment (see also Singer, 1994). Yet though feminist correctives to the disembodied individual agent of contract theory emphasize the importance of integrating sexual difference and embodied modes of being to models of agency, nonetheless, in Diprose's view, the nature of these are assumed. Moreover, though some feminists have emphasized that the exercise of choice and rationality is shaped by social relations and context, they do not explain 'how the significance of the body becomes the ground for exclusion from social exchange' (1994: 14). Hence, Diprose accuses feminist ethical argument of a tension between the claim that the self is an embodied self, developed in and through specific social relations and contexts and the perpetuation of a 'self-present disembodied individualism'. The implication of this claim is that the specificities of female embodiment are shaped in and through social relations that are patriarchal. This undercuts any potential for the assertion of female embodiment shaped through non-patriarchal relations and contexts.

Diprose is persuaded by Foucault's claim concerning shifts in the form of power in modern bureaucratic states and emphasis on its productive nature. This shift is most clearly seen in his analysis of biopolitics in which new knowledges (for instance, sociology, psychology and education) intersected with and contributed to new political interests concerning healthy populations. There is a vast body of work detailing and elaborating Foucault's analysis of biopolitics; its impact on the family (Donzelot, 1980); the development of disciplines, agencies and knowledges (Hewitt, 1983); and practices of surveillance that have established the body as open to public scrutiny through supervision, data collection and sanctions (Armstrong, 1983, Nettleton, 1992). On the whole, feminist theory does not engage with this literature. Nonetheless, Diprose claims that the kind of body established as the target for surveillance was the reproductive body (though biomedical surveillance has targeted the female body in a range of non-reproductive ways, Howson, 1998). She argues that an expanded investment in the surveillance of mothers, their child-care practices and children themselves (see also Donzelot, 1980; Turner, 1987; Armstrong, 1995) defined the maternal body in the new, emerging public order as the 'site of the reproduction of the social body' (1994: 26). However, though the pregnant body is endlessly monitored, 'it does not get absorbed into the labour market it reproduces' (ibid.). Hence for Diprose, in the expanded surveillance of the reproductive body, the differential treatment of women is established.

However, the surveillance practices to which Diprose refers do not become entrenched forms of monitoring in Scandinavia and the Anglo-American world until the post-war period as part of a more concerted attention to disease prevention in the Anglophile world (Stone, 1986; de Swaan, 1990) in which social medicine and public health were supported by the state in policing a moral and social order (Wear, 1992). Moreover, the expanded surveillance of women and children is part of a more general expansion of welfare citizenship, which cannot wholly be seen as excluding the specificities of female embodiment. Disease prevention practices (ante-natal screening, child monitoring) – or surveillance – were part of a package of reforms that symbolized a collective good by embodying a notion of social citizenship (Freeman, 1992) as well as social control (Lewis, 1986). They emerged in welfare states that operated, in the post-war period, with a model of social citizenship (Marshall, 1963), which, while uneven in its development (Mann, 1987), nonetheless established a 'feminized' project in which the principle of care was implicitly embedded (Holmwood, 1993).

Moreover, women have been instrumental in the development of welfare states (Wilson, 1977) and the surveillance practices it generated, not necessarily as 'power brokers' (Hernes, 1987) but as workers and lobbyists. Women were differentially marked out within and through the prevention practices that form the kinds of surveillance identified by Diprose, as mothers and guardians (Graham, 1979; Nettleton, 1992), as paid and unpaid carers (Gamarnikow, 1978; Finch and Groves, 1983) and as 'watchers' over themselves and others (Stacey, 1988). Hence, though the experience of being welfare citizens may be different and contradictory for women (Marshall, 1994), nonetheless welfare states have provided a material basis for citizenship for women (Walby, 1995) which, contrary to Diprose's claims, did in fact contribute to the absorption of women (the reproductive body) into the (poorly paid, low status, public sector) labour market via maternity pay and benefits. Thus, some acknowledgement of the complexity of surveillance in welfare contexts is important in relation to Diprose's subsequent argument concerning discourse.

Following Foucault, Diprose argues that there cannot be subjectivity outside the discourses that constitute it, nor can there be modes of embodiment beyond the meanings and values assigned to them in discourse. In contrast to perspectives that draw distinctions or gaps between body metaphors and lived experience, Diprose asserts that such a distinction is itself discursively constituted. She uses her characterization of the surveillance of the maternal/reproductive body to argue that the embodied ethos of the pregnant body is produced through normalizing practices that ensure its public scrutiny and the healthy reproduction of the social body. As others have argued concerning neo-liberal citizenship (especially Rose, 1990), health in general is viewed as a positive goal in which people invest through complicity in practices that subject them to surveillance and differentiation.

Embodied ethos represents an orientation towards achieving the goals of 'healthy pregnancy' – there can be no ethos outside this context. Diprose emphasizes that power relations operate on the material body in ways that do not rely on conscious knowledge: we can be subjected thoroughly (to a discourse of healthy pregnancy) and not realize it and orient our actions and practices towards achieving the goals articulated within such a discourse. Hence, within this view, there can be no alternative consciousness or mode of being that lie outside subjection. In particular, differentiated embodiment cannot be the source of new modes of subjectivity because the body is the target of subjection. In short, difference is constituted in relation to the female body through discourses and practices and there can be no basis for difference other than that constituted in discourse. However, as I have already pointed out, surveillance discourses, of which the discourse of health pregnancy is surely part, are themselves complex. They are not seamless webs of power and practice in which women are positioned in undifferentiated ways. Women may welcome the monitoring that attends the surveillance of the reproductive body through their subjection to neo-liberal discourses that emphasize choice, individualism and conscious knowledge. However, women may also be profoundly critical of such practices and display an alternative (racialized, classed) embodied ethos that requires substantive engagement from feminists.

Rather than pursue such substantive engagement, however, Diprose pursues the argument that politically resourceful difference does not stand outside the discourses that constitute difference in dichotomous terms, but can be developed from within, because discourse is never self-contained or complete. There is a (presumed) distance between the lived body and the discourses through which the lived body is constituted, in which lies the potential for non-dichotomized difference. Hence, feminists need to examine the discourses and practices that constitute (sexual) difference and invest in Butler's (1990) assertion that to be constituted by discourse is not necessarily to be 'determined' by it. However, Diprose's discussion of politically resourceful difference shifts from the transformative potential of power/knowledge to a concern with the gaps or spaces in the imaginary fashioned by appeal to a post-Lacanian psychoanalytic framework, particularly as developed by Judith Butler.

Butler develops this observation in the context of self–other constitution and how it produces what she terms as 'excess of difference' (1993). As Diprose sees it, this is developed through a relational understanding of identity that emphasizes habitual practice (or performativity) with the potential for open spaces or 'excess'. For Diprose, 'intersubjective embodied existence' or the ongoing actualization of the embodied self is accompanied by ambiguities that are concealed within and by discourse. The identification of excess or ambiguities may thus occur via feminist critique of the social discourses that constitute women as other to men, and the ways such discourses exclude the specificity of female embodiment from 'the benefits of social exchange'. Thus, feminist critique is clearly defined as textual and tactical. Though such discourses operate in conditions that produce the male as norm, there may be residual space from which an ethics for women could emerge. The body (culturally defined) can *talk back* through the spaces of excess to which Butler refers rather than from the primordial ontology implied in some feminism. Hence, though Diprose espouses a Foucauldian position accompanied by consideration of practical ethos, she ultimately appeals to the psychoanalytic frame as the key tactic for academic feminism through which to deconstruct the socially constituted embodied self as a resource for identifying sexual difference. However, as Chapter 4 will make more apparent, knowledge of the imaginary space/gap that suggests an 'excess of difference' can only be understood through knowledge of text rather than through substantive knowledge derived from observations and understandings of bodily experience rooted in material locations and practices.

Leaky bodies: Margrit Shildrick

The 'excess of difference' taken up by Diprose is defined by Margrit Shildrick as a leaky body (1997) in her intervention in the development of new feminist philosophies of the body and considerations of embodied subjectivity. Her goal is the disruption of 'masculinist philosophy' through a tactic she refers to as an interdisciplinary application of 'bricoleur' derived at least in part from a sympathetic encounter with the deconstructive practices associated with the work of Jacques Derrida (1974). For Derrida, in language there are no fixed positions, only differences, and concomitantly no transcendental signified that can evade representation by signs, hence no underlying truth that has been distorted but could be recovered. What is considered real takes its meaning from a trace, thus, there is no originary source for what exists in language/representation but only ever supplementation. There is only difference in being or *différance*, an allusion to a movement that is not in attendance in a substantial sense but is a differentiating movement that makes difference possible (McNally, 2001). Thus, language, signs, being *presuppose* something or some condition that makes difference possible.

However, we cannot think outside language or conceive of being prior to difference, or rather, *différance*, the elusive reference to what there is before language but which we cannot know. Indeed, language is what makes it possible to think and talk about *différance* at all, albeit involving an endless play of reference through signs. *Différance* is both undecidable and 'the condition of possibility of that undecidability' (McNally, 2001: 59), a condition that leaves 'traces' in language and in the differences that constitute language. Woman is undecidable for Derrida, lacking substance and specificity, but the undecidability of *différance* is precisely what is hopeful for feminists by alluding to the possibility of challenging and changing signs (deconstruction). Following Derrida then, deconstructionist analysis presupposes that language acquisition involves the 'internalization of a patriarchal symbolic order' (Currie and Raoul, 1992: 15) and analysis involves destabilizing logocentricity by rethinking oppositional, binary categories. Analysis focuses on spoken and written text, typically seen as unified, yet which construct binary oppositions that confer symmetry or hierarchies. On the one hand, deconstruction exposes the oppositional categories embedded within texts and how they create meanings. On the other hand, deconstruction focuses on the ways that linguistic meaning shapes a wider cultural landscape. Hence, feminist analysis consists of deconstructing the binary oppositions between 'man' and 'woman' and feminists have used this approach to demonstrate how women come to embody difference.

Deconstruction thus offers a critical tactic for Shildrick to show how the binary 'other' is always the suppressed 'supplement' or the difference inscribed within a term, such that there is no 'decidable term'. Since difference is so limiting for women, deconstruction makes a virtue out of a refusal to equate sexual difference with binary oppositions (Ebert, 1996). In common with other feminist theorists who advocate a discursive form of materialism, Shildrick takes the dissolution of the subject as axiomatic in her pursuit of an ethics that acknowledges and corporealizes difference. Shildrick develops a reading of Irigaray that 'anticipates a distinction between men and women' and 'points to a female specificity beyond binary dualisms' (1997: 9). Specificity here is defined as 'fluid' yet is linked by the 'in-common experience of a specific body form'.

However, Shildrick swiftly dispels any potential for essentializing the notion of experience here by insisting on the instability of the material boundaries of the body. This manoeuvre not only deflects analysis from the bodies of women to cultural constructions of female bodies (especially within modern biomedical practice) but also from a materially inflected approach to experience that locates actual bodies in contexts from which cultural constructions are derived. Her approach privileges text and language without attention to the corporeal *con*text in which language is developed and uttered. Shildrick defends her manoeuvre on the grounds that she is not denying materiality but what she views as its authority and certainty (ibid.: 14). Ultimately for Shildrick, the 'act of representation is the moment of materialization' since we only know our bodies through the discourses that make them available to us.

However, there is surely an analytic tension here for Shildrick and those sympathetic to her work, associated with the degree to which we accept or reject the possibility of a form of knowledge unmediated by discourse imparted by the body itself. Though Shildrick's approach to subjectivity and moral agency admits the body, it nonetheless privileges a cognitive subjectivism that implies bodily knowledge as the outcome of reflective thought. This stands in contrast to the phenomenological proposition of a continuous and possibly unutterable relation between body and self and isolates language and text as the constituent of subjectivity. Moreover, though Shildrick's substantive focus – biomedicine – is historically located in terms of its contribution to the effacement of corporeality and the fragmentation of the body into constitutive parts, her approach fails to allow for the continual production and application of language in particular contexts through speech acts. The impulse of deconstructionism is to displace linguistic hierarchies in order to render the linguistic organization of society less authoritative and enable marginal signifiers to establish presence, however, this displacement and the politics of subversion it signals need a broader political and critical social project that links discourses to institutional and organizational frameworks (Seidman, 1994).

In contrast, alternative forms of discourse analysis seek to account for the ways in which language reflects and sustains institutional and cultural arrangements and accomplishes social action through particular kinds of use in particular social contexts (Fairclough, 1992). Thus, focus on 'talk-in-text' as social accomplishment and practice would appear to circumnavigate the impasse evident in 'broad brush' discourse and textual analysis favoured by new feminist philosophies of the body. Shildrick's location of language and discourse in the cultural sphere compromises any potential for developing an approach that *accounts* for language and its role in the constitution and maintenance of experience and material reality (in the form of institutions, structures, practices as suggested, for instance, by Frank (1991). Ultimately, Shildrick's focus on sexual difference through embodiment, ethics and discourse is pitched much too abstractly to offer the kind of specificity warranted by the valorization of corporeality. As a result, it obscures that which it seeks to make visible – embodied specificity.

Imaginary bodies: Moira Gatens

Though Gatens's substantive focus is on ethics as a particular form of practice, her collection of essays that span a decade, *Imaginary Bodies*, explores the philosophical underpinning of symbolic representations of 'sexed difference'. Her argument is that there is an unbroken line between representation and metaphysics that is manifest in epistemology, moral and social theory and which has 'material effects on the manner in which we conduct ourselves ethically and politically' (Gatens, 1996: vii). Gatens reads a range of philosophers with feminist eyes and is particularly interested in those texts that provide a means of locating knowledge and ethics in embodiment and conceive of knowledge as a 'mode of being'. This kind of claim underpins her generally anti-cognitive stance. For instance, though she acknowledges the part played by consciousness-raising in the development of feminism as a social and political movement, she rejects it as too wedded to the Enlightenment categories of reason that have hitherto imprisoned feminist thought.

Her work in this collection of essays focuses on the representation of human embodiment in ways that both efface women from the philosophy of humanity and privilege men as representative of the human body. Her analytic focus is on what she terms 'imaginary bodies' which are those 'ready-made images and symbols through which we make sense of social bodies and which determine in part, their value, their status and what will be deemed their appropriate treatment' (ibid.: viii). Her approach is eclectic, draws freely on a range of theorists and philosophers and substitutes the term imaginary for that of ideology. This signals her distance from both the unitary Marxist and materialist uses of ideology of which she is generally critical and from Irigaray's concept of imaginary as a form of 'paramount reality' from which women are effectively excluded. Nonetheless, following Althusser's appeal to Lacan's theory of the unconscious, Gatens argues that the historical 'cache' of philosophy constitutes an imaginary body, yet philosophical practice rarely reflects on the uses and sources of these images. This 'cache' helps to construct the subjectivity of the student of philosophy, which in turn, 'marks' the student with the 'corporate body' of the discipline.

Her particular focus is the deployment of the human body as an allegorical device to represent the body politic and political corporation. As Pateman (1988) has argued, the neutral body of the liberal state is in practice a male body, though it stands for what is in reality a complex and diverse body. Moreover, Western understandings of the liberal individual and of the body politic are premised on images of 'unity and independence from women and nature' (Gatens, 1996: 22), which she glosses psychoanalytically as a reflection of 'the infantile wish for independence from the maternal body', since the image of the modern body politic establishes male autonomy from women and from the maternal body (ibid.: 55). Women are incorporated into the political body rather than made part of it by contract in ways that service the 'artificial man' (body politic) 'preserving its viability, its unity and integrity, replacing its body parts, without ever being seen to do so'. Thus, the stakes of political imagery are high for women and Gatens seeks to open up the philosophical imaginary to scrutiny and 'to develop a notion of embodiment that posits multiple and historically specific social imaginaries' (ibid.: x).

There are two principal targets for Gatens: the limits of the sex/gender distinction and the implications for women of the relationship between representations of the human body and the body politic. Though she acknowledges the political purpose of the sex/gender distinction so central to feminist theory from the 1970s to the late 1980s, she is critical of it. Though her critique is too sustained and elegant to do justice to here, in short, she argues, like other feminists, that the body in this distinction was reduced to sex, defined in turn as a neutral platform for the inscription of gender identity. Gender is too extensive a term and cannot adequately specify the characteristics, social and political relations and social roles that are asked of it. Though the sex/gender distinction was particularly important as a tactic to break the 'arbitrary connection between femininity and the female body' (ibid.: 4) especially for the liberal feminist project, it over-emphasized the significance of socialization processes and tacitly accepted a Cartesian view of the subject that neutralizes the body.

Since Gatens is especially critical of the way that the Cartesian view of subjectivity that privileges a rational mind was influenced by the social environment and allocates the body to biology, she is unequivocal about the transformative capacities of resocialization and consciousness raising that was advocated by feminists in the 1970s and early 1980s. Moreover, she rejects a distinction between sex and gender on the grounds that the body is marginal within it to transformation processes. In her view, any feminist philosophical project needs to begin from the body, not only because the body is integral to female lived experience, but also because perception and action occur in and through the body in general. Hence, drawing here on Merleau-Ponty, reason is not disembodied but 'active and embodied precisely because it is the affirmation of a particular bodily existence' (ibid.: 57). The human subject for Gatens is not then passive and based on a neutral body, but is actively constituted through both thought and action and thus, an adequate philosophical appreciation of female subjectivity would need to take the body into account.

At this point in her claim, Gatens moves from gender to sex to assert that the female subject is already always a sexed subject (or the subject is always sexed). This is because, in her view, particular aspects of female embodiment are likely to become 'privileged sites of significance' in ways that differentiate it from male lived experience. These sites of significance may vary across time and place, as feminist historians have indeed demonstrated (e.g. Jordanova, 1989; Oudshoorn, 1994), yet there may be tensions between the social value attached to particular body parts/processes and the lived experience of such value attachment. Again, drawing on the philosophy of embodiment (Merleau-Ponty, 1962), she asserts that the significance accorded particular body parts/processes has a bearing on how female experience is lived. Hence, while men who believe themselves to be female may 'have social experiences that are socially coded as feminine' they nonetheless 'must be qualitatively different from female experience of the feminine' (Gatens, 1996: 10). In this way, conduct associated with femininity will be read differently if performed by those with bodies socially coded as male.

The various ways in which bodies come to be coded in terms of gender, however, are not addressed, nor is the observation that there must be some distinction between extra-discursive experience and the performances with which they are associated. It is difficult to not read Gatens as arguing here that lived experience is qualitatively – ontologically – distinct for men and women. MacInnes (1998) puts this ontology distinctly. He insists that though post-structuralist and ethnomethodological claims conceive of bodily difference principally in terms of meaning (Bordo and Jaggar, 1989) and processes of classification, two material classes of sex exist in a reality independent of processes of classification. These material classes of sex imply not only differences in meaning but also of experience, that 'remain the preserve of category members men and women' (Stanley and Wise, 1993: 199). As Wrong puts it in distinct contrast to Foucault, 'in the beginning there is the body' (1961: 129). However, the example of transsexualism (Garfinkel, 1967; Ekins and King, 2001) and the physical reconfiguration of body parts implied in sex changing in order to rectify the feeling of being in the 'wrong body' calls into the question the ontology implied by Gatens.

Though Gatens explicitly sees gender as an abstract term that that fails to address the 'lived experience' of 'embodied being' (1996: 30), her argument is underpinned by at least a partial notion of gender as a set of traits and/or characteristics to which one potentially has access but never fully possesses. This conceptualization of gender, she argues, informed feminist theorists who espoused degendering (e.g. Chodorow) and tried to envision a utopia devoid of gender. Understood in this way, gender could never capture the connections between sex and gender nor could it examine the conditions and experiences of living in the West, in a context 'divided and organized by sex'. The body materializes in the sex/gender distinction as a biological or anatomical body (though as Birke, 1999, notes, feminists have skirted around the meaning of the biological body rather than confronted it) rather than a body that is lived in particular ways. For an analysis of the lived body, feminists need a theory that originates from an understanding of the connected relationship between sex and gender, which is, Gatens asserts, embedded within phenomenological claims concerning embodiment. Hence connections between the body and gender are necessarily contingent because of the historically and culturally specific ways in which these connections are made. Gender is not an entity that people possess in varying amounts but a form of signification (imaginary) which has been historically linked to the biological body. Consciousness is itself embedded within and produced through a habitually lived body situated within a complex set of social and material structures, of which gender itself is but one aspect.

However, while histories and subjectivities may be constructed, the embodiedness of gender means that it cannot be shrugged off, as is implied by both those feminists who continue to view gender as the social component of sex (which is taken as a biological given) and those who see sex as also constructed. The construction of gender requires an embodiment which reflection or performance alone will not necessarily transform as her brief discussion of transsexualism/transgendering suggests. Thus, we do not necessarily have the 'freedom' to become whom we might wish to become (1996: 105) or as she puts it 'past contingencies become the materials of present necessities.' Here she is arguing for an 'ethics of difference' which would acknowledge the processes through which people become embodied in particular ways (an acknowledgement of their genealogies) without locking people into those differences in intransigent ways.

To reiterate, Gatens's critique of the sex/gender distinction and her attention to the significance of the body in this distinction are a critique of the implicit dualism reproduced within feminist theories of gender. This dualism equates sex with biology and gender with the social and cultural. The consequence of this separation between sex and gender has been that feminists have tended to develop political correctives such as re-socialization, that privilege the transformation of the rational mind to the exclusion of embodied experience. For Gatens, feminist inquiry needs to start from examining and accounting for the relation between sex and gender and in particular, the processes through which bodies come to be lived in gendered ways. Though Gatens implicitly draws here on Foucault, it is really to psychoanalysis and phenomenology she turns to develop her linking concept of the imaginary body.

The imaginary body (or as she sometimes puts it, the psychical body, drawing on Schilder's notion of body image) enables connections to be made between a historically and culturally specific image of the body in general. This general image, as Merleau-Ponty (1962) notes, is constructed through shared language, the significance given to body zones and parts, and 'common institutional practices and discourses (for example, medical, juridical and educational) which act on and through the body' (Gatens, 1996: 12). It is this general image of the body that informs the development of a psychical body and enables a conceptual connection between sex (understood as a material body) and gender (understood as a lived awareness of sexed identity). Thus understood, the experience of one's own body cannot be separated from the 'meaning and significance of the sexed body in culture' (ibid.: 31) and presumably, there can be no distinction between ontology and epistemology.

In order to comprehend the connection between the imaginary body and psychical body, Gatens turns to a Lacanian psychoanalytic framework that privileges the image of the body as a whole in the development of self. Like feminists in the 1970s who looked to psychoanalysis to build up accounts of gender identity, Gatens too subscribes to an understanding of gender identity based on a developmental sense of self. Though she acknowledges the scholarship of object-relations feminists, Gatens argues that the significance of the body in the emergence of the self has been under-estimated. Though object-relations theory prioritizes connectedness to the environment in the development of the self rather than separation from it, it does so by privileging a body already fragmented into parts that are accorded cultural and social significance in explaining processes of internalization. In contrast, she favours theories that in her view conceive of the body as a whole, such as those espoused by Lacan.

Gatens notes that in Lacan's account of the development of a child's self-consciousness, the body of both self and mother is seen as a whole before it is felt. It is this *act* of seeing, which 'constitutes' the child's own identity as separate and whole. Though feminists (especially Irigaray) have criticized Lacan for privileging vision over tactility Gatens redefines seeing as an active, embodied process. Drawing on Merleau-Ponty, she asserts that the passive process of perception that is implied in Lacanian psychoanalytic theory needs to be placed in the social and cultural context in which it occurs. Self-image is developed in both *context* (time and place) and in *relation* to embodied others, and not, as she claims is implied in object-relations theory (though this interpretation is to prematurely dismiss the work of both Melanie Klein and Karen Horney), something that can be constructed discretely via rational thought. Hence, Lacan is simultaneously invoked and criticized as Gatens has to move outside the psychoanalytic in order to redefine the mother/child dyad in ways that allow for interaction and relationality.

The phenomenological view emphasizes self as a product of intercorporeality, which Gatens refers to as investment in one's own body and the bodies of others. As evidence for the first point, she refers to accounts of the removal of body parts or limbs that appear not to enter consciousness. The example of limb removal and phantom limb pain is typically referred to as evidence of the indivisibility of mind and body (Leder, 1990; Rothfield, 1997). As evidence for the second, and in an impoverished interactionist move, she points to the ways in which people mimic the gestures, speech and habits of others in a 'network' of bodies. Though identification is based on the recognition of corporeal similarity, this similarity is not biological but emerges through shared cultural understandings of corporeality (or habitus) which themselves are open to change.

Gatens offers here a faithful reading of Merleau-Ponty's discussion of consciousness. People are not always already conscious of themselves as particular kinds of selves but as Crossley (2001) notes look out onto the world from a particular location that is our own 'blind spot'. Therefore, self-consciousness is developed first, in communicative interaction with others and second, by standing back from that interaction and from experience of the world and comparing it with what we know of the experiences of others (or by objectifying self and experience). This is distinct from the 'tacit sense of self within our corporeal schema' (Crossley, 2001: 142) that informs spatial awareness and motility (in terms of body shape, height and weight and how this informs our physical movement) and places more emphasis on experience of ourselves as particular kinds of embodied agents derived from relations with and comparisons to others and dominant cultural norms. Moreover, our sense of ourselves as particular kinds of selves develops as 'we come to see ourselves through the eyes of others' (ibid.: 143).

However, in order to emphasize the bearing of others on the development of self-consciousness, Crossley supplements Merleau-Ponty's development of self-perception through action with a reading of symbolic interactionism that emphasizes bodily competence, embodied performance and corporeal management in the production and presentation of self. He draws heavily on Mead's social psychological (1967 [1934]) account of play as the process through which children develop a sense of themselves literally by 'being', or copying the actions of others around them. For the symbolic interactionist perspective spear-headed by Mead and developed by Goffman, self emerges and is established by taking on the perspective of others and using those perspectives to not only look at oneself but also, through games: 'develop a pre-reflective corporeal "map" of the positions of the social world and its "place" in it' (Crossley, 2001: 146). Hence, self comes into being in and through *communicative* action and interactions with others who are needed for the recognition and affirmation required, enabling one to move beyond the limits of the corporeal self (Bakhtin makes a similar point). The corporeal map developed by the child in the Merleau-Pontian scheme is developed further in Bourdieu's emphasis on the durability of habitus. The consequences of repeated play and the taking on of the perspectives of others involved are twofold. First, play establishes a dialogue and capacity for reflection upon self such that one can become an object for oneself. Second, the cognitive and mental process associated with reflection are also embodied, in the sense that to 'put oneself in another's shoes' is a metaphor that invokes bodily action and mimicry to the extent that such action may be 'habituated' within the corporeal schema of the child (Jackson, 1986; Crossley, 2001).

This interpretation of Merleau-Ponty's philosophy of embodiment stands in some contrast then to Gatens's underdeveloped version of a relatively static and visual strand of phenomenology that, perhaps despite her intentions, emphasizes body image rather than bodily action. For Crossley, the sense of self as an individual is developed not through a cognitive notion of reflection but via bodily action in the world through which habits are formed. We can, as Crossley's development of Mead's work suggests, acquire a sense of self (I) conscious of itself (me) through the 'habit' of reflection (2001: 148). But the process of reflection described by Mead is one rooted in bodily action. It involves taking on the role of the other (not only via cognitive knowledge of what the other is about but also some understanding of the corporeal competence associated with that role) in ways that contribute to self-objectification (ibid.: 149).

Such a relational and contextual view of self-development could allow Gatens to hypothesize how the embodied self becomes gendered. However, instead she turns back to a Lacanian framework that contends the 'other' is incorporated in sexual difference such that each gendered body image contains within it the 'antithesis of and complement to' the other. In other words, selfhood involves recognizing the other in a conflictual link. The development of a gendered self depends on a process of 'body doubling' that incorporates and invests the image of the other into the image of self. These images are themselves socially constructed; there is 'complicity between self and other which is based on the necessary interconnectedness of our (social) images of ourselves' (1996: 38). This means that the social construction of body images requires the complicity of 'both men and women in the maintenance of a certain kind of "gendered" body image'.

Gatens uses this discussion of imag(in)ery to develop an account of the body politic and the effects for women of their invisible and unacknowledged incorporation. Liberal notions of neutrality mask and maintain sexual difference (Diprose, 1994) and the hidden character of the bodies of women preserves an image of political unity so that the (presupposed) different qualities of female embodiment do not need to be acknowledged. Hence, the metaphor of the body politic functions to restrict Western political vocabulary and preclude the articulation of difference. That is, if we accept, as Gatens does, that speech is itself an act that requires a particular bodily engagement with the world. Formulated thus, speech embodies difference (Merleau-Ponty, 1962), though this presupposes that the difference embodied is primarily sexual difference. Yet, even though the body politic has now been 'invaded' by the excluded as a consequence of the dismantling of many formal barriers to equality, the women admitted to the body politic still speak from a different (distinct) body (place). Thus, women's position within and entry to the body politic are accompanied by an intransigent limitation to what they can say and the authority with which they can say it.

According to Gatens, when women attempt to contribute to the body politic, there are two strategies for ensuring their bodies are re-incorporated. The first silencing and concealing tactic involves 'animalization' and the differentiation of the speaker from the human body politic. The second is to reduce the speaker to 'sex' such that what is spoken is the product of uncontrolled elements of female embodiment (hysterical women). Hence the metaphor reminds us of the difference between male and female bodies and between men and women. Concomitantly, feminists need to analyse how exclusions of women's bodies (e.g. informal sanctions against breast feeding in public spaces) define the body politic and how the experience of female embodiment might contribute to 'other' ways of being 'political and ethical'. Hence Gatens identifies the distance between her project and that of liberal feminist projects that address particular issues and rights in relation to the female body. Though women have acquired access to many of the political and public spaces of liberal democracies, their physical presence does not preclude exclusion, since women can be physically present yet silenced and made invisible. Moreover, women's entry to liberal institutions has occurred on the basis of sameness rather than difference, on their ability to emulate the capacities associated with male privilege.

Though this is a seductive argument, there are instances (admittedly few) in which difference *has* been the basis of inclusion. State feminism, for instance, in New Zealand has proceeded on the grounds that women's political incorporation provided one means of eroding the 'male' system from within precisely by emphasizing difference (O'Regan, 1992). While it is undoubtedly the case that women's entry to participation in the public sphere via equal opportunities policies has been disappointing because many women emulate the capacities associated with male privilege, women have made some difference to political activity and governance. In Scotland's devolved parliament, for instance, women have been key players in establishing the framework for parliamentary operations, the political process within parliament and are most active in negotiating change in parliamentary committees. Moreover, to acknowledge the dualisms inherent in the imag(in)ery of the body politic makes no difference to material issues concerning pay, employment rights and welfare entitlements. Finally, while the imagery of the body politic outlined by Gatens may hold for some states, it is not necessarily a universal image. In welfare states women's entry into citizenship has been *through* welfare rather than via employment and participation in the labour market. While there are a range of issues concerning women's relation to the state and the body politic in such an arrangement, it has nonetheless been suggested by some feminists (notably Walby, 1995) that a shift from private to public patriarchy has occurred, which in Gatens's schema, would imply some alteration in the imag(in)ery of the body politic.

What potentially marks Gatens from her contemporaries is her attempt to locate the development of disciplinary consciousness (or imaginary) within a concept of social practice derived from Pierre Bourdieu. Though she draws heavily on Lacan's notion of the imaginary, she also develops a concept of the social imaginary located within unconscious habits or practices that come to form a kind of second nature or 'embodied habit'. She reads Bourdieu as a theorist of the body who provides a means of demonstrating the crucial link between the forms of thought associated with particular social groups and their consequences for the wider body politic. As Bourdieu puts it, habitus is 'spontaneity without consciousness or will' (quoted in Gatens, 1996: xi) and 'is what makes it possible to inhabit institutions, to appropriate them practically, and so to keep them in activity … but at the same time imposing the revisions and transformations that reactivation entails' (from *The Logic of Practice*). Yet her appeal to Lacan imposes a reading of Bourdieu's sociological rendering of spontaneity through a psychoanalytic eye that understands transformation as primarily psychic.

Conclusion

This chapter has considered the emergence of the corporeal turn in feminist analysis. The paradigm shift in academic feminism from materialist analyses of gender towards gender as a cultural category has been under-pinned by postmodernist and post-structuralist ways of thinking, an emphasis on representation and on the 'micro-politics of difference' that largely privilege deconstructive tactics rather than explanatory develop-ment (Rojek and Turner, 2000). Although the impact of postmodernism and post-structuralism has been uneven across disciplines (Barrett, 1992), and is most visible in philosophy and literary theory, it is also evident in other disciplines that share a concern with issues of agency, identity and subjectivity such as human geography and sociology.

As Chapter 2 outlined, the move towards issues of representation and difference that are at the core of the development of feminist approaches to the body are underpinned by the rejection of a singular explanation for and conceptualization of gender. Gender is now deemed a set of unfixed relations rather than as a stable identity – or subjectivity – and fixed subordination (Flax, 1986). Both 'woman' and 'women' have been deprecated as a unitary category (Riley, 1988) and the claims of post-colonial argument (Said, 1993) have reinforced feminism as a partial per-spective (Spivak, 1990) that cannot provide a definitive account of gender relations or subjectivity. Hence, gender has become sexual difference and difference matters because of its potential to essentialize gender. Alongside deconstruction and discourse analysis, particular versions of psychoanalysis have provided a tool for the project of deconstructing sex-ual difference, its inscription in the social domain and the ways in which subjectivities become differentiated.

As argued in Chapter 2, feminism emerged as a movement that viewed the body as a site of subordination, exploitation and alienation. Following the influence of Foucault's work on Anglo-American feminism, the body is perceived as a site of resistance. Post-Foucauldian feminist scholarship utilizes the relational character of power and resistance and the situated character of subjectivity. While the body in early Foucault was developed as a docile body (Bordo, 1989), in later Foucault, the female body is discursively produced through practices of self (Deveux, 1994). This shift in feminist appropriations of Foucault has emerged from work-ing through Foucault's own equivocation between regulatory and disci-plinary power (discussed in Chapter 1), and notions of embodied agency and subjectivity. In this later work, Foucault returns to and reworks Enlightenment categories through his theory of practices of the self and his increasing emphasis on reflexivity grounded in bodily practices (McNay, 1992). Feminists have built on this interpretation of Foucault in order to develop an understanding of embodied subjectivity and open up the potential for analysis of process, practice and experience.

However, though the body is present in this work as a material focus for technologies of power, and though the Foucauldian optic denies the body the kind of ontology typical of earlier feminist scholarship on experience, the Foucauldian frame has been criticized for its tendency to over-invest in docility at the expense of agency. Moreover, though the Foucauldian approach offers an analysis of how the body is constituted materially via practices and discourses, it does so by harbouring a distinction, however implicit, between subject and object and latterly, as is discernible in the work of feminist ethicists in particular, by reducing the meanings of discourse to non-social discursive practices that privilege text. This has led feminist analysis of embodied agency to psychoanalysis in ways that recast experience in terms of a local, ethical subject of pleasure (Ebert, 1996) in which it is difficult to identify any body.

four

Mirrors, lips and other metaphors: feminism, the body and psychoanalysis

Introduction

The female body has occupied an equivocal presence within feminism. Though feminist activism more willingly engaged with the body at the level of experience, Anglo-American academic feminism, until the 1980s, did not generally equate the subordination of women with concerns about the body. While certain dimensions of female embodiment were central to radical feminist debates about women's subordination, female embodiment was not the focal point of academic feminism. However, the body has become the focus of substantive and theoretical treatment across feminisms in the social sciences and humanities and academic feminism has turned its gaze more explicitly on embodiment and the divisions that accompany it between the material and the discursive, the actual and the virtual. A range of concepts has been developed to correct what are identified as malestream, abstract accounts of the body with more specific accounts of lived, embodied experience. This scholarship forms the corporeal turn which is, however, a turn from experience to subjectivity and to theory that privileges the theme of sexual difference as the centrepiece of feminist scholarship.

The corporeal turn has implications for the goals of academic feminism. It is a turn that avows text and textuality through its endorsement of deconstructive and psychoanalytic practices. The growing emphasis on post-Lacanian psychoanalytic frameworks has generated an approach to theorizing the body that privileges writing and textuality, even in the work of those who seek to challenge this privilege. In examining the body as a theoretical object, and *inter alia* its significance as a grounding for feminist politics, academic feminism has substituted text for the rational, autonomous individual (mind) of which it has been so critical. As this chapter explores, the scrutiny of matter and materiality that characterizes the corporeal turn has generated a body suspended in space and time, a body without change and a body devoid of context. The chapter develops this claim by examining a selection of key feminist work that is continually cited across disciplinary boundaries and which, therefore, can be said to have had a significant impact on feminism's treatment of the body. I begin by outlining the general thrust of Lacan's work in order to lay the ground for looking at key feminists who have been influenced by this work. The feminist work examined here is influenced by many theorists and indeed, the hallmark for inter-disciplinarity is the way in which feminist academics are seen to pull together a considerable range of writing in consideration of their topic. However, my interest is in the pre-eminence of a particular psychoanalytic frame and in the way in which such a frame, despite its claim *for* materiality pushes against matter and pushes the body out of its frame.

Feminism and post-Lacanian psychoanalysis

The development of psychoanalytic theory has integrated notions of language as social and as the 'pure sign' of inner life by 'theorizing culture as the symbolic enactment of psychical realities' (Ian, 1993: 168). Psychoanalytic theory adds edge to feminist conceptions of subjectivity by emphasizing multiplicity, plurality, difference and the body as a lived, specific and conceptually open site, rather than as a biologically given entity. Feminist appropriations of psychoanalytic theory express a preference for the concept of *sexual difference* over gender identity (Segal, 1990). Where gender theorists have hitherto prioritized social and cultural processes of differentiation, sexual difference theorists privilege processes of identification and internalization (Braidotti, 1998: 298) within the subject. Yet psychoanalytic theory is extensive and dense. Emerging initially within feminism as an extension of feminist consciousness-raising practices in the Anglophone world (Brennan, 1998), psychoanalysis has developed broadly in Anglo-American and French directions. Though many feminists, including Kate Millet, Eva Figes and Simone de Beauvoir were sceptical of and condemned Freud's legacy, others championed Melanie Klein's (1975) subsequent treatment of Freud. American feminists were particularly interested in using this legacy to explore and explain why women appeared to accept the social and political arrangements that oppressed them. Feminists such as Dorothy Dinnerstein and Nancy Chodorow drew on versions of Freud that de-emphasized biological determinism and focused instead on the pre-Oedipal period of mother/child intensity. Chodorow in particular combined this with a reconstructed historical materialism that promised a means to explain the development of gender identity; to examine the connection between psychic and social worlds; and to undercut a view of sexuality as a 'natural' given.

Despite these initial sociologically modulated appropriations of object-relations theory in Anglo-American feminism, the main tendency within the psychoanalytic trope is the reconstruction of everyday life as 'eternal interpersonal conflicts unfolding outside of time, place, culture and in particular, the power relations of gender' (Segal, 1990: 77). Given the materialist traditions in which they developed, British feminist sociologists in particular have been reluctant to invest too heavily in psychoanalytic theory. Moreover, though feminist treatments of object-relations theory dominated several agendas in the 1980s (such as feminist studies of science), it has largely fallen out of favour and been superseded by the work of Jacques Lacan, brought to English-speaking feminists primarily through the translations of Juliet Mitchell and Jacqueline Rose.

Lacan trained as a psychiatrist and established his own school (having been thrown out of orthodox bodies) through which he delivered public lectures on Freud's psychoanalytic technique and from which the texts developed (mainly *Écrits* – written in a baroque style, see Macey, 1988) that have become the main source for feminist scrutiny concerning the unconscious, gender construction and the development of the subject. Lacan's biographer notes how his work was influenced by a Nietzschean crisis of modernity that saw mothers in a role of 'domestic tyranny' in the family at a historical point when patriarchal values and paternal authority were in decline, threatened by the expansion of women into and by the feminization of the public sphere (Roudinesco, 1997).

Although Lacan advocated a 'return to Freud', he did so through an emphasis on a post-Saussurian notion of language that begets speech and turns the subject into 'the captive of language' (Ian, 1993: 222). Language for Lacan is an autonomous, self-contained and self-reproducing whole where signs – whose meanings are generated by relations of difference (Seidman, 1994) – have value as part of a formal system that is also the privileged medium in which sexual difference is reproduced. This framework enabled Lacan to turn psychoanalysis into a system by investing in the 'rationalisation of the linguistic structuralists' (Kerrigan, 1989) which treated the unconscious as a 'site of mediation comparable to that opened by the signifier in the realm of language' (Roudinesco, 1997). For Lacan, subjectivity is based on the unconscious, which nonetheless has no final grounding or anchor. Thus, the notion of a conscious, unified self for Lacan is an illusion (Klages, 2001).

The acquisition of language is critical to entry into the Symbolic and structures the constitution of the subject (the child's subjectivity) in terms of 'positionality', in terms that is, of a specific relation to the mother and the father in the patriarchal family context. Lacan's account emphasizes sexual difference as the foundation of the Symbolic Order, which in turn is built on Lévi-Strauss's claim that kinship is a general structure driven by unconscious laws and 'regulated by a series of interrelated signs, roles and rituals' (Brennan, 1998: 220). This Order must be internalized through language by the child in order to function adequately and as long as the child speaks the language of this Order and adopts its roles, individuals will be regulated and society will reproduce itself. The Symbolic Order precedes the individual and its reproduction depends on unconscious acceptance and internalization of it by proceeding through various stages of development (the unconscious itself is structured like the language of this Order).

As the child passes through the various stages of development, outlined by Freud and developed by Lacan over a long period of time by revisiting not only Freud but also by incorporating a range of social and philosophical theories to reduce his reliance on Freud's biological materialism (Roudinesco, 1997), it recognizes itself to varying degrees as separate from significant others and from family members.

There are three phases that are critical to Lacan's framework and to the feminists who have taken up his work. In the first pre-linguistic phase, (the psychic place of the Real), the child is unaware of boundaries between his own body and that of his mother's, which offers a state of oneness with the world or abundance. As the infant begins to sense its separateness from the mother (though not as yet as a discrete self), it makes (psychic) demands (for a return to the oneness represented by the Real) that cannot be fully satisfied (Klages, 2001). In the second, mirror phase, the child experiences himself as fragmented since only parts of his body are within his field of vision at any one time, yet he also begins to recognize himself as a self via a process that involves both real and metaphorical mirrors. In the first sense, when the child first sees an image of himself in a mirror, the image is confused both with his own self and that of the adult holding him (assuming one is). Gradually the child realizes that what he sees is actually an image of himself that at the same time lacks something. Lacan uses this observation to contend that the process of becoming a self involves becoming two or a splitting. One understands oneself as a separate self by seeing an image reflected back to oneself. This process of reflection is for Lacan a model for all relations: the self finds itself through reflections in the Other, but is based on a misrecognition, an 'I' that incorporates a loss (Sprengnether, 1990: 184) that is recognized and signalled as desire (for what is lost) through communication.

The third Oedipal phase follows a process of separation between child and mother in which the child recognizes himself as separate from her rather than as part of her, and simultaneously becomes aware of her limitations to fulfil his desires. During the Oedipal phase, in which desire for the mother is accompanied by realization that self is neither at one with the world nor at the centre of the mother's attentions (Thurschwell, 2000), the child encounters a crisis which is shored up by antagonisms towards the father, who also has the mother's attention. The castration complex (associated with the discovery of genital pleasure for Freud) institutes a fear of symbolic castration (for boys – for girls the castration complex is associated with recognition of what has already been lost) as a punishment for continuing to desire the mother, at which point the child capitulates towards the father and acquires language as a medium of communication.

For Freud, entry into subjecthood occurs via the Oedipus complex (Wolff, 1990), through which differentiation between men and women is effected. However, this differentiation designates 'woman' or the feminine as a weaker image of the masculine rather than as distinctly different. In Western thought and in Freud in particular, the feminine is conceived of only in inferior, negative terms, as lack (where the feminine refers only to sexuality). Yet where for Freud, the castration complex and incest prohibition are bound to the father's penis, in Lacan, the father becomes a structuring principle of the Symbolic Order at the centre of which is the phallus (Klages, 2001). The phallus alone is the mark of sexual difference that separates the child from the experience of maternal plenitude and 'reveals the basis of differentiation in language' (Sprengnether, 1990: 196). As Vice puts it, by entering the Symbolic, 'the child is catapulted at once into the symbolic world of language, law and sexual difference' (1998: 196). Such catapulting comes with a cost, and the regret every subject feels for lost unity with the mother in the pre-Oedipal realm is what constitutes the unconscious. Language functions to 'plug up the hole at the centre of being' (Brennan, 1989: 274) and communication through language enables interaction, which fills in this emptiness in a limited and temporary way. Yet, for Lacan there are distinctions between what we want to say and what we actually say, that correspond to the gap between need and demand. This gap represents the psychical reality of desire, residing in the space between the biological and the social and mediating all relationships, events and interactions.

For Lacan, just as for Freud, boys and girls experience this entry into the Symbolic (language) differently. For boys, in Freud, identification with the father in the Oedipal phase is made on the basis of shared anatomy, but Lacan presents the phallus as the privileged – arbitrary – signifier that represents both a differentiated position in language and an illusion of wholeness. The phallus is thus a reminder of the absence of pre-Oedipal experience and 'the elusive signified in language' (Sprengnether, 1990: 196). However, while boys enter into subjecthood and individuality through language, girls enter the Symbolic on the side of lack, do not fully internalize the Symbolic Order and therefore escape categorization (Sprengnether, 1990). As a result, girls are both excluded from the Symbolic and repressed within it, because the only language women have is the language of the Father and sexual difference is a by-product of the child's entry into language (Sprengnether, 1990).

The implication of sexual difference for women is thus double loss, grounded on the apparent absence of language for women to express their experience and affect. Women, then, for Lacan as for Freud, 'cannot completely resolve the Oedipal complex', hence 'the feminine does not and cannot exist within the Symbolic Order' and as (Tong, 1994: 222) puts it, women are 'permanent outsiders'. The project of knowing women, for Lacan, can only be accomplished by examining a theorized position beyond the phallic economy – that of feminine sexual pleasure (*jouissance*). However, this cannot be known – only glimpsed – since it too lies outside phallic language (though Lacan's presumption about and position to *jouis-sance* are notably not discussed). Yet if *jouissance* were to be expressed, it might hold the potential to challenge or disrupt the Symbolic Order.

Mitchell (1984) introduced Anglophone feminists to Lacan's concept of the phallus as a symbolic representation of the Law/patriarchal power and shifted emphasis from the anatomical body to an imaginary body. Mitchell generally accepted Lacan's intepretations of Freud and endorsed his explanation of sexual difference as non-essentialist in three ways. First, a Lacanian framework viewed femininity (or sexual difference) as a non-biological construction, predicated on the absence of the phallus (which represents power). Second, it enabled critique of the concept of the unified subject by foregrounding processes of subject differentiation; and, third, it alluded to the availability of femininity to both men and women (Brennan, 1989).

Lacan appealed to structural anthropology, particularly Lévi-Strauss's study of kinship and post-Saussurian linguistics to argue that the unconscious was structured in topographical terms (or structured like a language of topography), thus, the acquisition of identity occurs via the adoption of a sexed identity with reference to the phallus as the privileged signifier, like a reference point in a formula. For Lacan, the phallus acquires its meaning through its difference from other signifiers, not through any actual equivalence between language and the material world. The phallus has a symbolizing function that 'introduces the alienating effect of difference into the pleasurable and natural mother–infant dyad' (Ragland-Sullivan, 1986: 290, cited in Sprengnether, 1990: 199) and arbi-trarily symbolizes anatomical difference. Nonetheless, the phallus is, as Merck notes (cited in Segal), *the* mark of division precisely because the penis is prominent in copulation and because of the epistemological priv-ilege accorded to vision in modernity (that is, the penis is visible). Identity is constituted in relation to the phallus, which constitutes woman in terms of lack and man in terms of the threat of lack, creating not two sexes, but 'one and its other' (Segal, 1990: 87). However, as many commentators have noted (though conspicuously absent from most contemporary feminist discussions of Lacan in relation to the body) it is difficult to sustain Lacan's distinction between phallus and penis. Gallop (1985), for instance, notes that there is inevitably confusion about Lacan's use of phallus because it is a word already saturated with sexualized or biologized meanings (such as 'virile member', ibid.: 136). Similarly, Macey (1988) traces the persistent slippages in Lacan between the symbolic phallus and biological penis leading Sprengnether to comment that 'either the phallus collapses into the penis or it becomes completely arbitrary as a sign of difference and thus uncoupled from any necessary connection with patriarchy' (1990: 199).

Though Lacanian psychoanalytic theory has been influential within Anglo-American feminism, it has had more impact within literary theory and cultural studies than within psychology or sociology (Segal, 1990), inspiring feminist analyses of image and text that reinforce psychoanalytic claims about the universality and ubiquity of cultural phallocentrism. Important differences exist between Anglo-American and French feminist readings of Lacanian psychoanalysis. Where Anglo-American feminists have tended to defend Lacan's reading of Freud, French post-structuralist feminists have tried to address the male dominance implied in Lacan's 'symbolic' law (Brennan, 1989: 2). Post-structuralist feminism has largely been responsible for the recuperation of interest in Lacan's psychoanalysis which has the effect of characterizing patriarchy as a material structure based on how the world is imagined rather than on a structure of social relations (Connell, 1987: 202). Psychoanalysis has been deployed by feminist theorists of the body as a means of transcending body/mind dualisms, and the 'space' between the unconscious and the materialization of sex through gendered performance. As both Butler (1990, 1993) and Braidotti (1998) assert, psychoanalysis has provided a means of moving from a dependence on material*ism* to a focus on a materia*lity* established and encountered via imaginary categories.

Maternal-feminine language games: Luce Irigaray

A textual frame overtly informs the work of Luce Irigaray whose work is central – though contentious – to the development of new feminist philosophies of the body (Irigaray, 1985a, 1985b). The canvas on which Irigaray – a linguist and practising psychoanalyst – works is extensive. Her project examines the phallogocentric claims of philosophy since Plato and asserts that the binary philosophical constitution of matter is constituted on an exclusion of the 'feminine' (Butler, 1993: 35) that enables philosophy to posture as internally coherent (ibid.: 38). Irigaray similarly takes Freud to task for failing to theorize the mother/daughter relationship and side-lining the significance of the pre-Oedipal maternal body in his account of gender differentiation (Sprengnether, 1990), a body suggestive of excessive matter that cannot be accommodated within the philosophical or psychoanalytical frame (or unthematizable materiality). Moreover, she inverts the primacy accorded the phallus by Lacan and insists on the significance of the female body in a feminist project organized around sexual difference. Further, the notion of sexual difference registers an anti-realist/anti-foundationalist note that forsakes concrete reference points beyond systems of representation and thus privileges representation as the key site of analysis. In this sense, the term sexual difference carries an abstract quality that allows the psychoanalytic frame in which Irigaray operates to work against divisions between the real and the represented.

Following Lacan, Irigaray focuses on contrasts between the

Imaginary and the Symbolic and on dissimilarities between the pre-Oedipal, pre-linguistic phase and entry into the Symbolic Order. Where self-realization depends on visualizing oneself in order to make distinctions between self and other, entry into the Symbolic Order is dependent on the acquisition of the 'I' of language. Like Lacan, Irigaray too notes differences between male and female entry into culture and in particular the absence of imagery or language that reflects relations between mother and daughter. The absence of such imagery constitutes a 'lack' that is, Irigaray suggests, at the root of women's sense of melancholy or longing, though women do not know what it is they mourn (Brennan, 1989). In such a claim, the influence of Freud rather than Lacan is noticeable. Yet in contrast to Lacan, Irigaray suggests critical differences in the consequences of male and female relations to the Imaginary. Where the Imaginary may be a prison (characterized by illusory, uncertain images) from which boys will be liberated into selfhood, attachment to it may be a potential source of power for women. Irigaray suggests that the Imaginary has been described from the point of view of men who are unable to define woman as anything other than a reflection of the masculine. However, there *may be* a non-phallic feminine Imaginary that could provide women with the means to selfhood. Crucially, Irigaray does not define this feminine, since to do so is itself an exercise in phallogocentricity (Davidson and Smith, 1999).

Irigaray's particular focus is on the ways in which women are represented and symbolized in Western patriarchal culture and perhaps also, the way in which 'the phenomenology of bodily experience' is constructed through such representation (Grosz, 1990). Becoming a sane subject depends on finding a place within culture, since that is what gives the psyche leverage (Brennan, 1989), thus for Irigaray, women can only move forward as subjects when they recognize themselves as part of a tradition in which they have a place. While 'maternal powers' are exalted in Western culture, matricide 'is the foundation of the male psychosocial contract as well as femininity', thus the mother is confined to 'symbolic insignificance' (Braidotti, 1998: 301). This insight provides for Irigaray a starting point for a reappraisal of the 'maternal as a site of empowerment of woman-centred geneologies' as a route towards an 'alternative female symbolic system' (ibid.: 301). As sexual difference forms the basis of women's oppression so it suggests a solution that requires the exposure of the 'maternal-feminine' inherent within Western philosophy through specific tactics that exaggerate these characteristics. Thus, Irigaray engages in a multi-dimensional project that is suggestive of a 'feminine imaginary' – an imagined imaginary – that seeks to reverse traditional psychoanalytic views of the feminine via a sustained emphasis on female embodiment. Though many feminists, especially philosophers, have welcomed her project, critics are wary of the status of the body within it, the notable erasure of distinction between body/language and the reluctance to name the 'excessive matter' in phallogocentrism as the 'absent *mater*' – the maternal body as the body of difference of the psychoanalytic frame.

Irigaray first proposes that women develop a language of their own based on their experiences as embodied female subjects and in doing so she makes use of female genital anatomy ('by our lips we are women'). Language is fundamental because it denies difference through its distancing and masculinizing capacities. Hence she arouses women to write and speak in an active voice that owns the words it speaks as a means of constituting a non-phallic language that privileges difference, not sameness. She advocates a (linguistic and philosophical) writing project that disrupts syntax and messes up sentence ordering to thematize an attitude about sexual difference. This project shares affinities with Cixous's (1986) attempts to retrieve a maternal body as 'contained otherness' through writing that subverts linguistic categories and orthodoxies based on the valorization of imagined phenomenological capacities. The centrality of the (maternal) body in the process of knowing allows the development of a knowing based on 'passion and empathy' that in turn integrates knowledge and action (Tomm, 1992: 211). This process entails the development of a self-awareness of the body (as reality) and ordering that awareness 'in a language that reflects and nourishes our female subjectivity' (ibid.: 212). Irigaray seeks to challenge the prevalence of the phallus and the 'male economies of desire' (Stanley and Wise, 1993) constituted through the possession and exchange of women's bodies. She does so via advocacy of exploring the plurality of sexual possibilities implied in female anatomy and through labial touch (through which women's sexuality 'is not one'). Finally, women must 'mime the mimes men have imposed on women' (Brennan, 1989: 228) by reflecting back to men the images men have created of women in 'magnified proportions', or, mimes as Butler (1993: 45) puts it, 'the origin only to displace that origin as an origin'.

Attention to embodied specificity is crucial to Irigaray's project, which is, quite apart from anything else, read by feminist theorists of the body as a thorough rejection of liberal feminism. In Irigaray's terms, the Symbolic Order denies the possibility of women's specificity and affirms their exclusion from culture, hence the pursuit of equality is a ruse. However, Irigaray's work attracts opposition and assent in equal measure from feminists. On the one hand, Irigaray's claims are interpreted as essentialist. Though even critics acknowledge the positive evaluation to the female body Irigarary's rhetorical strategy brings by 'speaking the unspeakable' (Stanley and Wise, 1993: 198), they are also wary of the way it privileges the female body through the notion of sexual difference (Poovey, 1988). A troublesome consequence of this valorizing is the way it potentially underscores the immutability of anatomy as an originary source, a point Irigaray herself seems diffident about.

On the other hand, commentators who are sympathetic to her strategy argue that her emphasis on essence and on the body is figurative rather than literal (Fuss, 1990), the body inferred is morphological rather than material. Whitford points to Irigaray's use of metaphor (especially 'two lips' speaking together) as serving a 'figure for women's relationship to language and utterance' (1991: 170). Such metaphors are deployed as part of her overall strategy and function as a textual tactic through which to represent female sexuality in positive, non-phallic terms (Grosz, 1990). The symbolic interpretation of the female body as idealized morphology is a necessary component of her strategy to speak about that which has no name in patriarchal culture (Gallop, 1988). Mimesis for Irigaray suggests a 'feminine "capacity" … to evoke the disruptive excess' that nonetheless operates within the binary of sexual difference (Cornell, 1991) or, in other words, offers 'a way of discovering things in oneself that are already there', animating and charging them with meaning in order to highlight a certain difference (Jackson, 1986: 343). Thus, Irigaray 'shows' how 'morphology interacts with linguistic definitions' and that 'female morphology [is] a privileged site of production of forms of resistance to the phallogocentric code' (Braidotti, 1998: 301).

Though Irigaray concedes that mimicry as a tactic of subversion could be interpreted as self-contradiction, nonetheless it is a tactic that challenges what she views as the logical, linearity of phallogocentrism, and is taken up by others, for instance, Margrit Shildrick (1997) who rejects a view of corporeality as essentialist yet valorizes and reclaims corporeality as a specifically feminine form of knowledge. Irigaray's emphasis upon the body should be viewed as a means to resist the extent to which women are subject to 'masculine imprinting and socialisation' within patriarchal culture (Fuss, 1990: 61). It is a cultural tactic/intervention rather than an attempt to create an ontological 'theory of women'. However, it is notable that most attempts to honour Irigaray's work as a tactic do so in ways that either textualize (and make safe) the material(ity) that grounds it or make an extra-discursive move that requires some conceptualization of the social as the context in which matter and text become indissoluble.

The suggestion of anatomical language and unresolved debates about whether it is essentialist or metaphorical reinforces the imprecision of relation between language and materiality. In part, the undecidability in/of Irigaray is an effect of her complex style. Even Butler, herself no stranger to complex style, concedes that Irigaray's grandiose mimicry requires a 'close, careful' reading to 'get' the 'disruptive movement or the speculative excess' (1993: 36). Nonetheless, a solution to this imprecision suggested by Davidson and Smith (1999) is that of a language-game through which feminist readings of Irigaray might situate her at the borders of dominant structures in order to 'engender a respect for difference'. Davidson and Smith reconcile the essentialist with the metaphorical

Irigaray via Wittgenstein's notion of 'forms of life', which lends a sense of embeddedness to language and sets it in place in ways that require a community to create meaning. This philosophical tactic (i.e. the re-reading of Irigaray through Wittgensteinian concepts) allows Davidson and Smith to pull the social back into the Irigarayan frame by way of Wittgenstein's socially and practically embedded concept of language-games. This tactic, though focused on language, is attentive to the social and material contexts in which language is developed and used, or as Wittgenstein puts it, the forms of life in which language occurs. In this way, Davidson and Smith absolve Irigaray of accusations about essences and see in her emphasis on embodied experiences and bodily language an attempt to recover the body as constitutive (not determinant) of experience and to view 'labial politics' as a 'form of life'. However, what is discernible in the kind of response represented by Davidson and Smith is that it registers the need to move beyond the text and return the text to the social.

Evoking the maternal body

Though there are distinct differences between the work of Julia Kristeva and Irigaray, the former is credited with emphasizing the significance of pre-Oedipal maternal materiality and abundance (Moi, 1986). Kristeva adheres broadly to Lacan's framework but places emphasis on the semiotic as precursor to the Symbolic, rooted in or characterized by the unorganized, pre-linguistic bodily rhythms of the 'chora' that appeal to maternal materiality (Ian, 1993). Where Lacan sees severance from the connection to the maternal body as the necessary precondition of entry into the Symbolic, Kristeva sees this Imaginary/semiotic connection as a resource for creativity and knowledge production. All subjects potentially have access to the pre-linguistic, pre-reflective internal rhythms of the semiotic from within the symbolic, but the chora's urges and desires need to be articulated in ways that are derived from and will be understood within culture or the Symbolic Order in order to be transgressive. In this sense Kristeva differs from Irigaray's insistence on recovering a language associated with the Imaginary (Sprengnether, 1990).

Kristeva is linked to the project of *l'écriture féminine* and its offensive against the ways in which felt awareness and analytic reflection are separated in patriarchal culture. For Kristeva, the disruption between bodily feelings and critical thought requires reconnection in an individual's consciousness in order to challenge the thinking 'I' as privileged over the feeling 'me' (Tomm, 1992). Like Cixous, this connection might be potentially re-established through writing the self and through forms of creativity (or what Boyne, 1998, refers to as the capacity of the body to 'talk back'). In particular, Kristeva suggests that the semiotic (or repressed memories of the semiotic) is open to use by intellectuals and other marginalized groups in ways that have the potential to disrupt the symbolic. However, Kristeva differs from Cixous and Irigaray in the sense that the self so writing is decidedly immaterial and androgynous, 'as that which is marginalized by the symbolic order' (Tomm, 1992: 171).

Kristeva has been especially influential in cultural and aesthetic interventions that seek to emphasize maternal–child symbolic bonds as a basis for non-phallic knowledge production (Howson, 2005). However, as Sprengnether (1990) comments, even Kristeva's attempts to imagine a way out of the double bind for women in Western culture have to move beyond the maternal absence of the Lacanian frame towards a reflection of her own experience – in *Stabat Mater* (Moi, 1986) – of maternity in a way that collapses the semiotic/materiality interface that her work otherwise seeks to install.

Re-materializing the body: Judith Butler

As noted in Chapter 2, the sex/gender distinction is the (liberal) legacy of de Beauvoir's rejection of Freud's body as the explanatory basis for differences between men and women because of its naturalizing effects and political neutralization. While many feminists continue to retain a sociological view of gender and sex as social products of material relations, but are charged with disregarding the body, other feminists have disturbed the sex/gender distinction with quite singular versions of the material that allude to the body. This disturbance has been developed in different ways but generally re-emphasizes sex as neither a physiological/anatomical category nor as wholly constructed. The most obvious case here is the work of Judith Butler, which quite explicitly reworks the sex/gender distinction in order to make the matter of the body or the body's materiality visible as an object for theory through a focus on the 'sex of materiality' and which takes issue with the 'material irreducibility of sex' (1993: 28). *Gender Trouble* develops the concept of performativity to side-step biologically or anatomically reductionist models of the body and the pathologizing of women that such models reinforce. Butler *rewrites* the sex/gender distinction as: 'a *stylised repetition of acts* ... understood as the mundane way in which bodily gestures, movements, and styles of various kinds constitute the illusion of an abiding gendered self' (1990: 140; emphasis in original). In doing so, Butler seeks to circumvent the determinism of both essentialism and social constructionism, to install a version of embodied subjectivity that is not circumscribed by the material circumstances of everyday life (that is, a form of power 'fixed' by class relations or institutional structures) but operates through a non-specific discursivized/textualized form of power. Sex, in the earlier sense of the term (as the assignation of binary characteristics) is not matter, in the sense of providing an immutable (physiological, biological) foundation for identity or conduct. Rather, the 'materiality of the sexed body is discursively constituted' through the regulatory frame of (Western) reproductive heterosexuality (or in other words, through the dimorphic norms of two mutually exclusive, invariant and complementary sexes outlined by Garfinkel in 1967). Different sexes are enacted via the body both in compliance with and through disruption of norms. Nor is gender separate from sex, rather, it is implicated in the frame of reproductive heterosexuality and an illusion of stability and fixity is produced through repetitions and enactments (typically interpreted as habitual practice) that *make it seem* as though gender (as identity) is fixed and attached to sex (as in the 'sexed body').

Hence, for Butler, materiality is shaped by a 'process of materialization that stabilizes over time to produce the effect of boundary, fixing and surface' (Alcoff, 2000: 858) and is indissoluble from the regulatory norms and signification in language that govern it, so the body comes to be seen as matter (immutable) over time (Hughes and Witz, 1997) and performativity represents a form of reiterative power in which there is no determining subject but only discourse that 'produces the effects that it names' (1993: 14). *Bodies That Matter* provides more insight into the operations of discourse and how power constitutes materiality. Following Foucault, Butler argues that 'the moment materiality seems like a given, or "outside" discourse, is the moment power is most effective' though she does not specify *how* power operates beyond being the 'sedimented effect of a reiterated iterability' (1993: 34). Butler's work resolutely collapses matter and language on the grounds that there is no 'outside' to language (or text as Derrida would have it) and no way in which materiality can be grasped beyond the signifying processes that refer to it which are themselves (already) material (Butler, 1993). However, her emphasis on performativity later becomes a more pronounced discursive citationality and her emphasis on cultural norms (regulatory heterosexuality) implicitly reinforces language (discourse) as autonomous and self-producing, in ways that detach its use and (re)production from concrete social situations (McNally, 2001: 44) and reinforce the notion of an autonomous citing subject.

She notes in *Bodies That Matter* that there is no easy return to the materiality of either the body or sex. 'To return to matter requires that we return to matter as a *sign* which in its redoublings and contradictions enacts an inchoate drama of sexual difference' (1993: 49). Yet, by grading matter as sign, Butler nails her colours to the textual mast of post-structuralism. A core part of her argument in *Bodies That Matter* concerns establishing the relation between materiality and representation in order to claim that materiality and signification are bound together. In this text she provides extended discussion of matter via the Greeks, Aristotelian philosophy, Foucault, Marx and Derrida to secure her claim concerning the indissolubility of materiality/signification or how materiality is already invested in signification. The idea of matter for Butler points to patriarchal

authority and exclusions 'constituted through an exclusion and degrada-
tion of the feminine' (1993: 28). Matter – the body in this case – is typically viewed as prior to the sign, or rather, it is a process of signification that
effects this view of the body. Consequently, matter cannot *be* prior to the
sign since it is the sign or language that signifies its prior status in the first
place. Thus, matter (the body) becomes meaningful (for instance, as foundational) or distinct from language because language enables us to signify
in this way. There is, then, for Butler, an 'outside' to discourse/language
only because we can invent it, not because there is an ontologically distinct
outside: the 'outside' (or a body beyond language) is supplementary in the
sense that it presents a 'disruptive return' that constitutes what excludes it
(Ebert, 1996: 211).

Butler's work has prompted considerable debate in academic feminist communities and her work is often cited to support a (sociologically)
constructionist view of gender identity (e.g. Lorber, 1994) that is somewhat
at odds with her own terms of reference. Her influence is considerable and
there are numerous (in some cases, sycophantic) websites that
support/discuss her work. Her texts are set reading for undergraduate
courses in Women's Studies, Gender Studies, Feminist Theory and are
thus deeply implicated with the complex networks that constitute inter-
disciplinarity. A range of feminist scholars engages with her work as a way
of bringing the body back into sex, gender and theory. It is important to
remember, however, that Butler's project is located within a wider feminist
philosophical project that seeks to disclose the culturally mediated character of what has been naturalized within the philosophical frame (i.e. gender). In particular, that matter of the body stands for a contentious materiality as the ground of identity/subjectivity and it is this notion of materiality that invites (de)constructionist approaches. Yet feminist philosophers
(and feminists in other disciplines) have been critical of the ways in which
constructionist approaches to materiality *inter alia* exile experience, which
has hitherto been defined in corporeal terms. There is, therefore, a 'double
bind' (Alcoff, 2000) for feminist philosophers that Butler's work has been
seen as perhaps more successfully negotiating. However, the body
brought back in not only lacks a social dimension (Jackson and Scott, 1998)
but also reiterates what others have observed from within the sociological
field (for instance, interactionism – Goffman, 1968 – and ethnomethodology
– Garfinkel, 1967), which may have something to do with Butler's disciplinary location and which is forgotten by feminists. I would suggest that
Butler writes materiality out of a feminist consideration of the body in
relation to sex/gender in two main ways.

First, the conflation evident between materiality and its signification
is mirrored by a conflation between sex and gender. For instance, Butler's
discussion and revision of the concept of performativity (1990) highlight
the artifice entailed in 'doing gender'. She argues that the performance of

drag within queer culture takes the form of a self-consciously exaggerated presentation and parade of femininity that depend on a distinction between 'the anatomy of the performer and the gender that is being performed' (p. 137). Butler suggests that the pleasure and delight of drag is that the audience is never in doubt that the queen is (anatomically) a man. This observation leads her to question the sex/gender binary hitherto so valuable to feminists and to suggest that there is nothing self-evidently gendered about either bodily conduct or the sexed body. Gender (as identity/subjectivity) is actively produced or *materialized* through a 'stylized repetition of acts' that have come to be understood as natural – as sex – over time. In the example of drag, the exaggeration of what are recognized as conventional displays of femininity should encourage us to consider all gender displays as a kind of performance regulated by cultural norms. Many feminists would agree with this analysis and there is much social sciences scholarship that lends support to it (for instance, interactionist and phenomenological studies that emphasize gender, defined as femininity/masculinity as something that is done/performed in ways that reinforce not only gender but also sex/sexuality). However, Butler's notion of performativity is not only about 'acts' or material practices such as gesture, conduct, movement but also, and is increasingly read as speech acts/citationality that reproduce the effects named in discourse (1993).

Second, though she is engaged in a project of trying to discern ways for bodies to matter in philosophical discourse, the resolutely post-structuralist stance that insists on the indissolubility of materiality and representation (and language in particular) epiphenomenalizes materiality (Alcoff, 2000) in ways that have the effect of reducing the material to discourse. In seeking to assert the indissolubility of materiality and its signification in language, the former is subsumed in the latter by a methodological strategy that privileges deconstruction and emphasizes regulatory heterosexuality as a symbolic regime rather than a set of social practices associated with particular social formations (and there is no reason why regulatory heterosexuality cannot be analysed in relation to both, for instance see Connell, 1995, but Butler's textual deconstruction/power analytics approach precludes this). If language is 'the very condition under which materiality can be said to appear' (1993: 31), then logically only language can be the focus of analysis. Although the analysis of language and discursive construction has its place, those working within the humanities – and literary theory in particular – tend to view discourse in primarily linguistic terms (matter as *sign*). However, some feminists working in and across other disciplines have been more sensitive to Foucault's original meaning of the term, which included attention to *social practice*.

Butler clearly moves away from an emphasis on gender as performance in *Bodies That Matter* (Hughes and Witz, 1997; Jackson and Scott, 1998) and from a concern with action (as a 'specific modality of power as discourse', 1993: 187) in a what has been developed by others as a socio-logical sense of bodily movement and gesture, towards a linguistic notion of citationality. Through performativity, language brings forth that which it names and which is 'citational', in that language cites practices and norms that are familiar. Linguistic performances draw their authority from known conventions which are repeated through citation and which, in turn, have a regulative effect. Thus, for Butler, linguistic performativity is both normative and regulative. This is the process through which sex is 'materialized' but because it is not absolute in its effect, there are 'spaces' in which to break the constraining impact of performativity. It is on this argument that Rosalyn Diprose develops her framework of ethical embodiment (see Chapter 3). However, for the feminist sociologist, there is little in Butler to address how linguistic performativity is shaped and why such performativity consistently produces 'heterosexual hegemony' (Ramazanoglu, 1993).

Butler's primary and initial emphasis was on the 'surface appearance of gender effected through performance' (Jackson and Scott, 1998) although she subsequently tries to address the production of gendered subjectivity through what she sees as a productive and limiting psychoan-alytic framework that rejects a clear distinction between an inner psychi-cal core of femininity and an outer representation of that core. In *Bodies That Matter*, Butler takes from Freud his diffident emphasis on the 'theo-retical indissolubility of physical and imaginary injury' (1993: 58) and develops a post-Lacanian argument around the inseparability of the sub-ject from internalized objects (for instance, the body). Though the body is in language it is never fully of it – the materiality of the body cannot be taken for granted as necessarily distinct from other forms of matter (evok-ing Althusser's question) but should be understood as morphology based on linguistic rules of differentiation (invoking Lacan). For Lacan, the body is psychical totality, an effect of signification (or a fiction), a morphological schema in which the phallus is unattached to a particular body part. Moreover, the psyche is implicated in the formation of morphology (or body-image) and can thus be conceived of as 'somatizing' or constitutive of how we imagine and experience the body (which she concedes always has an 'undeniable materiality', ibid.: 66). Through this claim Butler seeks to question Lacan's attachment to the structural privilege of the phallus and develop subversion from within his framework and instigate 'an anti-heterosexist sexual imaginary' (ibid.: 262).

Sexual difference emerges from the intersection of psyche and appearance, where the former is partially unknowable but which, nonetheless, shapes bodily action and conscious thought. This concept of self and subjectivity, traced through psychoanalysis and located within a symbolic regime, is radically distinct from a sociological notion of subjec-tivity which recognizes space for the social, or as Jackson and Scott put it, as 'a reflexive, social, embodied self in interaction with others' (1998: 14). Social space and interaction between different aspects of embodiment are masked in psychoanalytically inflected feminist philosophies of the body. In contrast, Lindemann (1997) offers distinctions between three different but related aspects of embodiment. The 'objectified' body refers to the body as an object moving through space that is recognized by self and others as a body while the 'experiencing' body refers to the sensory body as the phenomenological medium of experience. Finally, the body 'experienced' denotes not only awareness and sensation of one's own body in particular states, such as pleasure, but also the unobtrusive and taken-for-granted experience of one's own body when we are not necessarily aware of it in any heightened way. Here the body simply is. While the 'objectified' and 'experiencing' body constitute the 'living body' they are not reducible to the objectified body. Put another way, Lindemann's conceptualization suggests that the ways in which bodies are presented does not necessarily correlate in a straightforward way to our embodied experience. To some extent, Butler later acknowledges this. Although for Butler there is no pre-discursive (or pre-social, though these terms are not interchangeable) 'I', the potential for self-reflexivity exists, though she does not say how, through an investment in Derrida and the idea of the 'undecidability of the relation between inner psyche and exterior performance' (1993: 14).

Though Butler's approach to sex/gender valorizes the body, it 'devalorizes gender' and the sociality of women the concept of gender pulled into the sociological imagination (Witz, 2000). Her concept of 'sexed bodies' alludes to a partial concept of gender that is concerned with identity/subjectivity differentiation without attention to the structural, relational and symbolic inequalities and outcomes to which subjectivities are tied (Acker, 1989). In particular, the materialization emphasized by Butler is individualized and psychicized, dependent on the wilful mastery over one's body, a sharply honed self-consciousness and reflexive self-management to achieve particular outcomes. In doing so, Butler's approach leaves aside sociologically inflected understandings of the social, such as change across historical time and across the lifecourse, the importance of context for not only performance but also recognition and interpretation of what is meant by such performances and the local and global social processes underpinning change. The problem with this devalorization, accomplished by the conflation of materiality and a linguistic understanding of discourse, is that it encourages a view of the body detached from experiences, and collaterally from the bodies of women.

While Butler's work is seductive – it carries all the hallmarks of hierarchical abstraction and density that require a close and careful reading in order to 'get' the meaning – it offers a deradicalization of feminist endeavour within the privileged space of higher learning. The deconstructive and psychoanalytic frames within which she works open up the idea of the symbolic to resignification and the idea of discourse to resistance from within but fails in its splendidly formed logic to specify what it is about materiality that offers the potential for disruption or displacement beyond writing as the creation of a non-specific form of material culture. The body for Butler becomes an 'empty sign' that comes to bear 'phantasmastic investments' (1993: 191) that offer an expectation of unity that cannot be accommodated within the terms of post-Lacanian psychoanalysis because the body is the object of Lacanian theory. The body is a thing Lacanian psychoanalysis cannot recognize *as* a thing and hold on to its posturing towards disciplinary integrity (Ian, 1993: 28). Finally, Butler's partial conceptualization of gender compromises any political force that academic feminism might deliver beyond the context of the academy itself and undermines the potential for sincere inter-disciplinarity among feminists by privileging as her audience those working primarily within a textual frame who need to read closely and carefully in order to 'get' the text.

Corporeal feminisms: Elizabeth Grosz

In his book *Bodies of Meaning*, McNally (2001) notes that 'in talking about "the body" in a generic, non-gendered way' he may be accused of 'ignoring what so much feminist theory has tried to teach us: that we are not all of the same body, that the female body (and some female bodies more than others) experiences a unique sort of repression within the dominant relations of modern society'. He notes that 'a growing current within feminist theory is taking up many of the concerns with embodiment and the materiality of social practices that form my point of departure' (ibid.: 11). The body of theory to which he points includes the work of corporeal feminists such as Vicki Kirby and Elizabeth Grosz, with whom he credits as insisting on 'a turn to real, natural-historical bodies' (ibid.: 208n) as well as the work of avowedly materialist feminists such as Dorothy Smith. What is puzzling about this description is that he reads Kirby and Grosz as insisting on a return to the real when both authors effectively 'disappear' the body.

Feminist philosophers working in the continental tradition have increasingly returned to the specificities of the female body as a means of addressing metaphysical questions and of transcending binary oppositions that create ordinate/subordinate positions. Elizabeth Grosz is one of the main expositors in an emergent trajectory of 'corporeal feminism' and begins from the question of 'What constitutes a body?' She argues that feminist philosophers need to restate the question in different terms that destabilize the very notion of 'the body' as one thing or another. Her starting point is also a reconsideration of materiality through a re-reading of texts characterized by attention to the specificities of the lived body, that may enable the development of new metaphysical concepts of embodiment that offer neither essentialist nor discursive understandings of the body. Hence her project is concerned with 'destabilizing' oppositional categories, 'upsetting' binaries and installing indeterminacy as the principal tactic for developing feminist theories of the body. Like her peers, Grosz's work presents feminist treatments of a considerable range of (male) philosophers and theorists, but, like the work of Judith Butler, tends to be read by non-philosophers as a form of theory rather than *as* philosophy (Alcoff, 2000) and her work has been taken up by feminists across disciplines (and some non-feminist theorists) as a toolkit for engendering a 'non-dichotomous understanding of the body' (Grosz, 1994: 21).

Grosz picks up the Irigarayan challenge of using psychoanalytic theory to make women visible as philosophical subjects, to identify the ways in which the female body is 'spoken through' by representational practices (Grosz, 1999) and to confront the neutrality embedded in liberal concepts of subjectivity (see Hekman, 1992). Her method involves confronting the dualistic tendencies within such concepts and refusing any ontological distinction between a 'real' material body and its various representations, on the grounds that representational practices and discursive frameworks constitute the body. With a nod to Merleau-Ponty, Grosz presupposes the organic incompleteness of the body and its openness (Grosz, 1994: xi). This presupposition buttresses her claim that the body exceeds the disciplinary discourses through which it is understood (such as biomedical and academic discourses), though these undoubtedly have 'tangible effects on the bodies studied'. In making such a claim, Grosz reinforces the importance for feminists of locating their work on borderlands, and of moving across disciplines to find ways of addressing sexual difference from women's specific locations. However, such crossing rarely occurs in her own work and when it does so, it is unidirectional, moving in the direction *from* the more empirically modulated disciplines *towards* the formal theory to which Grosz contributes.

Grosz's method involves the substitution of dualistic models that separate mind and body with more a complex, psychoanalytically derived model that recasts sexual difference in corporeal terms. Though she too draws primarily on Lacan's work on the imaginary anatomy, she also concedes the value of Freud's understandings of the ego, sexual drives and psychical topography (see also Falk, 1994; Craib, 1998) and of how the body functions 'as a psychical, lived relation', and of the psyche as 'a projection of the body's form' (1994: 27). A main aim in her work is to secure the body's indeterminacy as a strategy through which to upset the binary opposites in which the body is conventionally understood (or later as she puts it, to create new models and metaphors in which to understand the significance of the body). Of particular concern, is the way that women have seldom been conceptualized as 'knowing subjects' within the philosophical optic and how, concomitantly, the body's relevance to knowledge production has been discarded. Though there is some variation in this regard, the body has in general been viewed within philosophy as a constraint on reason (Blaikie et al., 2003). Hence, she is engaged in a particular project that addresses not only feminist concerns but also the field of philosophy and she lays out a range of credible tactics that may contribute to this overall aim.

First, she stresses the need to develop accounts of the subject that avoid polarizations of mind and body and resist dualisms. Terms such as 'embodied subjectivity' or 'psychical corporeality' signal an insistence on rethinking materiality in terms that acknowledge not only physical matter but also the materiality of language and the ways in which particular discourses of the body are privileged (such as biomedical/biological discourses). It is worth quoting Grosz here to see the magnitude of her project:

> We need an account which refuses reductionism, resists dualism, and remains suspicious of the holism and unity implied by monism – a notion of corporeality, that is, which avoids not only dualism but also the very problematic of dualism that makes alternatives to it and criticisms of it possible. The narrow constraints our culture has imposed on the ways in which our materiality can be thought means that altogether new conceptions of corporeality – those, perhaps, which use the hints and suggestions of others but which move beyond the overall context and horizon governed by dualism – need to be developed, notions which see human materiality in continuity with organic and inorganic matter but also at odds with other forms of matter, which see animate materiality and the materiality of language in interaction, which make possible a materialism beyond physicalism (i.e. the belief that reality can be explained in terms of the laws, principles, and terms of physics), a materialism that questions physicalism, that reorients physics itself. (1994: 22)

There is much in this programmatic passage to examine but what is especially striking is the scale of the project Grosz promotes and the complexities that a feminist concept of the body needs to articulate in order to contribute to 'autonomous modes of self-understanding' (ibid.: 19) for women. What is also striking is that a programme that begins with a declaration about the need to retrieve the specificities of the female body as a vital element of that project moves rapidly towards a theoretical concept of the body that is everything and nothing. Moreover, while she places materialism and materiality outside or beyond either the materiality of biology/physics or language (as a non-reductive ontology), as holding the key or potential for resistance, her methodology – textual analysis of theorists as disparate as Merleau-Ponty and Deleuze and Guattari – means that materiality ends up as that which is textually constituted. Yet her detachment from scholarship that closely examines the bodily specificities to which she points as imperative to the development of feminist theory undercuts the force of her argument and proscribes discussion of the social as a concrete, discernible space in which bodies work, play, copulate, live and breathe.

Second, corporeality needs to be viewed as a concept that addresses both women and men and needs to be used as an inclusive concept that accounts not only for sexual difference, but difference in general. As is evident in her discussion in Chapter 6 of *Volatile Bodies* of the censorship of seminal fluids, writing women's embodiment into philosophy/theory should not be undertaken in ways that reinforce disembodied men as the rational actors of the public stage (see also Rahman and Witz, 2003). Finally, she advocates terms that imply relationships and articulations between the biological and the psychological (inside and outside) and in particular, between the 'psychical representation of the subject's lived body as well as relations between body gestures, posture, and movement in the constitution of processes of psychical representations' (1994: 23).

Though Grosz's work addresses a range of philosophical concerns, it is mainly read by non-philosophers (feminists and otherwise) as a theory of relations between soma and psyche. Or, as Grosz herself puts it, psychoanalytic theory provides a framework through which to explore how 'the subject's corporeal exterior is psychically represented and lived by the subject' (1994: xii). Grosz credits Freud for foreshadowing an understanding of the interaction between biology and psychology (soma and psyche) in his discussions of how perception reaches consciousness. In his view, as Grosz sees it, 'the psychical cannot be unambiguously separated from the perceptual' (ibid.: 30). Indeed, ego and id are only distinguished from each other via the impact of perceptual stimuli on the surface of the body. In particular, skin provides a kind of screen between ego and id that synthesizes an array of sensations gathered from other sense organs and directs these towards the ego, which operates as a kind of internal screen (bodily ego). Thus formulated, the ego may be seen as an inner representation of an outer surface that is in contact with its immediate environment. The idea of skin as cultural border is not new in the field of social criticism. For instance, the art critic John Berger has written about the Mexican painter Frida Kahlo's use of skin, where her canvas acts as a form of skin on which the painter inscribes images and thus mirrors the way that the social and emotional is inscribed on human skin (and see, more recently, Benthein, 2002). Nonetheless, Grosz develops Freud's materialist understanding of the unconscious (as neurologically stimulated) to reject ideas about the body as a neutral body implied by medical, scientific and conventional discourse, since it is invested with a particularity and a positionality between nature and culture from which the ego develops.

Lacan pursues a similar notion of bodily ego in his discussions of its emergence from the mirror stage of development in which the child becomes fascinated with the externalized image of its own body. Again, Lacan's body is not the anatomical or physiological body but 'an imaginary outline or projection of the body ... insofar as it is imagined and represented for the subject by the image of others (including its own reflection in a mirror)' (1994: 39). 'Imaginary anatomy' connotes 'an internalized image or map of the meaning that the body has for the subject, for others in its social world, and for the symbolic order conceived in its generality' (ibid.: 40). Psychic structure in Lacan is not concurrent with biology as with Freud, but is redefined as morphology, or as 'enfleshed, experiential understandings of the bodily self' (Braidotti, 1998: 300). However, as Irigaray also claims, the issue of gender differentiation associated with the externalized image of one's body is at stake. This is particularly so because both Freud and Lacan adopt a male view in their discussions of the Oedipus complex and avoid the impact of female morphology on self-conception.

Lacan stresses the power of the phallus in constituting how the subject views oneself, and Grosz concedes that it may be plausible that male body morphology influences how boys see others prior to their understanding of anatomical differences (i.e. as phallic). However, she argues that in order to argue this for girls, the phallus needs to be accorded *a priori* privilege in the constitution of the body image (1994: 59). Indeed, this is what Lacan implies in his claims that for girls, the pre-Oedipal development of body image is one that is castrated; hence girls are required to 'accept castration long before the castration complex'. As other feminists have observed, both Freud and Lacan assert that 'the condition under which patriarchy is psychically produced is the constitution of women's bodies as lacking' (1994: 60). Yet, the 'lack' referred to in the psychoanalytic frame is not necessarily ontological but morphological and imaginary. Thus, though Grosz acknowledges the limits of psychoanalytic theory, it remains potentially productive for a feminist project as a means of identifying the processes through which bodies are inscribed at a number of levels (anatomical, neurological, physiological) and at a number of stages in development. Moreover, she insists that the psychoanalytic frame, like that of Merleau-Ponty's philosophy of embodiment, implies a body that is open-ended and pliable rather than fixed and durable. Thus formulated, Grosz prepares the way for a feminist reading of imaginary anatomy that involves challenging the ways in which the body is socially and culturally represented and privileges cultural/textual deconstruction as the key goal for academic feminism.

Grosz develops Lacan's brief reference to the Möbius strip in his 1966 lecture *The Language of Criticsm and the Sciences of Man* as a conceptual means of integrating body and mind. This is a three-dimensional figure of eight in which mind and body are 'not two distinct substances or two kinds of attributes of a single substance but somewhere between these two alternatives' (1994: xii). Her model emphasizes the flow and fusion between mind and body and the analytic difficulties of separating one from another. The model itself is based on Lacan's fascination with a branch of mathematics – topology – that deals with the properties of geometric objects (surfaces and solids) that remain unchanged when deformed but not torn. Sokal and Bricmont's (1998) wicked parody of Lacan and other post-structuralists refers to a joke about a topologist as someone who is unable to tell the difference between a donut and coffee cup because both are solid objects with a single hole, in order to raise a more serious question about the implications of using geometrical modelling to metaphorize relations between soma and psyche. Grosz's development of corporeal feminism offers a means of integrating 'lived experience' and its production and interaction with cultural categories. She argues that the body can be understood as: 'the site of the intermingling of mind and culture; it can also be seen as the symptom and mode of expression and communication of a hidden interior or depth' (1994: 116). Grosz's project, while identified with post-structuralism, seeks to ascertain how the body may be inscribed in ways that could contribute to women's independence and autonomy. Her aim in this regard is decidedly derived from an Enlightenment impulse to transform women's experience and is rooted in the development of a theory of the body that acknowledges difference and specificity without reducing women to 'other', to provide a means of emancipation and value that does not reduce femininity to immanence. Her work circulates across disciplines, is much cited by feminists and non-feminists, philosophers and non-philosophers (e.g. Burkitt, 1999) who seek to embody gender and gender the body in their work.

Yet Grosz has been criticized by feminists for addressing theoretical questions which have little connection with everyday experience. Despite her insistence on specificity, there is little that is specific in her work. For instance, she writes in general terms about 'men' and 'women' that fail to acknowledge shifts in their social position and experience in late modern contexts in terms of for example, pay, parenting and sexuality. A similar feature of generality is also evident in her work on cities (1995), which has been especially influential in feminist geographers' attempts to rethink places and space. However, her speculations on relations between the body, place and space (in which the city 'seeps' into corporeality and leaves its traces) seem uninformed by detailed empirical and experiential scholarship around such issues (for instance, the work of Jane Jacobs in the USA or Liz Bondi in the UK). This unawareness of scholarship is also evident in her discussion of medical discourses about sexual difference and her observation that feminists need to historically trace these discourses because of their status as an index of cultural attitudes about sex and sexuality. In fact, this is precisely what Thomas Laqueur (1991) offers in his meticulously researched *Making Sex*. While there are blind spots or gaps even in the most rigorous academic studies, what makes the absences so absorbing in Grosz's case is her interdisciplinary status and her insistence on particularity and specificity.

Despite her insistence on a model that purportedly collapses boundaries between dualisms, the psychoanalytic frame and the topological model of the Möbius strip have a tendency to create a space in which the body is textualized in ways that privilege mind, or as Marshall puts it: 'body vanishes into the self and interior is privileged over exterior' (1996: 254).

Though there exists considerable scholarship that seeks to demonstrate the material inscriptions of culture on the body (e.g. Burnett and Holmes, 2001) and though the concept of corporeality signals acknowledgement of the physical body, it is nonetheless psychoanalytically derived, and thus loses the materiality (lived experience) of difference by its insistence on textual metaphors of inscription (Burkitt, 1999). And though the concept of corporeality developed in Grosz's work appears to emphasize 'actual social relations' (and the practices and connections embedded within such relations), the psychoanalytic timbre constantly works against a fuller elaboration of the relations and practices in which inscription occurs. Though Grosz concludes that masculinity and femininity are coded as different as a corollary of psychoanalytic difference, a difference inflected differently according to class, context, race, history, her failure to specify these differences makes the social significance of difference unclear. Moreover, the psyche is privileged in a way that reflects the habitus of academic feminism and philosophy in particular and the concession to the autonomous subject that continues to characterize liberal institutions such as the academy.

Though the Möbius strip offers a model in which mind and body are interlaced, neither Grosz, nor those who favour her model (e.g. Williams and Bendelow, 1998), have as yet been able to demonstrate the value of such a model in the context of examining substantive issues. The model raises the epistemological question of how individuals develop a consciousness of the interconnection of mind and body and concomitantly, how researchers can 'know' about the body when it may not be 'known' by individuals themselves (Scarry, 1985). For instance, in empirical research there is some evidence that when researchers look for evidence of such interaction they often do not find it, i.e. people only become aware of their bodies when asked about it and are forced to 'articulate' embodiment in ways that typically make reference to dominant metaphors and discourses about the human body (Marshall, 1996; Cunningham-Burley and Backett-Milburn, 1998).

Finally, though feminist philosophers attempt to reveal the 'culturally mediated and changeable character' of those aspects of life that are naturalized through the body, they also aspire to reappraise philosophies that ignore corporeality (Alcoff, 2000). Yet, their attachment to and sympathy with constructionist approaches effectively write against the grain of materiality and of experience (Hughes and Witz, 1997). The epiphenomenal status of materiality within philosophy and the absence of engagement with experience may be discerned in the following. Even though Grosz's immanent critique offers a *model* of corporeality that promises the dissolution of boundaries between entrenched philosophical binaries, feminist and non-feminist discussion gets locked into a dialogue about the intrinsic value of the model, rather than *how* it might be applied to substantive concerns. Thus, the starting and finishing point for feminist philosophies of the body is theory rather than experience and the epistemological insights that are developed through this work are translated into *writing* as a form of cultural/political intervention. As with the grand narratives of the master philosophers before postmodernism, feminist theories of the body seek to establish an explanation for sexual difference prior to (and as a substitute for) identifying the substance and consequences of difference. Such an exercise would require engaging with experience and materiality beyond the text, and as such, would presumably be antithetical to the project of rewriting the body in which feminist philosophers of the body are engaged.

Telling flesh: Vicki Kirby

Kirby offers an intellectually and stylistically complex work in her book *Telling Flesh* (1997), which also draws on a body of writing that spans a decade and addresses what she views as the problem of surreptitious reassertions of Cartesian divisions in the work of feminist theorists even as they struggle to challenge these divisions. In particular, Kirby argues throughout against an understanding of difference (between, for instance, mind/body or real/represented) as a distance. Rather, the relation between oppositional concepts such as real/represented can be viewed as a 'productive entanglement'. To support her argument, she draws on both Saussure and Derrida, and in particular the latter's assertion that 'there is no outside of text' in order to demonstrate the inseparability of substance and representation (ibid.: 61).

Derrida describes 'flesh and bone' as text. The deconstructive scene of writing itself, claims Kirby, includes the perceived density and immediacy of lived experience together with the critique of such empiricist truth claims. The empirical fact of the body is not simply rejected by a deconstructive gesture: rather, it is complicated and rewritten within the weave of these 'paradoxical implications' (ibid.: 69). This interpretation of Derrida pitches his deconstructionism close to a form of dialectical critique in which writing and the trace are 'reminders of the inescapably material character of language and thought' (McNally, 2001: 56). Using this, then,

Kirby argues for an approach to the body that refuses the divisibility of matter/language, that reads the body as text, where text assumes a more critical and complex definition than 'merely' documents or utterances. For Kirby, the generalized writing of culture through the body evoked by Derrida's notion of the body as 'the scene of writing' offers a 'corporeography' through which body can be grasped as text and through which text becomes embodied.

Kirby asks provocative questions about the goal of academic feminism but suggests that even in the destabilizing work undertaken through academic feminism's mobilization of interdisciplinarity, the female body, as a flesh and blood body, occupies a 'danger zone' from which feminist writing seeks to protect itself and corporeality is viewed as involving 'a difference that cannot be known' (1997: 154). One of her main points is the irony that feminist writers who occupy theoretical positions largely in opposition to each other share the same 'theoretical investments' in a body located beyond or outside language (or patriarchy) since the beyond in which the body is located is effectively excluded from 'the scene of production' or writing in phallocentrism (ibid.: 99). Referring to Irigaray's work, for instance, she notes how the body that occupies this work is made safe for feminist theory/theorists by being identified as a metaphorical rather than literal body. This bracketing out of matter – what feminist sociologists might view as a 'flesh and blood' body (Witz, 2000) – by feminist theorists of the body, occurs in different ways, outlined in Kirby's detailed excursions through the work of those she identifies as key feminist theorists of the body, namely, Drucilla Cornell, Jane Gallop, Luce Irigaray, Gayatri Spivak and Judith Butler.

For instance, for Cornell, matter is inaccessible since it occupies a location beyond language and can only be grasped indirectly through language, which becomes the reality of matter (Kirby, 1997: 89). For Kirby, such a view offers an understanding of matter as both something distinct from language and rendered intelligible through language. Though Butler's position is complex, she too suggests that there can be no access to bodily life prior to or beyond the language that names it, such that language and materiality are embedded in each other though radically different (ibid.: 103). However in Butler's work, the body as matter is bracketed out since it exceeds representation and thus, argues Kirby, Butler's position ultimately reinforces a view of matter as outside language (ibid.: 115). Similarly, Gallop conceptualizes matter as illusory since it is constituted *as* matter through language (ibid.: 74). Although on first reading this position may seem close to Kirby's own refusal of separation between matter and language ('representation is a material expression through and through', ibid.: 115), Kirby is critical of Gallop's argument on the grounds that the illusory nature of matter effectively closes off a means of engaging with how language is implicated in matter, because of the way in which psychoanalytic takes on subjectivity 'veil' the body 'before or behind language' (ibid.: 156).

Kirby is sceptical of correctives that seek to displace old theories with new (better) ones and respectful of the feminist body of work on which she develops her own position. Indeed, she repeatedly avows her membership of the same categorical positions in which much of this work is located and asserts her attempt to push the indivisibility of matter and language further than has been possible in the work of theorists. This indivisibility is repeatedly emphasized through assertions that word and flesh are 'utterly implicated', are both always becoming, are inseparable, in which flesh, blood and bone are literate matter that 'never ceases to reread and rewrite itself through endless incarnations' (ibid.: 127). Here, Kirby is reiterating Derrida's notion of the 'irreducible materiality of history' implicated in the scene of writing though Derrida himself avoided explicit reference to matter as substance, reference, context beyond text. However, it is difficult to identify the nature of flesh implicated in language.

Like many other feminist theorists, for Kirby, 'the body' is typically used interchangeably with biology, anatomy, interiority or morphology. That is to say, even in the complex understandings of the relation between matter and language dissected by Kirby, understandings of what the human body is are restricted to these terms. To be fair, Kirby herself acknowledges the restricted way in which the body is materialized in feminist theory (ibid.: 116) or limited to 'specular reflection'. Yet her insistence on the mutual implication of matter and language in the 'other' does little to identify a body that could be recognized as distinct from language or as materiality. Indeed, she makes the extraordinary claim in her introduction to a chapter on cyberspace and virtual bodies that 'in the closing years of the millennium the *self-evidence of the corporeal* can no longer be assumed' (ibid.: 127; my italics), yet at no point does she discuss the specific ways in which the corporeal has hitherto been deemed 'self-evident'. These might include common-sense understandings of the human body, metaphors, taboos, biomedical understandings, understandings framed in terms of experience, and so on. Hence, though Kirby is critical of the bracketing out of matter effected by the repetition of Cartesian divisions in feminist theory, it is difficult to identify what sort of matter matters in Kirby's work.

The more serious problem for feminists interested in thinking through the body, and the contribution to this project that feminist theories of the body could make, is how to retrieve matter not only in a way that matters for theory (as in Butler and Kirby's projects), but also to retrieve matter in a way that women recognize as matter that matters for a more pragmatic politics grounded in the everyday. The body variously identified as biology/anatomy/morphology is a conceptual body fixed in space and time. For instance, as Kirby observes, while Butler attempts to reassure readers that she is not theorizing away the 'unavoidable facticity of bodily life' (ibid.: 101), nonetheless, the bodily life to which she refers is one characterized by appeal to facts. These facts include sleep, ingestion, pain and illness as primary and irrefutable experiences that 'can be seen as limiting horizons' (ibid.: 101). Where, for Butler, the facts of bodily life proffer limitations for the consideration of human subjectivity and the theorization of the politics of identity, for her critics, 'even if the construction of reality is conceded, the pressing facts of bodily existence endure' (ibid.: 101).

There are two issues here for Kirby, one that concerns how bodily existence comes to take on the factual status that results in its bracketing out and one that concerns how constructionism is viewed within feminist theories of the body and exemplified by Butler. The view of constructionism that informs Butler's work is one that is avowedly linguistic. Language and discourse are typically used interchangeably and come to mean the same thing in Butler's texts. Yet, as has been well documented, this collapse of discourse to language excludes an appreciation of discourse as an active production of the social and the cultural through not only language but also non-linguistic practices. Moreover, what is constructed through language in Butler's thesis is culture as something that either stands in opposition to the social or which subsumes the social.

Kirby rejects the oppositional inevitability of Butler's thesis but remains locked into an asocial understanding of language because of her own reproduction of Cartesianism and, one suspects, a refusal to seriously consider the 'necessarily mediated character of all phenomena' (McNally, 2001: 56). While she repeatedly argues for a notion of the specific, of matter as a located corporeography, she is diffident about her own concept because of the potential for the unity of the subject implied in notions of the local, situation and positioned. Hence, the specificity implied in her concept of corporeography disappears from her text, because of the way in which the female body is repeatedly referred to as 'the body'. This reference reproduces the Cartesian notion that the subject *has* a body of which Kirby is so critical and fails to recognize that within other perspectives (such as phenomenology), the subject *is* already embodied. The deconstructive impulse of repetition forgets the body and, according to McNally, 'fetishes text in an endless circuit of ideas emptied of substance' (2001: 74), a consequence of the refusal to concede the idea of a foundation to self that sets limits to thought. The embodiment of the subject offers the potential for addressing the corporealization of the subject through text only where text not only refers to documents and written forms of life, but also contexts, actions and practices.

Theorists such as Kirby avoid specifying the corporeal because of the way in which attention to specificity demands attention to particular experiences, but the category of experience has been denigrated within feminist theory. Kirby alludes to this denigration in a footnote that explains how trenchantly Joan Scott has analysed the 'intellectual paralysis that results when "experience" is taken as the last word in an account of the politics of identity' (1997: 171). However, it does not make sense to advocate a theory of the specific or the particular, as the concept of corporeality claims to capture, without being able to identify and describe the specificity and particularity so claimed.

Conclusion

This chapter has provided a critical overview of the key theories developed within new feminist philosophies of the body and of corporeal feminism in particular. Though these theories differ in many respects, in terms of their substantive emphases, they have a number of elements in common. First, the psychoanalytic framework developed by Lacan and subsequently by others is key to exploring relations between the body and (differentiated) subjectivity. Sexed subject positions are constructed principally via language though they are not necessarily fixed and stable and, thus, offer a potential, imagined site of resistance though resistance is limited to textual interventions that write the body in provocative ways.

Second, sexual difference theory is oriented towards addressing difference as other than non-masculine and is conducted largely within the field of theory, though feminists engaged in this project do acknowledge the importance of material inequalities and the specificities of lived, embodied experience. Yet the acknowledgement of inequalities and specificities is partial and limited. In practice, feminist adoption of psychoanalytically derived notions of sexual difference reorders concern with social and political issues to questions of 'theoretical exactitude' (Brennan, 1998: 279) where theory is endlessly elaborated and the body is troped (Ebert, 1996; Rojek and Turner, 2000).

However, many feminists continue to seek ways of addressing the relationship between the experience and significance of female embodiment and the wider contributions of female embodiment to the social devaluation of women. For liberal feminists (e.g. Friedan, 1963) and materialist sociologists (e.g. Jackson and Scott), sexuality is overemphasized and sexual difference occludes gender (Witz, 2000). This has particular implications for feminist sociologists who seek to identify and explain inequalities and differences that stand outside but have a relation to the psyche. Clearly the challenge for contemporary feminism has been to do so without *opposing* the body (sex) to the symbolic (gender). However, though the project of corporeal feminism bears more than a family resemblance to feminist standpoint theory, it differs to the extent that where standpoint begins from the materiality of the body, corporeal feminisms begin by calling materiality into question. The methodological strategy of writing fetishizes text and accords analytic privilege to representations of the body in ways that not only collapse divisions between the real and represented but also privilege the feminist theorist as best placed to read, write and culturally decode the body. Hence, materiality has become 'the site at which a certain drama of sexual difference plays itself out' (Butler, 1993: 49) but it was not always thus. The new feminist theories of the body that privilege deconstructionist and psychoanalytic tactics occlude earlier theories that seek not only to make visible materiality but also to make some material difference.

five

Embodying gender/gendering the body

Introduction

While many feminists are sympathetic to the expressed concern for 'bringing the body in' to scholarship, the body has never been fully absent, yet, paradoxically, in recent attempts to embody theory, the body is not fully present. Chapter 1 suggests that while sociological scholarship has been concerned with the historical and material production of the body, the emergence of somatic society and its attendant practices and relations, efforts to gender the body have over-subscribed to feminist theories underpinned by a Lacanian psychoanalytic framework. In such a framework, particular aspects of female embodiment are transcribed into a general theory of the body that places sexual difference at its core. While the explication of sexual difference is a strategic goal for academic feminism, new feminist theories of the body framed by sexual difference cannot be uncritically grafted into sociological theories that seek to gender the body. In the passage from feminist theory, bounded by Lacanian discussions of sexual difference, to the field of sociology, the body escapes specification. Yet this escape works against other legacies within both feminism and sociology.

Chapter 2 makes the claim that analysis of the politics of the body was especially important for both radical feminists in the 1970s and materialist analyses in the 1980s in ways that have had an impact on subsequent body theorizing. Feminists in many disciplines continue to generate pragmatic materialist research on a range of substantive issues concerning female embodiment but these tend to be located within a particular field – for instance, the sociology, anthropology or geography of health and illness – and defined as specialist knowledge in ways that fail to be incorporated into interdisciplinary work by theorists (Ebert, 1996). The feminist conceptions and interventions associated with women's health activism and body politics in the 1970s engendered a range of feminist organizations in the UK, the USA, Australia and New Zealand that are increasingly global in scope, are embedded within state bureaucracies (Broom, 1991) and address the implications for women of specific events or interventions (in relation to reproduction, health surveillance or hormone replacement therapy). Hence, the kinds of activism stimulated by concerns for women's bodily experiences continues to thrive, influenced by and interconnecting with feminist scholarship and debates about difference, conflict and multiple standpoints, yet these exemplify feminist knowledges that are marginalized by theory (Clarke and Olesen, 1999).

Chapter 3 focuses on the emergence and development of the corporeal turn and the various ways in which feminism has tried to embody theory and in so doing embody gender. The legacies of Foucault, Merleau-Ponty and Lacan are distinct in this scholarship yet there are tensions between the focus on embodiment as a condition and constituent of agency evident in Foucauldian and phenomenological approaches and the body as the focal point of Lacanian theory. In particular, feminist interventions in ethics that begin by drawing on arguments associated with Foucault and Merleau-Ponty begin to move more explicitly towards a post-Lacanian psychoanalytic framework that privileges the imaginary over imagery, and textual tactics over social practices.

Chapter 4 suggests that while the process of embodying theory has been increasingly central to feminism, the body has not been fully present. Rather, it has occupied an ethereal presence in the theorizing that takes place through textual and psychoanalytic categories in the name of inter-disciplinarity. As discussion of key feminist work argued, the scrutiny of material/ity that characterizes the corporeal turn has generated a body suspended in space and time, without change and devoid of context. Despite the claims made by those working within a psychoanalytic framework *for* materiality, such a frame pushes embodiment out of its frame.

Embodying Gender concludes by situating new feminist (and sociological) theories of the body in the context of inter-disciplinarity and psychoanalytic theory. The critical threads spun out across Chapters 1 to 4 are reconnected and body concepts are considered that offer the potential for building 'reliable knowledge'. This chapter argues that this project could ensue by revisiting the category of experience, hence, the discussion proceeds by reconsidering materialist accounts of experience in an attempt to retrieve an approach to the body – or rather, embodiment – that retains a pragmatic concern for the social and cultural contexts in which embodiment is lived and in which it becomes politically significant.

The postmodern/post-structuralist academy and inter-disciplinarity

The development of cultural and literary studies as the core reference point for contemporary feminist theory is part of a more general geo-political shift in Western social sciences and humanities away from discipline-centred scholarship towards a style of social philosophy that asserts a decentred subject and denounces grand narratives. These inclinations are derived from the intellectual crisis associated with the demise of Western Marxism and the turn against materialist analysis as both political practice and as a theory of socio-economic change (Rojek and Turner, 2000), the displacement of science as the basis for emancipation (Lyotard, 1984) and aesthetic modernity's emphasis on language and representation as constitutive of reality (Ian, 1993). However, these post-structuralist inclinations place an ironic limit on the capacities of inter-disciplinarity to fulfil its undertaking.

Academic feminism has developed unevenly across disciplines and acquired more strength in some disciplines than others, depending on the modes of apprenticeship and openness of scholarship within particular disciplines (Stanley, 1997). For instance, the attraction of sociology for many of its practitioners – perhaps especially women – is its eclectic character and methodological pluralism. In contrast, twentieth-century philosophy has operated along more closed, guarded lines. This unevenness, combined with the practical difficulties of doing feminism in academic environments already reshaped by education cuts in the neo-conservative political climate of education from the 1980s, and a political commitment to shared knowledge production, has contributed to academic feminism's confrontation with disciplinary boundaries as a product of a rigidly male conception of knowledge. Inter-disciplinarity may also be understood as a partial solution to persistent inequalities associated within Western academic institutions, in that relatively few women are in promoted positions or institutional positions of influence and there continue to be inequalities in pay between men and women across grades. Furthermore, while some disciplines may be more likely to have women in tenured or secure positions, women in other disciplines are much more likely to occupy marginal positions because of their part-time and/or temporary employment status. These differences contribute not only to divisions between male and female academics but also among female academics and have implications for the forms of scholarship in which they (are able to) engage.

There are – often unacknowledged – problems with inter-disciplinary ethos. Though feminists generally favour interdisciplinary approaches to the production of knowledge, the disciplinary apprenticeships that academic feminists invariably serve encourage assumptions about what disciplines view as their objects of study and the appropriate methodologies for examining them (Stanley, 1999). Though academic feminists may see themselves as both feminists and as academics within a particular discipline, as members of that discipline feminists may be said to share certain disciplinary assumptions that presumably influence how they conceptualize the subjects who are the focus of feminism (Oakley, 1998). These assumptions also have methodological implications since disciplines constitute boundaries of inclusion/exclusion and we cannot safely assume that key concepts will translate across disciplines (Howson and Inglis, 2001). In short, it is unclear whether methods and techniques from one discipline can simply be imported to another without attention to what happens to them in the process of importation. Moreover, conceptual boundaries are no longer clearly defined and objects of study previously claimed by one discipline are increasingly viewed as within the realms of possibility of another. Accordingly, academic feminism's orientation towards inter-disciplinarity may compromise the extent to which feminists are able to explicitly engage with the main debates within their own discipline, which as we have seen, encourages non-feminist members of disciplines to ignore discipline specific feminist knowledge in consideration of particular fields (such as the body).

The sharing of substantive issues is particularly evident in relation to the body. Feminist theorizing on the body has developed its own specialists, who are widely cited, and who engage much more with theoretical concerns and concepts than with the significance of the body in everyday life. As Stanley (1999) puts it, the data on which feminist philosophies of the body are based are other texts, which engage with abstract concepts of the body while simultaneously acknowledging the continued importance of addressing the 'woman in the body'. However, as I have argued, the body in the text assumes an aesthetic quality that renders it distinct from the bodies of women. Indeed, as sociology and other disciplines have focused more intently on the body as grounding of experience and/or action, feminists have contributed to the consolidation of the body as an object of theory.

Academic feminism's initial ambivalence towards the female body has been transformed into a decisive espousal of the body as the conceptual centrepiece of feminist theory. Stirred by postmodern and post-structuralist intellectual currents, academic feminism has been at the forefront of the critique of the universal subject (Pateman, 1988), and has criticized the attendant ways in which women have been obscured by the Enlightenment model of the subject (McNay, 1992), though feminism itself as a social and political movement is a creature of the emancipatory imperative within modernity (Marshall, 1994). However, feminism's attempts to incorporate women have not only attenuated differences between women (Barrett, 1992) but also have highlighted how the Enlightenment self has been a disembodied self (Hekman, 1992) that is now invariably understood as a fragmented self (Flax, 1986). Consequently, epistemological questions concerning the basis of knowledge about the constitution of self and subjectivity are at the forefront of current feminist inquiry (Barrett and Phillips, 1992). These questions inform the turn to the 'politics of ambivalence' evident in feminist textual interventions that aim to rewrite the body for feminism as part of a critique of subjectivity. For some feminists the conundrum here is that while the critical tools of Enlightenment thinking have made women theoretically visible (that is, visible in the field of theory), the women made visible as theorists implicitly abandon the tools through which their visibility has been made possible (Fraser and Nicholson, 1990).

This conundrum seems most apparent in the field of the body. The shift towards theory is as Barrett (1992) has observed, a shift from things to words, in which the former are seen to acquire their meaning solely through the discourses in which they are constituted as particular kinds of objects. Post-structuralist approaches to social reality deconstruct the practices and words through which reality is perceived and constituted while simultaneously disavowing any boundary between real/represented. The analytic emphasis of this approach is on process rather than on producing definitive accounts that 'tell it like it was or is', because of the difficulties of establishing universal criteria of judgement as a consequence of the demise of grand narratives as the basis for claims of authority and through which social phenomena are explained. Yet, though new feminist philosophies of the body eschew the materiality of the body because of the universalizing and essentializing tendencies with which materiality has hitherto been associated, such theories nonetheless attribute subversive qualities to the female body by viewing it as an epistemological resource through which to challenge patriarchal knowledge, meanings and values (Currie and Raoul, 1992). Despite the best of feminist intentions, it is difficult not to read such attribution as a re-assertion of grand narrative expressed in feminist theory as an art form, through a repetitious focus on texts as though they themselves possess significant form (Ian, 1993). Though feminists in a range of disciplines are engaged in substantive projects that speak to and of embodiment at various levels and through diverse conceptualizations of experience, feminist theory has been concurrently grouping itself around the body as its centrepiece and the textual practices associated with the field of the body tender a disciplinary apparatus that holds the various and diverse elements and fissures of feminist theory together. The insertion of the body into feminist theory thus offers an integrative field in which many feminists locate themselves as *theorists* and which may be an effect of the challenges of explicitly working within and towards an ethos of inter-disciplinarity.

Inter-disciplinarity is compromised in two main ways. First, the textual methodologies underpinned by abstract analytical categories dependent on detailed readings of post-structuralist texts are accorded a privileged place within academic feminism. They are treated thus because of the ways in which abstraction represents cultural capital in a knowledge hierarchy (Bourdieu and Passeron, 1990) and the institutional and disciplinary advantages it confers on feminists who develop the skills to interpret and produce such texts. Yet, such methodologies potentially blunt the critical bite of feminist theories of the body by reinforcing an inward form of critique impelled by textual politics and practice rather than interventions to examine and explain the material conditions of women's lives. While it may be that many feminists have abandoned the latter form of endeavour as discourses of neo-liberalism concerning agency, the individual subject and writing as invention displace praxis (Ebert, 1996), this may be a luxury that few women can afford; indeed, it may be a luxury accrued only by the relative institutional security of tenured academics in prestigious research universities. Moreover, the focus on text to the exclusion of matters beyond the text offers a narrow horizon for a politically relevant feminism and publicly engaged academic endeavour.

Second, the status associated with abstraction *as* methodology means that those feminists best skilled in its deployment are more likely to be heard within academic (and publishing) communities than those whose methodological commitments place them closer to strategies associated with pragmatic research agenda. Theory is privileged and viewed as uniquely authoritative within knowledge systems. This privilege is reinforced by the drift in publishing towards theory as a form of non-disciplinary language that claims to reach wider audiences. The textual politics generated by textual methodologies means that academic feminists now have to skill themselves up as rhetoricians in order to compete in an interdisciplinary community that simultaneously underscores yet effectively undermines freedom of exchange. While textual practices are seductive, they are also potentially divisive in the sense that they sustain a feminist hierarchy based on techniques of representation that are themselves socially designated practices of a particular habitus (Bourdieu and Passeron, 1990): forms of grand theory that treat text as a static authority. The skills required to 'get' the text (as Butler puts it in relation to Irigaray) effect closures rather than openings and forget that feminists themselves are part of the textual apparatuses they engender and to which they commit. Such skills are associated with the development of the autonomous self/thinking subject as a discrete individual contemplating an outer world from which she is detached (Elias) but are quite specifically the product of privilege and specific historical circumstances. However, the current forms of inter-disciplinarity within which theory dominates generally mask the location of feminist knowers and the relations of privilege in which theorists operate (Skeggs, 1997).

The reading of new feminist theories of the body offered here and the ways in which they circulate and are adopted within academic feminism suggest that dialogue among feminists in the interdisciplinary community takes place in a restricted space in which certain feminists are heard and accorded prestige and others are not. It is not necessarily the case, as Ebert (1996), for instance, argues in her searing condemnation of what she sees as *ludic* feminism, of which new feminist theories of the body are part, that only historical materialist feminist voices are unheard, but rather, in my view, it is the case that increasingly voices that speak outside the immanent critique of textual politics are muted. While many feminists engage with the theories of body feminism, such theories rarely consider feminist scholarship beyond the boundaries of formal theory. As an *academic* endeavour, perhaps such theories do not need to seriously engage with empirical work. After all, the distance between formal theory and messy data is hardly a new phenomenon since the academy in general is the 'native land of textual practice' (Connell, 2001). One might expect such a distance to be most pronounced within disciplines characterized by attention to immanent criticism and conceptual development, such as philosophy or literary theory. However, if academic feminism wishes to continue to develop as a *political* endeavour committed to building reliable knowledge with the potential to explain if not transform women's lives, new feminist theories of the body, such as those outlined here, need to rethink their relationship to other forms of feminist scholarship, including and perhaps especially, those committed to methodologies that support a pragmatic approach to the analysis of embodiment.

Sociology and psychoanalysis

While, as Lupton (1997) comments, Freudian psychoanalytic theory is notably absent from contemporary sociology, there is nonetheless a discernible tradition in sociology of integrating psychoanalytic categories to analyses of the social. For instance, psychoanalytic theory was particularly influential in early twentieth-century attempts to develop sociologically modulated accounts of the development of the self as open to influence through social relations with others (Cooley, 1902; Mead, 1934). Winnicott (1987) too developed a more socially inflected process of development that concedes both active social interaction and responses between infant and carer and the corporeal presence of the mother. Freud's legacy was similarly important for Parsons's (1964) theorizing of medical encounters and his treatment of personality; and for the reconstructed Marxism of the Frankfurt School which developed psychoanalytic insights to explore and demonstrate the repressive impact of capitalism on the psyche (especially Herbert Marcuse, Karl Mannheim and Wilhelm Reich).

Of particular influence in the immediate post-war period was Freud's (1957) thesis that the 'civilizing process' entailed the collective renunciation or repression of instinctual aspects of human development and experience. This historical renunciation is repeated at the level of the individual through the process of psychosexual development and Freud's work presented a sustained effort to discern the ways in which the human body is repressed and regulated by the structures of modern Western society (Blaikie et al., 2003). Hence as Connell (1987) puts it, nature is rendered social by Freud, whereby aspects of nature deemed inappropriate for modern society are civilized across both historical time, on a macro-social level, and across the life course of the individual. This process is made possible because of the common psychic experience associated with two key motifs Freud drew from myth: the taboo of totemism and the Oedipal drama.

Similar elements within these two motifs (that of killing or supplanting the father and marrying the mother, or women in the same totem group) provided Freud with a basis for claiming the Oedipal complex as a cultural universal. Freud interpreted these presumed shared elements as an indication of a 'memory of a common mythic past', reproduced across time and place as a collective inheritance connecting present with earlier generations (Sydie, 1987: 130). Hence Freud's work provided a crucial reference point for sociological attempts to link unconscious processes – understood in both material (e.g. neurological) and psychic terms – and the social, by psychoanalyzing the latter and sociologizing the former within a methodological framework of historical materialism.

However, the post-Freudian legacy associated with the work of Jacques Lacan latterly influenced the development of sociological theory, concerned not only with the deeply rooted forms of power and domination associated with capitalism but also the lived relationships of subjects to their historical conditions of existence. In keeping with a long linguistic turn in the twentieth century, Louis Althusser (1971) in particular focused on representations, myths and images and built on Lacan's psychoanalysis to both specify the relation between ideology and subjectivity and to develop a critique of the 'unified' subject (Barrett, 1992: 92). Barrett claims that Althusser's framework offered a sociologically inflected version of Lacan's concept of the 'imaginary' that referred to 'lived' emotion in ways that had some resonance for feminists working towards analyses of the conditions under which one becomes a subject (e.g. Williamson, 1978). While Althusser has been considered but rejected by feminist sociological accounts of subjectivity, his work has been influential in explaining the relation between psyche and the social without relinquishing emphasis on the significance of the material conditions of human life. Nonetheless, for feminists, the main difficulty in integrating psychoanalytic approaches with historical materialism was the explanatory weight accorded class, rather than the unconscious, in shaping subjectivity, conscious thought and experience (Scott, 1992).

In contrast, Lacanian psychoanalytic approaches to subjectivity bypass attention to the material conditions of existence in order to focus exclusively on the unconscious as the (desolate) location of (illusory) subjectivity. Lacan offers a philosophical rather than a clinical reading of Freud to develop a theory of the unconscious that is structured like a language, and hence, can be revealed only through analysis of language as a universal force shaped by relations of difference that generate meaning (Waters, 1994). Lacan has been interpreted by feminists contra Freud as arguing against the existence of a pre-social stable or foundational body, and in support of the claim that the body can only be known through language, though the interaction between the individual's image of her own body, and that of the body of the (various) 'other'. The imaginary order

for Lacan is understood in relation primarily to the symbolic and in particular to the cultural processes through which subjects are constituted.
The metaphorical topography described by Lacan (outlined in Chapter 4)
corresponds to 'orders of signification': Real–Imaginary–Symbolic
(Roudinesco, 1997). Language is not the mediator of experience but its
chief constituent and provides the means through which meaning is
imposed upon anatomy. Influenced by structural linguistics, Lacan
argued that the symbolic order seeks to make sense of the imaginary
order via linguistic signs that are generated by their relations of difference (Seidman, 1994).

Though there has been considerable debate within feminist theory
concerning the advantages or disadvantages of psychoanalytic theory,
feminist sociologists have been in general rather more circumspect about
its value than feminists in other disciplines. Caution about the value of
psychoanalytic approaches is associated with its grounding – about which
feminist theory has surprisingly little to say. Compared to his contemporaries, Lacan published few clinical cases to support his theories, allowing
him to develop the distinctive theoretical framework subsequently read as
social philosophy (Roudinesco, 1997). Indeed, many contemporary practising psychoanalysts and psychiatrists are scathing of Lacan and suggest
that contemporary Lacanian theory is a mix of muddled thinking (Sokal
and Bricmont, 1998) and 'evidence-free assertions' (Tallis, 1997).

Similarly, feminist sociologists have been cautious about the value of
Lacanian psychoanalysis on the grounds that while feminist theory has
recovered Lacan as a post-structuralist thinker, it has done so in ways that
overlook the ways in which his writings have become detached from a
clinical (and potentially attestable) context of psychoanalysis. As a practising psychoanalyst, Lacan's theory of (illusory) subjectivity led him to
reject the customary assumption that the goal of psychoanalysis was to
encourage the restoration or adjustment of patients (Waters, 1994).
Moreover, contemporary re-readings of his work that simultaneously
attempt to re-write his observations concerning difference in ways that do
not exile women, nonetheless represent his theories as a holistic form of
cultural enquiry that obscures his relation to both essentialist and speculative psychoanalytic traditions (Barrett, 1992; Eagleton, 1996).

There are difficulties for feminist sociologists with how psychoanalytic theory and method – detached from clinical encounters and contexts
– handle the unconscious and presupposes its contents, though there
exists considerably more sympathy among British feminists for object-
relations approaches that allow for analysis of encounters and relationships (Craib, 1998; Vogler, 2000). For instance, the post-structuralist
emphasis on metaphor and aporia in the Lacanian framework leads feminist writing into an impossible corner since metaphors need to be analysed
in some kind of context (Lakoff and Johnson, 1980). Yet questions of con-

text are largely antithetical to the post-structuralist framework in which feminist psychoanalytic theories of the body have developed, and which work against the demands of pragmatic inquiry. Similarly, where Foucauldian and more general postmodern (Bauman, 1994) approaches to subjectivity emphasize historical contingency and cultural specificity, psychoanalytic accounts of subjectivity tend towards the universal typically reducing certain kinds of phenomena to psychic dramas (Segal, 1990). Psychoanalytic *theory* (though not necessarily practice) has a tendency to normalize and reproduce essentialist and universal assumptions about gender, ethnicity and sexuality (Foucault, 1988). As Barrett and McIntosh (1982) put it, psychoanalysis proceeds from the assumption that 'original' family experiences are central to interpretations of the unconscious, where original is interpreted in a singular fashion. It is this latter normalizing tendency that is most discernible in the methodology of psychoanalytically inflected theories of the body.

Similarly, writing from the standpoint of post-colonial perspective, Spivak (1990) notes that psychoanalytic theory in its development of sexual difference reproduces the disregard for ethnicity found in other forms of feminist theory. In particular, its emphasis on the importance of culture at the expense of society is problematic. For instance, the concept of the 'post-colonial subject' is understood more in symbolic and subjective terms rather than in social, economic and political terms (Barrett, 1992: 213). The conflation of culture and society is not peculiar to post-Lacanian psychoanalytic theory but is part of a more general collapse of boundaries by post-structuralist and postmodern forms of analysis between what might previously have been viewed as discrete spheres (Habermas, 1975). Although this conflation has flourished within feminist theories that seek to work across disciplinary borders, it is a move that compromises pragmatic analysis of the social. This conflation is especially problematic for feminist sociologists in relation to questions of method and the methodological convergence on language and text as the focus for analysis.

Lacan's absent body

Those who work with psychoanalytical concepts derived from the work of Lacan are interpreted as being at the cutting edge of literary and visual theory. Despite the fragile basis of Lacan's work and although he was disowned by the regulating body for practising psychoanalysts, his work has moved into a sphere that enables him to be valorized as a theorist. This may have something to do with the aura which Lacan himself cultivated and manipulated (Tallis, 1997) – he was wealthy, courted fame and was sexually voracious. Concomitantly, he attracted a circle of followers who adhered to his work (his biographer's acknowledgements reads like a who's who of twentieth-century philosophers and social theorists), which might explain his appeal during his lifetime. However, this cannot explain his continuing appeal to a new generation of writers and thinkers, particularly feminists, who continue to develop his work as an unyielding basis for theoretical elaboration.

There are limits to the application of Lacan's *œuvre* to feminist and consequently sociological approaches to the body. Lacan's approach was largely indifferent to historical context or approach and this indifference is reproduced in new feminist philosophies of the body that advocate textual analysis as the key tactic of a 'politics of ambivalence'. Text in this approach is without *con*text and is both timeless and placeless (Rojek and Turner, 2000). Feminist appropriations of psychoanalysis in theories of the body focus on deconstructing categories to the exclusion of the contexts that give such categories meaning. Given the influence on sociological approaches to the body of Elias's scholarship on the civilizing process, it is difficult to see how Lacan's psychoanalytically derived corporeality could be reconciled with a view of corporeality that insists on temporal and spatial context. There are considerable tensions for feminists between using psychoanalysis as an explanatory tool for gendered or sexual difference and approaching psychoanalytic theory as an ineluctable theory that they desire to comprehend (Brennan, 1998). The impenetrability of psychoanalytic theories has its own seduction that is premised on the importance that masculinist ideas continue to hold in academic contexts. Considerable weight continues to be attached to theory as an enterprise with its own momentum that does not need to engage with the material world. For Lacan, the body is not and does not matter.

A further irony of post-structuralist inclinations is that the reliance of new feminist theories of the body on an ostensibly Lacanian psychoanalytic framework licenses form over substance. Culture – the academy – is the privileged sphere in which feminist theory operates and thus feminist theories of sexual difference are lined up within the Symbolic in ways that efface the consequences of such difference through the textual practices via which theory reproduces itself and excludes the body. The particular ways in which feminists use text and develop textual practice admit the texts of women to the academy but do so in ways that make it difficult to talk (of a) beyond the text. In part, this difficulty is linked to the (Nietzschean) legacy of aesthetic modernity that collapses materiality and representation (language) in ways that have made it increasingly difficult to talk about an 'outside' to language/discourse, especially when harnessed to the established *œuvre* of Jacques Derrida and the ways in which the stories that people tell are supplementary to Lacanian psychoanalysis. This approach cedes an equivalence to representation, views language as symbolic of itself, its 'referentiality' to an empirical world erased in ways that fetishizes text 'as if it possesses a power or agency that particular human subjects themselves lack' (Ian, 1993).

Deconstructive and textual practices distance analysis from social practices, contexts and lived bodily experiences and thus effect an enclosed, circular form of immanent critique. Such practices are derived from an intellectual bourgeois habitus that dematerializes thought, forgets the body (McNally, 2001) and makes it difficult to see theory as a particular form of situated knowledge. Textual practices typically interpret embodied experiences in terms of cognitive or linguistic modes of meaning, subjugating the somatic to the semantic (Jackson, 1986). Yet conceptual thought is not necessarily inherently tied to language or text, as practical or embodied knowledge can exist without speech or text. Moreover, the formal emphasis on language and text that inheres in new feminist theories of the body tends to congeal *parole* or cut off the particularity and inter-corporeal exchanges of the speaker in ways that detach communication from the concrete activities and contexts associated with voices, gestures, bodies and speech that animate language and text.

In new feminist theories of the body, the body becomes theory's 'other' rather than a site of particular experiences and current applications of psychoanalytic theory by feminists have a tendency to abstract and detach bodies from their social context, 'empty bodies of meaning' and mystify embodied experience (Jackson and Scott, 1998: 18–19). Embodying gender/gendering the body needs more than attention to the unconscious and the materialization of sex, such as attention to the social components of performance of the unconscious (Lindemann, 1997), how gender performance/embodied subjectivity is supported through the acquisition of habits (Bourdieu, 2000) and through interaction not only with others but also space (Young, 1990) and material objects (Hartsock, 1987). Though feminist historians have assembled considerable evidence to substantiate claims concerning the contingency and specificity of the body's relation to the 'totality of the self', feminist philosophies of the body continue to efface the 'woman in the body'. Whereas new feminist philosophies tend to take the visibility of the body for granted, feminist sociologists argue that sociological treatments need to demonstrate how social practices and cultural meanings render bodies visible and knowable as gendered as well as in other ways (Delphy, 1993; Hood-Williams, 1996).

Finally, new feminist theories of the body emphasize gender as identity/subjectivity in ways that weaken its power to conceive of and relate sexual difference to material inequalities such as income differentials, occupational segregation, physical abuse and sex tourism. Sexual difference theory collapses key concepts in the feminist literature and absorbs other sources of difference such as ethnicity. The analysis of sexuality, sex, 'the domain of sexual difference' and 'the morphologies of bodies' (Grosz, 1994) sidelines gender as a concept concerned with social(ly produced) differences between men and women that have material effects (scarcity, need, inequality). This tactic attenuates all relations between and among men and women to sexual relations, which do not necessarily capture the full range of (sexual and non-sexual) hierarchical and relational divisions between men and women, as well as between women themselves. In contrast, feminist sociologists (Jackson and Scott, 1998; Witz, 2000) have insisted on gender as a central sociological concept that highlights social divisions between men and women in ways that are inclusive of but not reduced to (issues of) the body.

New feminist philosophies of the body that have turned to the insights of psychoanalysis reproduce their own conditions of existence by pursuing the finer points of analysis implied by that framework. They contribute to the development of disciplinary theory but not significantly to a feminist project that has at its heart the production of knowledge for women. Rather, the knowledge produced in this field is knowledge for feminists, knowledge that will no doubt contribute to the professional consolidation and advancement of feminism and raise its intellectual status. As a feminist *sociologist* it is difficult to argue against this: the academic world that we live in encourages this kind of pursuit and it is exceedingly hard to go against that grain. However, as a *feminist* sociologist, I have misgivings about the nature of the body project in feminism and its advantages for women who are not academics. In particular, current forms of the body project in feminism diminish the political potency of feminism and mask its relevance to women.

Material/ity

Reconnecting the particular bodies of subjects to contexts and concrete activities is no easy task, especially since a core concept in psychoanalytically inflected theories of sexual difference – material/ity – has been such a focus of contention and confusion. As outlined in Chapter 2, the concept of material/ity has existed in several versions. One version of material/ity offered second-wave feminism in the 1970s a way of challenging biological/naturalist suppositions by emphasizing gender as socially and culturally constructed. While this version left sex intact as the biological bedrock of gender, it nonetheless opened up the potential for the sociological analysis of hitherto naturalized aspects of women's lives. However, another emerging version of material/ity in the 1970s, associated with radical feminism, reclaimed the body as the basis for a particular form of consciousness that presented the potential for collective empowerment and change, particularly when harnessed to renderings of materialism. A third version of material/ity shifted focus from the biological body altogether onto social, economic and political practices and relations that constitute material contexts and circumstances that have actual consequences for women's lives.

As Rahman and Witz (2003) comment, while feminist materialism in the 1980s presented a strong constructionist version of gender as a social consequence of capitalist and/or patriarchal relations that sidelined the body matters of radical feminism's material/ity and foregrounded material/ity as forms of productive activity, materialist feminism 'stretched' the concept of material/ity to include analysis of productive activity *and* ideological/cultural practices that contribute to subject/identity formation. For Rahman and Witz, feminist materialism bestowed a narrow economic version of material/ity that failed to grasp cultural and experiential dimensions of gender whereas materialist feminist approaches defined material/ity in terms of social practices, discourses, interactions and institutions – everything in fact that might fall under the purview of what they refer to as the *social*, including culture. Hence, the stretched version of material/ity moves away from both confrontations with biology and overemphasis on economic issues to embrace the realm subsequently occupied by post-Lacanian psychoanalysis.

However, as Chapters 3 and 4 have argued, feminist uses of post-Lacanian psychoanalysis present a limited version of the cultural realm that emphasizes language, discourse and representation detached from the social contexts in which they emerge and hence, detached from the specific bodies that produce them. Just as feminist materialist/materialist feminist versions of material/ity have sought to be inclusive of something 'beyond' the economic or to include the ideological/cultural, new feminist theories of the body that rely on the textual practices derived from deconstructionism and post-Lacanian psychoanalysis, have inadvertently sneaked in a body 'beyond' culture, or beyond discourse/language/representation – the 'deferred ontology' of Butler or the imaginary maternal-feminine of Irigaray. Just as sociologists struggle to gender the body in ways that include all dimensions of life, so too do feminists struggle to embody gender in ways that not only secure a theory and politics of sexual difference but also do justice to the various ways in which sexual difference is lived. There are then various renditions of material/ity that include the economic (Barrett) or biological (Rich) as core; that embrace everyday social practices, actions and meanings (Young); that defer ontology (Butler, Diprose, Gatens); that present a stubborn immutability (Bordo, 1998) or residual facticity (Witz) that nonetheless is dynamic and non-linear (Hird, 2004). In the end, the insistence on material/ity may ultimately point to the *social* practices and relations in which embodiment is lived.

Appropriations of post-Lacanian psychoanalysis within new feminist theories of the body reframe gender primarily as a symbolic order rather than as either structurally determined positions or socially constructed arrangements. There has been a discernible shift towards dealing with the body's materiality and the materiality of difference via psychoanalytic categories that operate within a tradition that claims to dissolve boundaries between the material and the symbolic. Feminist philosophers working within this tradition have been trying to develop frameworks for theorizing the body: that is, they have been working towards developing frameworks that incorporate the (physical) body into sexual difference, which has emerged as the conceptual centrepiece of feminist scholarship.

Yet this feminist treatment of the body begins from theory and text, rather than from experiential or pragmatic realities. As identified in Chapter 2, though feminist writing began from and developed experience as an analytic category in the 1970s and 1980s, experience has been eclipsed by the concept of sexual difference, which is not mobilized as a means of revealing relations between the personal and political but of working through the undecidability of *différance*. A discernible feature of this scholarship is the way in which emergent theories of the body fail to name and specify the body about which it writes. As outlined in Chapters 3 and 4, feminist post-structuralist treatments of the body take many different forms that are subtly and elegantly distinguished from each other through an endless circuit of textual debate and immanent critique which attempt in their various ways to write the body into being through text.

However, the effect of this form of internal debate, and the way in which reference to something beyond language (what founds *différance*), or beyond the psyche is disqualified in this mode of practice, is that the body vanishes because of its separation from social/sensuous being, action and practice. Instead, the body is presented as a trope (Ebert, 1996) or as a conceptual space emptied of specific meaning in order to pursue a methodologically individualistic focus on theory and text. The starting point matters and feminist writing that begins from text and proceeds towards the body, though often stylishly presented and argued, is less serviceable to a pragmatic academic feminism and to a politically engaged feminism than analysis that begins with the particularities of embodiment and proceeds towards a body of theory. As Witz and Marshall (2003) put it, rather than establish a more central role for the body within feminist theory, feminist theorizing needs to proceed by 'disentangling the complex ways in which gender is embodied and bodies are gendered'.

Revisiting materiality and experience

There is a range of available ways in which the relation between materiality and experience could be revisited and productively deployed within a pragmatic feminist sociology that seeks to disentangle the complex ways in which 'gender is embodied and bodies are gendered'. A pragmatic critical materialism might be developed to disentangle and examine the complexity of relations between embodiment and language that returns text and speech to the body and views bodies as sites of meaning and meaning as embodied. Where Davidson and Smith (1999, see Chapter 4) argue for complementing Irigaray's textuality with Wittgenstein's forms of life, others have suggested developing the scholarship of Vološinov, Bakhtin and Benjamin to return words to the sensory world of things and objects in ways that locate speech in 'unique contexts of life and labour' and regard experience as part of transformative practice (McNally, 2001). In part, such a project retains its Marxist debt and commitment to materialism as a challenge to the autonomy of cognitive thought and as a 'defence against belief in the infinity of mind' (Horkheimer, 1972, in McNally, 2001: 74), but such a project is also consistent with a pragmatic sociology interested in returning problems of philosophy to human practical activity.

The sociological and anthropological scholarship outlined in Chapter 1 points to a range of non-linguistic/textual forms of expressiveness and communicative (inter)action to which embodiment is core. For instance, while both symbolic interactionists and critical theorists note that bodily expressions, postures and gestures 'give us away' (Reich, Bourdieu) or 'give off' information (Goffman) that do not need cognition for comprehension, phenomenologists observe that memories are typically experienced as bodily sensations (or housed memories) that precede the linguistic categories through which they are interpreted, hence meaning cannot be reduced to a sign that lies beyond the 'domain of an act', as put by Merleau-Ponty. Thus, bodily praxis – including speech and writing – may be intelligible in its own terms but at the very least is linked to movement, action and context and offers material origins for ideas.

While the post-structuralist approaches to embodied subjectivity outlined in Chapter 3 create a subject that appears to exist for self, phenomenological approaches present a subject who comes into being as such through communicative – embodied – interaction with others on the grounds that any notion of self that must not only take account of the embodied form of existence based on both being and having bodies but also the way in which we are perceptible to ourselves and to others. As Crossley notes: 'We fall within their perceptual field and, in this sense, they "have" us too. Our embodiment in necessarily alienated. We are never in complete possession of ourselves' (2001: 141). Moreover, phenomenological approaches, or approaches to embodiment that regard embodiment as the condition and constituent of agency (Howson, 1996) have the potential to enable a relational understanding of bodily experiences in the context of particular forms of practice, representations and metaphors. Examination of this claim might entail attention to the role of visual imagery in structuring bodily experience (Howson, 2001b) and the dialectical relationship between embodied experiences and the various forms of regulatory power as 'a complex strategic relation in a given society' (Gordon, 1980) directed towards the body.

Anthropologically inflected perspectives on the materiality of language are derived in part from phenomenology and begin from the premise that experiences are socially and historically constituted and mediated by activities, practices and ideas that appear external to them. Emily Martin's work has been important to the development of arguments that link forms of embodiment to experience. Taking up Foucault's challenge to demonstrate not only how forms of embodiment are shaped for specific purpose across time and place (Lowe, 1995), her work has highlighted how the relation between forms of embodiment and experience are mediated through image and metaphor. Martin's approach suggests that if we examine how the body is organized and managed we will learn about the sources and forms of power and domination in social life. Her method reveals something of the pervasiveness of images and their relation to embodiment and instigates a dialectic that neither denies the materiality of the lived body nor the power of image and metaphor to shape understandings and experiences of embodiment. It is therefore an important contribution to conceptualizations of the relation between matter and language that is based on substantive research and works hard to neither privilege one over the other, nor efface real bodies from language and life.

Experience

The concept of experience has been mobilized within feminism as an authoritative basis from which to challenge various knowledges concerning women's lives (especially biomedical knowledge) precisely because knowledge hierarchies and orthodoxies typically dismiss women's embodied experiences as non-authoritative. The modern, Western mode of thought has displaced 'carnal knowing' by 'cognitive apprehension' that privileges knowledge produced through mental endeavour (Mellor and Shilling, 1997). Modern forms of embodiment provide no means of validating knowledge because of the way the body is equated with senses and knowledge with a disembodied mind. Accordingly, 'experience' has become a buzzword for the 'individual, unique' (ibid.). Yet female embodiment and women's lesser distance from the 'grotesque' have, for some feminists (e.g. Shildrick, 2002) provided a potential means of access to 'carnal knowing' (or a 'wild zone', see Showalter, 1985) not perhaps shared by men. A recuperated concept of experience denotes the erasure of carnal knowing and of sensory understanding, of the division between body and mind, which modern forms of organization and relations create. However, while as argued in Chapter 2, the concept of experience has been displaced by new feminist theories of the body, other feminist trajectories such as phenomenology and Foucauldian scholarship imply the concept of lived/embodied experience, as an effect of social and political practices, contexts and relations could be developed to construct reliable knowledge in service of the broader conversation in society that pragmatism characterizes.

While experience has been exiled from the feminist canon (though not from empirical research) as essentializing, reductive and individualizing, feminist focus on experience within disciplines such as sociology, anthropology and geography has typically been deployed as a means to an end and the aim of focusing on women's experience(s) has been to develop a better and more reliable understanding of subordination and oppression (Stanley and Wise, 1993; Skeggs, 1997). In relation to theories of the body, the concept of experience has been argued to be a necessary corrective to the claims and partial visions of theory (for instance, see Nettleton and Watson, 1998; Williams and Bendelow, 1998). It is used as an analytical device to achieve some leverage on theoretical claims and begin the process of examining them more closely. The use of the concept of experience needs to be part of feminist writing on the body because it serves as a constant reminder of the historically contingent nature of mind/body dualism and therefore, provides a way of persistently highlighting the importance of the particular, the local and the pragmatic.

Raymond Williams (1975) in *Keywords* defines experience as '(i) knowledge gathered from past events, whether by conscious reflection or by consideration and reflection; (ii) a particular kind of consciousness, which can in some contexts by distinguished from reason or knowledge', which might include what some writers refer to as 'embodied knowledge'. Scott's (1992) discussion of experience notes the centrality of the visual metaphor in Williams's definition, which is itself a product of historical change and like other feminists, is suspicious of epistemological confidence in the visual because it connotes a distanced, non-situated subject who plays the 'god trick', by creating an illusion of disinterested objectivity. However, as Gatens reminds us, Merleau-Ponty's philosophy of embodiment invites a consideration of vision as developed through and occurring within embodied, active orientations to the world. The production of knowledge in this way of seeing is tied to experience, where experience is understood as an active, embodied, particular engagement with the world and inseparable from the contexts and circumstances in which engagement takes place. Such an understanding of experience thus includes not only thought and reflection based on observation but also *feeling*. For Williams, feeling implies a sense of 'subjective witness', those 'immediate, true and authentic' responses to events and circumstances not only associated with 'inner' thoughts but also, perhaps as Burkitt (1999) would have it, derived from a material world.

Moreover, Williams's concept of 'structures of feeling' tried to capture actively lived and felt social experience as it interacts with and defies conceptions of formal, fixed and official social forms. For Williams, 'structures of feeling' denoted a 'practical consciousness of a present kind' (Williams, 1977) and he was especially concerned in his analysis of subjectivity to avoid the reduction of specifically lived experience in the present to an account of social forms rooted in the past. He was concerned to establish a methodology that did not 'segregate' the social from the subjective and marginalize considerations of the 'living present' in all its compelling, intricate detail (Gordon, 1997). Thus, in Williams's work, an adequate materialist account of the social could only be enhanced by attention to the immediacy of experience, feeling and being.

As Chapter 2 noted, the analysis of experience has been central to feminist sociology as a counter to 'objectivity', which is premised on the exclusions of various 'others'. Those others include women, who, argued Dorothy Smith, have a particular standpoint distinct from that of men and are 'heard' within the discipline as marginal voices. *The Everyday World as Problematic* (1987) developed a different kind of sociology that includes those others and begins from she views as the local and particular. The 'sociological imagination' is premised on a view of society from the standpoint of male sociologists and their privileged place in the 'relations of ruling', which are characterized as much by patriarchy as by capitalism. Developing a union between materialist and phenomenological perspectives, Smith argues that the textually organized world of academia and the local world of domestic, familial life in all its absorbing particularity represent two distinct modes of being, which produce a sense of dislocation for women in sociology.

While the academic world reflects male abstract forms of knowledge, the domestic world reflects the local, particular standpoint(s) of women. Textually organized forms of knowledge seek to present the world in abstract form and in doing so, decontextualize the production of that knowledge. Smith's alternative form of knowledge production seeks to develop 'a way of seeing, from where we actually live, into the powers, processes, and relations that organize and determine the everyday context of that seeing' (ibid.: 9). In contrast to feminist sociological projects that add women's topics to established research agenda, Smith seeks to develop a feminist standpoint sociology 'that will look out at the world at large and not just those pieces of immediate relevance to women' (ibid.: 10). For her, a 'feminist mode of inquiry might then begin with women's experience from women's standpoint and explore how it is shaped in the extended relations of larger social and political relations' (ibid.: 10). While much of *The Everyday World as Problematic* seeks to develop a distinct feminist method within sociology, her discussion of experience, knowledge and consciousness foreshadows many of the concerns of current feminist theories of the body.

First, Smith defines experience 'as embedded within the particular historical forms of social relations that determine that experience' (ibid.: 49). She notes that women are alienated from their immediate, particular bodily experience through institutions – such as medicine and academia – which render women as other rather than as subjects in and for themselves. A 'line of fault' fails to acknowledge women's bodily experience as legitimate and relations of ruling (processes and institutions of social control) render women's experiences alien to themselves. Second, there is a fault line between women's consciousness of the academic world and their consciousness of the everyday. Drawing on Marx's and Engels's discussion of ideology, she notes that though consciousness ('how people think about and express themselves to one another') arises in the context of the immediate everyday, it is organized by 'external' images and ideas.

However, women's sensual ways of speaking, understanding and knowing have been replaced or submerged by the development of rationalized literacy. While Smith recognizes the essentializing tendencies embedded within the concept of experience, its development in the context of consciousness raising was used by the women's movement as a critical tactic in the process of (re)discovering and creating ways of speaking. The concept of experience is a reminder of the historical separation of mind/body; of the displacement of sensual or carnal understanding with rational knowledge; and of the division between mind and body that modern forms of organization and relations create (Mellor and Shilling, 1997). Hence, the critique of the women's movement provided a way of retrieving women's submerged bodily experience from the relations of ruling (Smith, 1987: 54). Experience stands for a conscious method of reflecting on the everyday or of 'discovering how to begin from ourselves' (ibid.: 58). It represents an acknowledgement that feminist accounts start from somewhere: from the places and spaces of the everyday as experienced by women themselves. The local and particular experiences of women can also be understood as a world known through the 'bodily mode' which is silenced within conventional forms of intellectual inquiry.

Hence, of particular importance to Smith is the development of methods that allow women to write sociology that makes visible and audible their experiences in a form that is recognizable to those who live and speak it. The concept of experience is a way of redirecting the focus of sociology from the general to the particular, from the abstract to the concrete. Though feminists have been critical of the universalistic implications of the concept of experience as *a priori* 'of woman', Smith's redirection points 'to an "embodied" subject located in a particular actual and historical setting' (ibid.: 108). Part of this standpoint is 'situated outside textually mediated discourses in the actualities of our everyday lives' (ibid.: 107), in part because women have been allocated marginal roles in the production of such discourses (Witz and Marshall, 2003) and because women's consciousness is characterized by a sense of bifurcation produced by the actualities of their experience.

Embodied experience as an 'everyday negotiation of the mundane' (Skeggs, 1997: 167) might then remain both a core struggle concept for academic feminism as a tool for identifying, naming and authorizing what might otherwise remain invisible to academic eyes and a concept for beginning the process of explaining the social practices and relations that give rise to what comes to be named as experience. The retention and development of embodied experience as a key concept for feminism's encounter with the body might then also enable the development of what Rahman and Witz (2003) refer to as a social ontology of gender, a means of identifying not only how gender is embodied and bodies are gendered but also of naming those aspects of the social that are unrecognizable as social precisely because the embodied experiences of women are excluded from them.

Hence, embodied experience need not be taken for an arbitrating source of knowledge but presents a space for making analytical sense of the material meanings and moorings of life. As Scott (1992) has remarked, what people claim as their experience is already an interpretation and in need of interpretation, a co-construction written up into texts such that 'private troubles' might be transformed into public issues (see also Bourdieu, 1977). While it may be that a 'residual facticity' or 'stubborn immutability' of material/ity pushes back at the feminist or sociological analyst, the analysis of talk and text and interpretative methodologies will doubtless remain core for feminist and sociological approaches to embodiment. These methodologies – narrative and discourse analyses, listening to subjects' stories, observational and visual methods – in contrast to the troping of Lacanian psychoanalytical categories epitomized by the work outlined here – remain sensitive to issues of authority and to the ways in which embodied experiences are located within particular local contexts (Bell, 1988) and embedded within particular ways of telling and historical moments in which experiences may be materialized (Denzin, 1988). In this way, analysis focuses on how immateriality – texts, ideas, constructs – is materialized in ways that become part of embodied experience/embodiment (Smith, 1990) and allows a sociological convergence on interactions between 'the' body, embodied experience and specific social practices and relations.

Conclusion

In part, the sociological imagination has been engaged in a modernist project of documenting and making visible the lives of the oppressed, the disenfranchised and the excluded, but it has largely done so by appeal to the voice of experience as a special form of authority. The voices of the oppressed and excluded have been heard by appealing to their experiences as the grounding on which their claims are made (notwithstanding any distinction between the claims such voices might make and claims made for them by sociologists). The problem with the modernist sociological imagination has been that the distance between knower and known is concealed and (made) invisible. The sociological imagination makes its claims by appeal to the criteria of science and hence the writing or translation of the voices and experiences of excluded others is dependent on concealing the relation that makes it possible to identify experiences in the first place.

The uncertainties associated with postmodernity make it possible to question the nature of relation between researcher and researched, between experience and knowledge, between what can be seen and what can be known. The process of interrogation about such relations is of course an uneven one. Though American 'West coast' sociologies are at the forefront of interrogative practice, drawing as they do on a form of anthropological reflexivity, there is a considerable body of sociological scholarship in both the USA and the UK that appears untouched by such considerations. Academic feminism is similarly though less sharply marked by unevenness, though on the whole, it is no longer tenable to assert the experiences of subjects (historically constituted as subjects) as unmediated and self-evident. Experience cannot be presumed to provide an authoritative foundation for knowledge because the very notion of foundation has itself been discredited. Yet, even (especially?) in these circumstances that reshape the production of knowledge, throw epistemological certainties into doubt and fracture the relation between experience and knowledge, experience continues to ask to be considered as a starting point for knowledge. Even though experience requires interpretation in sociological and feminist imaginations of the new world order that begin with postmodernist or post-structuralist epistemological and/or political commitments, experience surfaces as a silent referent that seeks to be admitted and demands attention beyond the (Lacanian) body.

six

Conclusion

Both sociology and feminism have had an uneasy relationship with psychoanalytic theory, yet feminism has increasingly turned to psychoanalytic theory in order to examine dualisms between mind and body, sex and gender and to incorporate the body into accounts of sexual difference. As a corollary, a range of concepts and metaphors have been developed to explore the 'space' between mind and body as a potential resource through which to challenge and subvert the phallogocentricity of the Symbolic. Yet the turn to psychoanalytic theory has moved feminist theory further from materialist conceptions of the body towards discursive concepts of the body that engage with texts in ways that reproduce an internal referentiality 'that deny reference to the human acts from which they emerged and refer only to themselves' (Scarry, 1985: 260). In writing about the body particular stories about embodiment are written out. For philosophical approaches to the analysis of life perhaps this is acceptable but it is anathema to the sociological imagination. At the same time, there is a discernible diffidence in current feminist theory about the implications of abandoning material conceptions of the body altogether. This book has tried to show that this diffidence is born of the reductive way in which Lacanian theories have developed within new feminist theories of the body, a reductionism reinforced by repetitious application of elements of his theories as an interpretative grid on the 'problem' of the female body (Howson, 2005). The integrative framework suggested by body theories works against the post-structuralist inclination to contextualize knowledge, issues and theories within local, particular, dispersed milieu.

A further problem with feminist philosophies of the body is that the situatedness of the storytellers is masked by the artifice of the story telling. Where feminists in other disciplines, notably geography and sociology, have begun to make a concern of the relationship between experience and knowledge and to highlight how writing itself is a practice that organizes the stories of situated others (Gordon, 1997), the tactics inspired by new feminist philosophies of the body conceal the situatedness of not only those about whom stories are told but also those who tell stories of the body. Moreover, though power ostensibly remains the focus for new feminist philosophies of the body, tactics of deconstruction and metaphorical elaboration obscure the processes and channels through which power operates in the production of knowledge and the ways in which feminism's uneven place within the academy reinforces a hierarchical notion of formal theory. While the legacy of postmodernism has produced episte-mological critique as the dominant form of academic feminism, a socio-logically informed feminism could combine this with a sustained critique of the forms of domination in postmodernity. It seems to me that though epistemological critique is clearly of importance to feminism, it is currently being pursued at the expense of empirically based, theoretically informed analyses of social phenomena, which would be mindful of the ways in which our own relations to those phenomena inform analysis.

The primacy of textual approaches to embodiment is possibly linked to the ways in which processes of professionalization within philosophy (Mills, 1964) have contributed to its detachment from a non-academic pub-lic and to the development of a tradition that separates thought from everyday life and 'sensible experience'. Thus, feminist philosophy and the new feminist theories it is used to support are relatively detached from a public forum. A feminist sociology live to Mills's sociological imagination cannot afford to lose sight of public fora as part of its endeavour to edu-cate and produce reliable knowledge about women's – and men's – lives. A pragmatic feminist sociology of the body is thus a sociology that approaches embodiment with an eye for the social implications of a range of differences, divisions and inequalities for women rather than through entanglement with the internal logic of theory and unremitting immanent critique. A pragmatic feminist sociology displaces conceptual transcen-dence with 'conceptual sketches' (as Mills would have it) to guide inquiry that is 'respectful of empirical realities' and work towards translating 'pri-vate troubles' into 'public issues' as part of a broader conversation in soci-ety with peers, students, and clients.

It would seem, rightly in my view, that feminism has fully taken on board the notion, also associated with the Chicago sociological tradition of which Mills was part, that claims to knowledge are contingent and provi-sional. In the field of the body, this is all too apparent yet there are contra-dictions here too. For instance, the category of sexual difference is at once a way of asserting differences between men and women in ways that resist the essentializing tendencies of sex. Yet it is also a reassuring category and part of the wider search for truth about self that is the legacy of modernity (MacInnes, 1998). However, through the concept of sexual difference the female body has been transformed into a 'bloodless category' within new feminist philosophies of the body, which write the body from a distance. Indeed, distance displaces experience as the authority on which claims to knowledge are based. Again, while this distancing may serve the intellec-tual agenda of contemporary philosophy, it cuts against the grain of a soci-ology that sees itself as part of project oriented towards the production of 'sensuous knowledge', a form of sociological inquiry, based on both American and British empirical traditions, that insists on a rich description and analysis of social life, a 'conjuring trick' (Taussig, 1993) or a profane illumination in which sociology is engaged in the production of 'fictions of the real' (Gordon, 1997). For feminist sociologists, new feminist philosophies of the body appear as a reductive practice that not only fails to capture the delicacy and fragility of lived embodiment but also resists animation through the mechanical reproduction of theoretical categories. Life's complications and 'things unseen' need to be conjured in ways that make them visible and amenable to analysis and in a sense this is sociology's gift, to 'unsettle the relationship between what is seen and what is known' (Berger, 1972: 10).

Sociological theories of the body substitute a concept of gender for that of sexual difference. In doing so, they relinquish a socially inflected approach to difference, which includes, as I have already asserted, attention to the material conditions of existence, and an emphasis on experience, however problematic this may be to conceptualize. Concomitantly, consideration of sexual difference in sociological theories of the body takes places through sociological readings of feminist appropriations of psychoanalytic theory that fail to offer sufficient emphasis on materiality. Consequently, there needs to be considerably more dialogue between social theories of the body and feminist sociological theories of the body, rather than with new feminist philosophies of the body. It is paradoxical that sociological theories of the body acknowledge feminist writing in disciplines other than sociology, and ignore feminist writing on the body within sociology. Accordingly, new feminist philosophies of the body need to acknowledge that feminist sociologies provide a means of engaging with the social, and that the social is the space in which the category of gender resides and which the concept of sexual difference conceals.

This book has argued that the tendency within new feminist theories of the body to privilege psychoanalysis as the core apparatus for embodying gender suffers from its emphasis on text, forgets the body and uses material/ity in ways that divorce texts and bodies from meaningful social contexts and concrete activities. *Embodying Gender* does not presume to throw the Butler out with the bathwater – feminists will continue to work productively with feminist theories of the body – but considered across the whole, new feminist theories of the body over-emphasize those aspects of Lacan that are most problematic for feminism: his disavowal of the social, his pessimism concerning the illusory nature of the subject with 'no appeal to tomorrow' and his denial of the particularity of the maternal body. Sexual difference theories, theories of the body, need to be taken into 'encounters with the real' and moved beyond the text (Brownlie, 2004) in ways that remember not only the bodies of those encountered in such a move but also keep in mind as O'Neill (1972) put it, that sociology is a 'skin trade' and that women *are* the text.

Bibliography

Acker, J. (1989) 'Making gender visible', in R.A. Wallace (ed.), Feminism and Sociological Theory. London: Sage.

Alcoff, L. (2000) 'Philosophy matters: a review of recent works in feminist philosophy', *Signs*, 26: 841–62.

Althusser, L. (1971) *Lenin and Philosophy and Other Essays (Notes Towards an Investigation)*. London: New Left Books.

Archer, M. (1982) 'Morphogenesis versus structuration: a critique of Giddens', *British Journal of Sociology*, 33: 445–83.

Armstrong, D. (1983) *The Political Anatomy of the Body*. Cambridge: Cambridge University Press.

Armstrong, D. (1984) 'The Patient's View', *Social Science and Medicine*, 18: 737–44.

Armstrong, D. (1987) 'Theoretical tensions in biopsychosocial medicine', *Social Science and Medicine*, 25(11): 1213–18.

Armstrong, D. (1993) 'Public health spaces and the fabrication of identity', *Sociology*, 27: 393–410.

Armstrong, D. (1995) 'The rise of surveillance medicine', *Sociology of Health and Illness*, 17: 393–404.

Arney, W.R. (1982) *Power and the Profession of Obstetrics*. Chicago, IL: Chicago University Press.

Arney, W.R. and Bergen, B.J. (1984) *Medicine and the Management of Living*. Chicago, IL: Chicago University Press.

Atkins, S. and Hoggett, B. (1984) *Women and the Law*. Oxford: Blackwell.

Atwood, M. (1986) *The Handmaid's Tale*. New York: Anchor Books.

Bakhtin, M.M. (1984) *Rabelais and his World*, trans. H. Iswolsky. Bloomington, IN: Indiana University Press.

Barrett, M. (1992) *The Politics of Truth: from Marx to Foucault*. Cambridge: Polity.

Barrett, M. and McIntosh, M. (1982) *The Anti-Social Family*. London: New Left Books.

Barrett, M. and Phillips, A. (eds) (1992) *Destabilizing Theory: Contemporary Feminist Debates*. Cambridge: Polity.

Bartky, S.L. (1988) 'Foucault, femininity and the modernization of patriarchal power', in I. Diamond and L. Quinby (eds), *Feminism and Foucault: Reflections on Resistance*. Boston, MA: Northeastern University Press.

Bartky, S.L. (1990) *Femininity and Domination*. New York: Routledge.

Bauman, Z. (1994) *Postmodern Ethics*. Oxford: Blackwell.

Bell, D. and Klein, R. (1996) *Radically Speaking: Feminism Reclaimed*. Melbourne: Spinifex Press.

Bell, S. (1988) 'Becoming a political woman: the reconstruction and interpretation of experience through stories', in A.D. Todd and S. Fisher (eds), *Gender and Discourse: the Power of Talk*. Norwood, NJ: Ablex.

Bell, S.E. (1994) 'Translating Science to the People: Updating the New', *Our Bodies Ourselves Women's Studies International Forum*, 17(1): 9–18.

Bell, V. (1993) *Interrogating Incest: Feminism, Foucault and the Law*. London: Routledge.

Benton, T. (1991) 'Biology and social science: why the return of the repressed should be given a (cautious) welcome', *Sociology*, 25: 1–30.

Benoist, J. and Catheras, P. (1991) 'The body: from an immateriality to another', *Social Science and Medicine*, 35: 857–65.

Benthein, C. (2002) *Skin: on the Cultural Border Between Self and the World*. New York: Columbia University Press.

Berger, J. (1972) *Ways of Seeing*. London: Pelican.

Berthelot, M. (1991) 'Sociological discourse and the body', in M. Featherstone, M. Hepworth and B.S. Turner (eds), *The Body: Social Process and Cultural Theory*. London: Sage.

Birke, L. (1999) *Feminism and the Biological Body*. Edinburgh: Edinburgh University Press.

Blaikie, A., Hepworth, M., Homes, M., Howson, A., Inglis, D. and Sarteen, S. (2003) *The Body: Critical Concepts in Sociology*. London: Routledge.

Bloor, M. and McIntosh, J. (1990) 'Surveillance and concealment: a comparison of techniques of client resistance in therapeutic communities and health visiting', in N. McKeganay and S. Cunningham-Burley (eds), *Readings in Medical Sociology*. London: Routledge.

Bologh, R.W. (1990) *Love or Greatness: Max Weber and Masculine Thinking – a Feminist Inquiry*. London: Unwin Hyman.

Bordo, S. (1989) 'The Body and the reproduction of femininity: a feminist appropriation of Foucault', in S. Bordo and A.S. Jaggar (eds), *Gender/Body/Knowledge*. New Brunswick, NJ: Rutgers University Press.

Bordo, S. (1992) 'Anorexia nervosa: psychopathology as the crystallization of culture', in D. Heldke and L. Curtin (eds), *Cooking, Eating, Thinking: Transformative Philosophies of Food*. Bloomington, IN: Indiana University Press.

Bordo, S. (1993) *Unbearable Weight: Feminism, Western Culture and the Body*. Berkeley, CA: University of California Press.

Bordo, S. (1998) 'Bringing the body to theory', in D. Welton (ed.), *Body and Flesh: A Philosophical Reader*. Oxford: Blackwell.

Bordo, S. and Jaggar, A.S. (eds) (1989) *Gender/Body/Knowledge*. New Brunswick, NJ: Rutgers University Press.

Bourdieu, P. (1977) *Outline of a Theory of Practice*, trans. R. Nice. Cambridge: Cambridge University Press.

Bourdieu, P. (1992) *The Logic of Practice*. London: Routledge.

Bourdieu, P. (2000) *Pascalian Meditations*. Cambridge: Polity.

Bourdieu, P. and Passeron, J.-C. (1990) *Reproduction in Education, Society and Culture*. London: Sage.

Boyne, R. (1998) 'Before the body: sociology and the subject', conference paper presented at BSA annual conference, April. University of Edinburgh.

Braidotti, R. (1989) 'The ontology of difference', in T. Brennan (ed.), *Between Feminism and Psychoanalysis*. London: Routledge.

Braidotti, R. (1998) 'Sexual difference theory', in A.M. Jaggar and I.M. Young (eds), *A Companion to Feminist Philosophy*. Oxford: Blackwell.

Braidotti, R. (2001) *Metamorphoses: Towards a Materialist Theory of Becoming*. Cambridge: Polity.

Brennan, T. (1989) *Between Feminism and Psychoanalysis*. London: Routledge.

Brennan, T. (1998) 'Psychoanalytic feminism', in A.M. Jaggar and I.M. Young (eds), *A Companion to Feminist Philosophy*. Oxford: Blackwell.

Brook, B. (1999) *Feminist Perspectives on the Body*. London and New York: Longman.

Broom, D. (1991) *Damned if We Do: Contradictions in Women's Health Care*. Sydney: Allen and Unwin.

Brown, B. and Adams, P. (1979) 'The feminine body and feminist politics', *m/f*, 3: 35–50.

Brownlie, J. (2004) 'Tasting the witches' brew: Foucault and therapeutic practices', *Sociology*, 38(3): 515–32.

Brownmiller, S. (1976) *Against our Will: Men, Women and Rape*. Harmonsworth: Penguin Books.

Brumberg, J. (1997) *The Body Project: an Intimate History of American Girls*. New York Random House.

Brush, P. (1998) 'Metaphors of inscription: discipline, plasticity and the rhetoric of choice', *Feminst Review*, 58(Spring): 22–43.

Buckley, T. and Gottlieb, A. (eds) (1988) *Blood Magic: the Anthropology of Menstruation*. Berkeley, CA: University of California Press.

Bunton, R. and Petersen, A. (1997) 'Introduction: Foucault's medicine', in A. Petersen and R. Bunton (eds), *Foucault, Health and Medicine*. London: Routledge.

Burkitt, I. (1999) *Bodies of Thought: Embodiment, Identity and Modernity*. London: Sage.

Burnett, K.A. and Holmes, M. (2001) 'Bodies, battlefields and biographies: scars and the construction of the body as heritage', in K. Backett-Milburn and S. Cunningham-Burley (eds), *Exploring the Body*. Basingstoke: Palgrave.

Bury, M. (1995) 'Ageing, gender and sociological theory', in S. Arber and J. Ginn (eds), *Connecting Gender and Ageing: a Sociological Approach*. Buckingham: Open University Press.

Butler, J. (1990) *Gender Trouble*. London: Routledge.

Butler, J. (1993) *Bodies that Matter: the Discursive Limits of Sex*. London: Routledge.

Charles, N. (2000) *Gender in Modern Britain*. Oxford: Oxford University Press.

Chodorow, N. (1978) *The Reproduction of Mothering*. Berkeley, CA: University of California Press.

Cixous, H. (1986) *The Newly Born Woman*. Minneapolis, MN: University of Minnesota Press.

Clarke, A.E. and Olesen, V.L. (1999) 'Revising, diffracting, acting', in A.E. Clarke and V.L. Olesen (eds), *Revisioning Women, Health and Healing*. New York and London: Routledge.

Classen, C. (1997) 'Engendering perception: gender ideologies and sensory hierarchies in Western history', *Body and Society*, 3(2): 1–19.

Connell, R.W. (1987) *Gender and Power*. Cambridge: Polity.

Connell, R.W. (1995) *Masculinities*. Cambridge: Polity.

Connell, R.W. (2001) 'Bodies, intellectuals and world society', in N. Watson and S. Cunningham-Burley (eds), *Reframing the Body*. Basingstoke: Palgrave.

Cooley, C.H. (1902) *Human Nature and the Social Order*. New York: Charles Scribner.

Corea, G. (1985) *The Mother Machine*. London: The Women's Press.

Cornell, D. (1991) *Beyond Accommodation: Ethical Feminism, Deconstruction and the Law*. New York: Routledge.

Craib, I. (1998) *Experiencing Identity*. London: Sage.

Crawford, C. (1984) 'A cultural account of "health": control, release and the social body', in J.B. McKinlay (ed.), *Issues in the Political Economy of Health*. London: Tavistock.

Crawford, R. (1994) 'The boundaries of self and the unhealthy other: reflections on health, culture and AIDS', *Social Science and Medicine*, 38(10): 1347–66.

Crossley, N. (1995a) 'Body techniques, agency and intercorporeality: on Goffman's relations', *Public Sociology*, 29: 133–50.

Crossley, N. (1995b) 'Merleau-Ponty, the elusive body and carnal sociology', *Body and Society*, 1: 43–63.

Crossley, N. (1996) 'Body–subject/body–power: agency, inscription and control in Foucault', *Body and Society*, 2: 99–116.

Crossley, N. (2001) *The Social Body: Habit, Identity and Desire*. London: Sage.

Csordas, T.J. (1990) 'Embodiment as a paradigm for anthropology', *Ethos* 18: 5–47.

Csordas, T.J. (1994) *Embodiment and Experience*. Cambridge: University of Cambridge Press.

Cunningham-Burley, S. and Backett-Milburn, K. (1998) 'The body, health and self in the middle years', in S. Nettleton and J. Watson (eds), *The Body in Everyday Life*. London: Routledge.

Currie, D. and Raoul, V. (1992) 'Dissecting sexual difference', in D. Currie and V. Raoul (eds), *The Anatomy of Gender: Women's Struggle for the Body*. Ottawa: Carleton University Press.

Daly, A. (1991) *Women Under the Knife: a History of Surgery*. London: Hutchinson Radius.

Daly, M. (1978) *Gyn/ecology: the Metaethics of Radical Feminism*. Boston, MA: Beacon Books.

Davidson, J. and Smith, M. (1999) 'Wittgenstein and Irigaray: gender and philosophy in a language (game) of difference', *Hypatia*, 14: 72–96.

Davis, A. (1981) *Women, Race and Class*. New York: Random House.

Davis, K. (ed.) (1997) *Embodied Practices: Feminist Perspectives on the Body*. London: Routledge.

de Beauvoir, S. (1972) [1949] *The Second Sex*. Harmondsworth: Penguin.

de Landa, M. (1997) *A Thousand Years of Non-Linear History*. New York: Swerve Publications.

de Swaan, A. (1990) *The Management of Normality*. London: Routledge.

Delphy, C. (1984) *Close to Home: a Materialist Analysis of Women's Oppression*. Amherst, MA: University of Massachusetts Press.

Delphy, C. (1993) 'Rethinking sex and gender', *Women's Studies International Forum*, 16(1): 1–9.

Denzin, N. (1988) *Interpretive Interactionism*. London: Sage.

Derrida, J. (1974) *Of Grammatology*, trans. G.C. Spivak. Baltimore, MD: Johns Hopkins University Press.

Deveux, M. (1994) 'Feminism and empowerment: a critical reading of Foucault', *Feminist Studies*, 20(2).

Diprose, R. (1994) *The Bodies of Women: Ethics, Embodiment and Sexual Difference*. London: Routledge.

Donnisson, J. (1977) *Midwives and Medical Men: A History of Interprofessional Rivalries and Women's Rights*. London: Heinemann.

Donzelot, J. (1980) *The Policing of Families*. London: Hutchinson.

Douglas, M. (1966) *Purity and Danger: An Analysis of the Concepts of Pollution and Taboo*. London: Routledge & Kegan Paul.

Douglas, M. (1970) *Natural Symbols: Explorations in Cosmology*. New York: Pantheon.

Douglas, M. and Wildavsky, D. (1982) *Risk and Culture*. Oxford: Basil Blackwell.

Doyal, L. (1979) *The Political Economy of Health*. London: Pluto Press.

Doyal, L. (1983) 'Women, health and the sexual division of labour: a case study of the women's health movement in Britain', *Critical Social Policy*, Summer: 21–33.

Doyal, L. (1987) 'Infertility – a life sentence?', in M. Stanworth (ed.), *Reproductive Technologies*. Oxford: Blackwell.

Dreifuss, C. (1978) *Seizing Our Bodies: The Politics of Women's Health*. New York: Vintage Books.

Duden, B. (1993) *Disembodying Women: Perspectives on Pregnancy and the Unborn*. Cambridge, MA: Harvard University Press.

Dyck, I. (1996) 'Body troubles: women, the workplace and negotiations of a disabled identity', in R. Butler and H. Parr (eds), *Mind and Body Spaces: Geographies of Illness, Impairment and Disability*. London: Routledge.

Eagleton, T. (1996) *The Illusions of Postmodernism*. London: Blackwell.

Ebert, T.L. (1996) *Ludic Feminism and After: Postmodernism, Desire and Labor in Late Capitalism*. Ann Arbor, MI: University of Michigan Press.

Edwards, S.S.M. (1993) 'Selling the body, keeping the soul: sexuality, power, the theories and realities of prostitution', in S. Scott and D. Morgan (eds), *Body Matters: Essays on the Sociology of the Body*. London: Taylor and Francis.

Ehrenreich, B. and English, D. (1973) *Witches, Midwives and Nurses: A History of Women Healers*. Old Westbury, NY: Feminist Press.

Ehrenreich, B. and English, D. (1974) *Complaints and Disorders: the Sexual Politics of Sickness*. London: Compendium.

Ehrenreich, B. and English, D. (1979) *For Her Own Good: 150 Years of the Experts' Advice to Women*. London: Pluto Press.

Ekins, R. and King, D. (2001) 'Telling body transgendering stories', in K. Backett-Milburn and L. McKie (eds), *Constructing Gendered Bodies*. Basingstoke: Palgrave/BSA.

Elias, N. (1991) 'Human beings and their emotions', in M. Featherstone, M. Hepworth and Bryan S. Turner (eds), *The Body: Social Process and Social Theory*. London: Sage.

Elias, N. (1994) [1978, 1982] *The Civilizing Process*, vols 1 and 2. Oxford, Blackwell.

Elshtain, J.B. (1993) *Public Man, Private Woman: Women in Social and Political Thought*. Princeton, NJ: Princeton University Press.

Fairclough, N. (1992) *Discourse and Social Change*. Cambridge: Polity Press.

Falk, P. (1994) *The Consuming Body*. London: Sage.

Featherstone, M. and Turner, B.S. (1995) 'Body and society: an introduction', *Body and Society*, 1(1): 1–12.

Finch, J. (1993) 'Conceptualising gender', in D. Morgan and L. Stanley (eds), *Debates in Sociology*. Manchester: Manchester University Press.

Finch, J. and Groves, D. (eds) (1983) *A Labour of Love: Women, Work and Caring*. London: Routledge

Firestone, S. (1971) *The Dialectic of Sex*. London: Jonathan Cape.

Flax, J. (1986) 'Gender as a problem in and for feminist theory', *American Studies*, 193–213.

Foucault, M. (1972) *The Archaeology of Knowledge and the Discourse on Language*. London: Pantheon.

Foucault, M. (1973) *The Birth of the Clinic*. London: Routledge.

Foucault, M. (1977) 'Nietzsche, Genealogy, History', in D. Bouchard (ed.), *Language, Counter-Memory, Practice*. Ithaca, NY: Cornell University Press.

Foucault, M. (1979) *Discipline and Punish*. London: Peregrine.

Foucault, M. (1988) *The Care of the Self*, vol. 3 of *The History of Sexuality*. New York: Vintage Books.

Foucault, M. (1988) *Madness and Civilization*. New York: Vintage Books.

Frank, A. (1990) 'Bringing bodies back in: a decade review', *Theory, Culture and Society*, 7: 131–62.

Frank, A. (1991) 'For a sociology of the body: an analytical review', in M. Featherstone, M. Hepworth and B.S. Turner (eds), *The Body: Social Process and Cultural Theory*. London: Sage.

Frank, A. (1995) *The Wounded Storyteller: Body, Illness and Ethics*. Chicago, IL: University of Chicago Press.

Frankfort, E. (1972) *Vaginal Politics*. New York: Quadrangle Press.

Fraser, N. and Nicholson, L. (1990) 'Social criticism without philosophy: an encounter between feminism and postmodernism', in L. Nicholson (ed.), *Feminism/Postmodernism*. New York and London: Routledge.

Freeman, R. (1992) 'The idea of prevention: a critical review', in S. Scott, G. Williams, S. Platt and H. Thomas (eds), *Private Risks and Public Dangers*. Aldershot: Avebury.

Freud, S. (1957) *Civilization and its Discontents*. Oxford: Basil Blackwell.

Freund, P.E.S. (1982) *The Civilised Body: Social Domination, Control and Health*. Philadelphia, PA: Temple University Press.

Freund, P.E.S. (1988) 'Bringing society into the body: understanding socialized human nature', *Theory and Society*, 17: 839–64.

Freund, P.E.S. (1990) 'The expressive body: a common ground for the sociology of emotions and health and illness', *Sociology of Health and Illness*, 12(4): 452–77.

Friedan, B. (1963) *The Feminine Mystique*. New York: Norton.

Fuss, D. (1990) *Essentially Speaking: Femininsm, Nature and Difference*. London: Routledge.

Gagnon, J. and Simon, W. (1973) *Sexual Conduct*. Chicago, IL: Aldine.

Gallagher, C. (1987) 'The Body versus the Social Body in the works of Thomas Malthus and Henry Mayhew', in C. Gallagher and T. Laqueur (eds), *The Making of the Body: Science and Sexuality in the Nineteenth Century*. Berkeley, CA: University of California Press.

Gallop, J. (1985) *Reading Lacan*. Ithaca, NY: Cornell University Press.

Gallop, J. (1988) *Thinking Through the Body*. New York: Columbia University Press.

Gamarnikov, E. (1978) 'Sexual division of labour: the case of nursing', in A. Kuhn and A. Wolpe (eds), *Feminism and Materialism: Women and Modes of Production*. London: Routledge & Kegan Paul.

Game, A. (1991) *Undoing the Social: Towards a Deconstructive Sociology.* Buckingham: Open University Press.

Gardner, K. (1982) 'Well woman clinics: a positive approach to women's health', in H. Roberts (ed.), *Women, Health and Reproduction.* London: Routledge & Kegan Paul.

Garfinkel, H. (1967) *Studies in Ethnomethodology.* Englewood Cliffs, NJ: Prentice-Hall.

Gatens, M. (1988) 'Towards a feminist philosophy of the body', in B. Caine, E.A. Grosz and M. de Lepervanche (eds), *Crossing Boundaries: Feminism and the Critique of Knowledge.* Sydney: Allen Unwin.

Gatens, M. (1992) 'Powers, bodies and difference', in M. Barrett and A. Phillips (eds), *Destabilising Theory: Contemporary Feminist Debates.* Cambridge: Cambridge University Press.

Gatens, M. (1996) *Imaginary Bodies: Ethics, Power and Corporeality.* London: Routledge.

George, A. and Murcott, A. (1992) 'Research note: monthly strategies for discretion: shopping for sanitary towels and tampons', *Sociological Review,* 40(1): 142–62.

Giddens, A. (1979) *Central Problems in Social Theory.* London: Macmillan

Giddens, A. (1984) *The Constitution of Society: Outline of the Theory of Structuration.* Cambridge: Polity.

Giddens, A. (1991) *Modernity and Self-Identity: Self and Society the Late Modern Age.* Cambridge: Polity Press.

Gilligan, C. (1982) *In a Different Voice.* Cambridge, MA: Harvard University Press.

Goffman, E. (1963) *Behaviour in Public Places.* London: Allen Lane.

Goffman, E. (1968) *Stigma: Notes on the Management of Spoiled Identity.* Harmondsworth: Penguin.

Goffman, E. (1971) *Relations in Public: Micro-Studies of the Public Order.* New York: Basic Books.

Goffman, E. (1972) *Interaction Ritual: Essays on Face-to-Face Behaviour.* London: Allen Lane.

Gordon, A. (1994) 'Possible worlds: an interview with Donna Haraway', in M. Ryan and A. Gordon (eds), *Body Politics: Disease, Desire and the Family.* Boulder, CO: Westview Press.

Gordon, A. (1997) *Ghostly Matters: Haunting and the Sociological Imagination.* Minneapolis, MN: University of Minnesota Press.

Gordon, C. (1980) *Power/Knowledge: Selected Interviews and Other Writings 1972–1977 by Michel Foucault.* London: Harvester Wheatsheaf.

Gordon, L. (1978) 'The politics of birth control, 1920–1940: the impact of professionals', in J. Ehrenreich (ed.), *The Cultural Crisis of Modern Medicine.* New York: Monthly Review of Books.

Gottlieb, A. and Buckley, T. (eds) (1988) *Blood Magic: The Anthropology of Menstruation.* Berkeley, CA: University of California Press.

Gouldner, A. (1970) *The Coming Crisis in Western Sociology*. New York: Basic Books.

Graham, H. (1979) 'Prevention and health: every mother's business', in C. Harris (ed.), *The Sociology of the Family: New Directions for Britain*. Sociological Review Monograph, vol. 28. Keele: University of Keele.

Greer, G. (1970) *The Female Eunuch*. London: MacGibbon and Kee.

Grosz, E. (1990) 'The body of signification', in J. Fletcher and A. Benjamin (eds), *Abjection, Melancholia and Love*. London: Routledge.

Grosz, E. (1994) *Volatile Bodies: Toward a Corporeal Feminism*. Bloomington, IN: Indiana University Press.

Grosz, E. (1995) *Space, Time and Perversion: Essays on the Politics of Bodies*. London and New York: Routledge.

Grosz, E. (1998) 'Bodies–cities', in H.J. Nast and S. Pile (eds), *Places Through the Body*. London: Routledge.

Grosz, E. (1999) 'Psychoanalysis and the body', in J. Price and M. Shildrick (eds), *Feminist Theory and the Body*. Edinburgh: Edinburgh University Press.

Habermas, J. (1975) *Legitimation Crisis*. Boston, MA: Beacon Press.

Haraway, D. (1991) *Simians, Cyborgs and Women: The Reinvention of Nature*. London: Free Association Books.

Haraway, D. (1999) 'The virtual speculum in the new world order', in A.E. Clarke and V.L. Olesen (eds), *Revisioning Women, Health and Healing*. New York and London: Routledge.

Hartsock, N. (1985) *Money, Sex and Power: Towards a Feminist Historical Materialism*. Boston, MA: Northeastern University Press.

Hartsock, N. (1987) 'The feminist standpoint: developing the ground for a specifically feminist historical materialism', in S. Harding (ed.), *Feminism and Methodology*. Bloomington, IN: Indiana University Press.

Hartsock, N. (1998) 'The feminist standpoint: developing the ground for a specifically feminist historical materialism', in J. Squires and S. Kemp (eds), *Feminisms*. Oxford: Oxford University Press.

Harvey, D. (1990) *The Condition of Postmodernity: An Enquiry into the Origins of Cultural Change*. Cambridge, MA: Blackwell.

Harvey, P. (1998) 'Feminism and anthropology', in S. Jackson and J. Jones (ed.), *Contemporary Feminist Theories*. Edinburgh: Edinburgh University Press.

Hawkesworth, M. (1997) 'Confounding gender', *Signs*, 22: 649–85.

Hekman, S. (1992) 'The embodiment of the subject – feminism and the communitarian critique of liberalism', *Journal of Politics*, 54: 1098–119.

Hepworth, M. (1995) 'Wrinkles of vice and wrinkles of virtue: the moral interpretation of the ageing body', in C. Hummell and J. Lalive D'Epinay (eds), *Images of Ageing in Western Societies*. Geneva: Centre for Interdisciplinary Gerontology, University of Genvea.

Hepworth, M. and Featherstone, M. (1982) *Surviving Middle Age*. Oxford: Basil Blackwell.

Hernes, H.M. (1987) *Welfare State and Woman Power: Essays on State Feminism*. Oslo: Norwegian University Press.

Hewitt, M. (1983) 'Biopolitics and social policy: Foucault's account of welfare', *Theory, Culture and Society*, 2: 67–84.

Hird, M.J. (2004) 'Feminist matters: new considerations of sexual difference', *Feminist Theory*, 5(2): 223–32.

Hogle, L.F. (1995) 'Tales from the cryptic: technology meets organism in the living cadaver', in C.H. Gray (ed.), *The Cyborg Handbook*. London and New York: Routledge.

Holland, J., Ramazanoglu, C., Scott, S., Sharpe, S. and Thomson, R. (1990a) 'Sex, gender and power: young women's sexuality in the shadow of AIDS', *Sociology of Health and Illness*, 12: 336–50.

Holland, J., Ramazanoglu, C., Scott, S., Sharpe, S., Thomson, R. (1990b) *Sex, Risk and Danger: AIDS Education Policy and Young Women's Sexuality*. London: Tufnell Press.

Holland, J., Ramazanoglu, C., Sharpe, S., Thomson, R. (1992) *Pressured Pleasure: Young Women and the Negotiation of Sexual Boundaries*. London: Tufnell Press.

Holland, J., Ramazanoglu, C., Scott, S., and Thomson, R. (1994a) 'Desire, risk and control: the body as a site of contestation', in L. Doyal, T. Wilton and J. Naidoo (eds), *AIDS: Setting a Feminist Agenda*. London: Taylor & Francis.

Holland, J., Ramazanoglu, C, Sharpe, S. and Thomson, R. (1994b) 'Power and desire: the embodiment of female sexuality', *Feminist Review*, 46: 21–38.

Holmwood, J. (1993) 'Welfare and citizenship', in R. Bellamy (ed.), *Theories and Concepts of Politics*. Manchester: Manchester University Press.

Hood-Williams, J. (1996) 'Goodbye to sex and gender', *Sociological Review*, 44: 1–16.

hooks, b. (1992) *Black Looks: Race and Representation*. Boston, MA: South End Press.

Horkheimer, M. (1972) *Critical Theory*, trans. M.J. O'Connell. New York: Herder and Herder.

Howson, A. (1996) *The Female Body and Health Surveillance: Cervical Screening and the Social Production of Risk*, Edinburgh Working Papers, no. 2. Edinburgh: Department of Sociology, University of Edinburgh.

Howson, A. (1998) 'Surveillance, knowledge and risk: the embodied experience of cervical screening', *Health*, 2(2): 195–212.

Howson, A. (1999) 'Cervical screening, compliance and moral obligation', *Sociology of Health and Illness*, 21(4): 401–25.

Howson, A. (2001a) 'Locating uncertainties in cervical screening', *Health, Risk and Society*, 3(2): 167–79.

Howson, A. (2001b) 'Watching you – watching me: visualizing techniques and the cervix', *Women's Studies International Forum*, 24(1): 97–110.

Howson, A. (2005) 'Feminist art and feminist sociology: new directions', in D. Inglis and J. Hughson (eds), *The Sociology of Art*. London: Palgrave Press.

Howson, A. and Inglis, D. (2001) 'The body in sociology: tensions inside and outside sociological thought', *Sociological Review*, 49(3): 297–317.

Hughes, A. and Witz, A. (1997) 'Feminism and the matter of bodies: from de Beauvoir to Butler', *Body and Society*, 3(1): 47–60.

Hunt, K. (1994) 'A cure for all ills? Constructions of the menopause and the chequered fortunes of hormone replacement therapy', in S. Wilkinson and C. Kitzinger (eds), *Women and Health: Feminist Perspectives*. London: Taylor & Francis.

Ian, M. (1993) *Remembering the Phallic Mother: Psychoanalysis, Modernism and the Fetish*. Ithaca, NY: Cornell Univeristy Press.

Illich, I. (1986) 'Body history', *Lancet*, 2: 1325–7.

Inglis, D. (2000) *A Sociological History of Exrectory Experience: Defecatory Manners and Toiletry Techniques*. Lampeter: The Edwin Mellen Press.

Irigaray, L. (1985a) *Speculum of the Other Woman*, trans. G.C. Gill. Ithaca, NY: Cornell University Press.

Irigaray, L. (1985b) *This Sex Which is Not One*, trans. C. Porter. Ithaca, NY: Cornell University Press.

Jackson, M. (1986) 'Knowledge of the body', *Man*, 18: 327–45.

Jackson, S. and Scott, S. (1998) 'Putting the body's feet on the ground: towards a sociological conceptualisation of gendered and sexual embodiment', conference paper presented at BSA annual conference, April. University of Edinburgh.

Johnson, M. (1987) *The Body in the Mind: The Bodily Basis of Meaning, Imagination and Reason*. Chicago, IL: University of Chicago Press.

Jordanova, L. (1980) 'Natural facts: a historical perspective on science and sexuality', in C. MacCormack and M. Strathern (eds), *Nature, Culture and Gender*. Cambridge: Cambridge University Press.

Jordanova, L. (1989) *Sexual Visions: Images of Gender in Science and Medicine between 18th and 20th Centuries*. London: Harvester Wheatsheaf.

Kaw, E. (2003) 'Medicalization of racial features: Asian-American women and cosmetic surgery', in R. Weitz (ed.), *The Politics of Women's Bodies: Sexuality, Appearance and Behaviour*. Oxford: Blackwell.

Kerrigan, W. (1989) 'Terminating Lacan', *South Atlantic Quarterly*, 88: 998–1000.

Kirby, V. (1997) *Telling Flesh: The Substance of the Corporeal*. New York and London: Routledge.

Klages, M. (2001) *Jacques Lacan* www.colorado.edu/English/ENGL2012Klages/lacan.html (last accessed 27/09/04).

Klein, M. (1975) *Envy, Gratitude and Reparation and Other Works, 1946–1963*. New York: Delacorte Press.

Koedt, A. (1970) 'The Myth of the Female Orgasm', in A. Koedt, E. Levine, and A. Rapone (eds), *Radical Feminism*. New York: Quadrangle Books.

Kroker, A. and Kroker, M. (1988) *Body Invaders: Sexuality and the Postmodern Condition*. Basingstoke: Macmillan.

Lacan, J. (1977) *Écrits: A Selection*, trans. A. Sheridan. New York: Norton.

Lakoff, G. and Johnson, M. (1980) *Metaphors We Live By*. Chicago, IL: University of Chicago Press.

Laqueur, T. (1991) *Making Sex: Body and Gender from the Greeks to Freud*. Boston, MA: Harvard University Press.

Latour, B. (1993) *We Have Never Been Modern*. London: Harvester Wheatsheaf.

Lawler, J. (1991) *Behind the Screens: Nursing, Somology and the Problem of the Body*. Melbourne: Churchill Livingstone.

Lawrence, S.C. and Bendixen, K. (1992) 'His and hers: male and female anatomy in anatomy texts for US medical students 1890–1989', *Social Science and Medicine*, 35: 925–34.

Laws, S. (1990) *Issues of Blood*. London: Macmillan.

Lawton, J. (1998) 'Contemporary hospice care: the sequestration of the unbounded body and "dirty" dying', *Sociology of Health and Illness*, 20: 121–43.

Leder, D. (1990) *The Absent Body*. Chicago, IL: Chicago University Press.

Lewin, E. and Olesen, V. (1985) *Women, Health and Healing: Toward a New Perspective*. New York: Methuen/Tavistock.

Lewis, J. (1986) *What Price Community Medicine?* London: Wheatsheaf.

Lewis, J. (1993) 'Feminism, the menopause and hormone replacement therapy', *Feminist Studies*, 43: 38–56.

Lindemann, G. (1997) 'The body of gender difference', in K. Davis (ed.), *Embodied Practices: Feminist Perspectives on the Body*. London: Sage.

Lloyd, G. (1984) *The Man of Reason: 'Male' and 'Female' in Western Philosophy*. London: Methuen.

Longhurst, R. (1995) 'The body and geography', *Gender, Place and Culture*, 2: 97–105.

Lorber, J. (1994) *Paradoxes of Gender*. New Haven, CT: Yale.

Lorde, A. (1983) 'The master's tools will never dismantle the master's house', in C. Moraga and G. Anzaldua (eds), *This Bridge Called my Back: Writings by Radical Women of Colour*. New York: Kitchen Table.

Lovering, K. (1997) 'Listening to girls' "voice" and silence: the problematics of the menarcheal body' in M. de Ras and V.M. Grace (eds), *Bodily Boundaries, Sexualised Genders and Medical Discourses*. Palmerston North: The Dunmore Press.

Lowe, D.M. (1995) *The Body in Late Capitalist USA*. Durham, NC: Duke University Press.

Lupton, D. (1994) *Medicine as Culture*. London: Sage.

Lupton, D. (1995) *The Imperative of Health: Public Health and the Regulated Body*. London: Sage.

Lupton, D. (1997) 'Psychoanalytical sociology and the medical encounter: Parsons and beyond', *Sociology of Health and Illness*, 19(5): 561–79.

Lyotard, J.-F. (1984) *The Postmodern Condition: a Report on Knowledge.* Minneapolis, MN: University of Minnesota Press.

Macey, D. (1988) *Lacan in Contexts.* London: Verso.

MacInnes, J. (1998) *The End of Masculinity.* Buckingham: Open University Press.

MacKinnon, C. (1987) *Feminism Unmodified: Discourses on Life and Law.* Cambridge, MA: Harvard University Press.

MacSween, M. (1993) *Anorexic Bodies: A Feminist and Sociological Perspective on Anorexia Nervosa.* London and New York: Routledge.

McCarthy, E.D. (1996) *Knowledge as Culture.* London: Routledge.

McNally, D. (2001) *Bodies of Meaning: Studies on Language, Labour, and Liberation.* New York: SUNY.

McNay, L. (1992) *Foucault and Feminism.* Cambridge: Polity.

Mafesoli, M. (1995) *The Time of the Tribes: The Decline of Individualism in Mass Society.* London: Sage.

Mann, M. (1987) 'Ruling Class Strategies and Citizenship', *Sociology*, 21(3): 339–54.

Mansfield, A. and McGinn, B. (1993) 'Pumping irony: the muscular and the feminine', in S. Scott and D. Morgan (eds), *Body Matters: Essays in the Sociology of the Body.* London: Taylor & Francis.

Marshall, B.L. (1994) *Engendering Modernity: Feminism, Social Theory and Social Change.* Cambridge: Polity.

Marshall, H. (1996) 'Our bodies ourselves: why we should add old fashioned empirical phenomenology to the new theories of the body', *Women's Studies International Forum*, 19: 253–66.

Marshall, T.H. (1963) *Sociology at the Crossroads.* London: Heinemann.

Martin, E. (1984) 'Pregnancy, labour and body image in the United States', *Social Science and Medicine*, 19: 1201–6.

Martin, E. (1989) *The Woman in the Body.* Buckingham: Open University Press.

Martin, E. (1990) 'Toward an anthropology of immunology: the body as a nation-state', *Medical Anthropology Quarterly*, 4(4): 410–26.

Martin, E. (1992) 'The end of the body?', *American Ethnologist*, 19: 121–40.

Mauss, M. (1973) [1934] 'Techniques of the Body', *Economy and Society*, 2: 70–88.

Mead, G.H. (1967) [1934] *Mind, Self and Society.* Chicago, IL: Chicago University Press.

Mellor, J. and Shilling, C. (1997) *Re-Forming the Body: Religion, Community and Modernity.* London: Sage.

Merleau-Ponty, M. [1962] (1995) *Phenomenology of Perception*, trans. C. Smith. London: Routledge.

Miles, A. (1992) *Carnal Knowing: Female Nakedness and Religious Meaning in the Christian West.* Boston, MA: Beacon Press.

Millet, K. (1970) *Sexual Politics.* New York: Doubleday.

Mills, C. Wright (1959) *The Sociological Imagination*. New York: Oxford University Press.

Mills, C. Wright (1964) *Sociology and Pragmatism: The Higher Learning in America*, edited with an Introduction by I.L. Horowitz. New York: Paine-Whitman Publishers.

Mitchell, J. (1974) *Psychoanalysis and Feminism*. London: Allen Lane.

Mitchell, J. (ed.) (1984) *Feminine Sexuality by Jacques Lacan*, trans. J. Rose. New York: W.W. Norton.

Moi, T. (1985) *Sexual/textual politics: Feminist Literary Theory*. London: Methuen.

Moi, T. (ed.) (1986) *The Kristeva Reader*. New York: Columbia University Press.

Moore, H. (1994) *A Passion for Difference*. Cambridge: Polity Press.

Morgan, D. (1986) 'Gender', in R.G. Burgess (ed.), *Key Variables in Social Investigation*. London: Routledge.

Morgan, D. (1993) 'You too can have a body like mine: reflections on the male body and masculinities', in S. Scott and D. Morgan (eds), *Body Matters*. London: Taylor & Francis.

Morgan, D. and Scott, S. (1993) 'Bodies in a social landscape', in S. Scott and D. Morgan (eds), *Body Matters: Essays in the Sociology of the Body*. London: Taylor & Francis.

Moscucci, O. (1990) *The Science of Woman: Gynaecology and Gender in England 1800–1929*. Cambridge: Cambridge University Press.

Mulvey, L. (1975) 'Visual pleasure and narrative cinema', *Screen*, 16(3).

Murcott, A. (1993) 'Purity and pollution: body management and the social place of infancy', in S. Scott and D. Morgan (eds), *Body Matters: Essays in the Sociology of the Body*. London: Taylor & Francis.

Nast, H.J. and Pile, S. (eds) (1998) *Places Through the Body*. London: Routledge.

Nettleton, S. (1992) *Power, Pain and Dentistry*. Buckingham: Open University Press.

Nettleton, S. and Watson, J. (eds) (1998) *The Body in Everyday Life*. London: Routledge.

Newton, T. (2003) 'Truly embodied sociology: marrying the social and the biological?', *Sociology*, 51(1): 20–42.

Nicholson, L. (1994) 'Interpreting gender', *Signs*, 20(1): 79–103.

Oakley, A. (1976) *Sex, Gender and Society*. London: Gower.

Oakley, A. (1980) *Woman Confined: Towards a Sociology of Childbirth*. Oxford: Martin Robertson.

Oakley, A. (1984) *The Captured Womb*. Oxford: Basil Blackwell.

Oakley, A. (1998) 'Science, gender and women's liberation: an argument against postmodernism', *Women's Studies International Forum*, 21(2): 133–46.

O'Brien, M. (1981) *The Politics of Reproduction*. Boston, MA and London: Routledge & Kegan Paul.

O'Neill, J. (1972) *Sociology as a Skin Trade*. London: Heinemann.

O'Neill, J. (1985) *Five Bodies: The Human Shape of Modern Society*. Ithaca, NY: Cornell University Press.

Ogden, J. (1995) 'Psychological theory and the creation of the risky self', *Social Science and Medicine*, 40: 409–15.

Ortner, S. (1974) 'Is female to male as nature is to culture?', in M.Z. Rosaldo and L. Lamphere (eds), *Women, Culture and Society*. Stanford, CA: Stanford University Press.

Osborne, T. (1992) 'Medicine and epistemology – Foucault and the liberality of clinical reason', *History of the Human Sciences*, 5: 63–93.

O'Regan, M. (1992) 'Daring or deluded? A case study in feminist management. Mary O'Regan in interview with Mary Varnham', in R. du Plessis (ed.), *Feminist Voices: Women's Studies Texts for Aotearoa/New Zealand*. Auckland: OUP.

Oudshoorn, N. (1994) *Beyond the Natural Body: The Archaeology of Sex Hormones*. New York and London: Routledge.

Parsons, T. (1964) *Social Structure and Personality*. New York: Simon and Schuster.

Parsons, T. (1966) *Societies: Evolutionary and Comparative Perspectives*. Englewood Cliffs, NJ: Prentice Hall.

Pateman, C. (1988) *The Sexual Contract*. Cambridge: Basil Blackwell.

Petechesky, R.P. (1987) 'Foetal images: the power of visual culture in the politics of reproduction', in M. Stanworth (ed.), *Reproductive Technologies: Gender, Motherhood and Medicine*. Cambridge: Polity Press.

Phillips, A. and Rakusen, J. (1971) *Boston Women's Health Collective Our Bodies Ourselves: A Health Book by Women for Women*. Harmondsworth: Penguin.

Piercy, M. (1979) *The High Cost of Living*. London: The Women's Press.

Pinker, S. (2003) *The Blank Slate: the Modern Denial of Human Nature*. Harmondsworth: Penguin.

Polhemus, T. (ed.) (1978) *Social Aspects Of The Human Body*. Harmondsworth: Penguin.

Poovey, M. (1987) 'Scenes of an indelicate character: the medical "treatment" of Victorian women', in C. Gallagher and T. Lacqueur (eds), *The Making of the Body: Science and Sexuality in the Nineteenth Century*. Berkeley, CA: University of California Press.

Poovey, M. (1988) 'Feminism and deconstructivism', *Feminist Studies*, 14: 51–65.

Radley, A. (1995) *The Body and Social Psychology*. New York: Springer Verlag.

Ragland-Sullivan, E. (1986) *Jacques Lacan and the Philosophy of Psychoanalysis*. Urbana, IL: University of Illinois Press.

Rahman, M. and Witz, A. (2003) 'What really matters? The elusive quality of the material in feminist thought', *Feminist Theory*, 4(3): 243–61.

Ramazanolgu, C. (ed.) (1993) *Up Against Foucault: Explorations of Some Tensions between Foucault and Feminism*. London: Routledge.

Rich, A. (1976) *Of Woman Born: Motherhood as Experience and Institution*. New York: Norton Books.

Riessman, C.K. (1992) 'Women and medicalization: a new perspective', in G. Kirkupp and L.S. Keller (eds), *Inventing Women: Science, Technology and Gender*. Cambridge: Polity.

Riley, D. (1988) *Am I that Name? Feminism and the Category of 'Women' in History*. London: MacMillan.

Rodin, M. (1992) 'The social construction of premenstrual syndrome', *Social Science and Medicine*, 35(1): 49–56.

Rojek, C. and Turner, B.S. (2000) 'Decorative sociology: towards a critique of the cultural turn', *Sociological Review*, 48: 629–48.

Rose, G. (1993) *Feminism and Geography: The Limits of Geographical Knowledge*. Cambridge: Polity.

Rose, G. (1997) 'Situating knowledges: positionality, reflexivities and other tactics', *Progress in Human Geography*, 21.

Rose, N. (1990) *Governing the Soul: the Shaping of the Private Self*. London: Routledge.

Rothfield, P. (1997) 'Menopausal embodiment', in P. Komesaroff, P. Rothfield and J. Daly (eds), *Menopause: Cultural and Philosophical Issues*. London: Routledge.

Roudinesco, E. (1997) *Jacques Lacan: Outline of a Life, History of a System of Thought*. New York: Columbia University Press.

Rowland, R. (1992) *Living Laboratories: Women and Reproductive Technologies*. Sydney: Pan Macmillan.

Ruzek, S. (1978) *The Women's Health Movement*. New York: Praeger.

Sachs, A. and Wilson, J.H. (1978) *Sexism and the Law*. Oxford: Martin Robertson.

Said, E. (1993) *Culture and Imperialism*. London: Chatto and Windus.

Sawicki, J. (1991) *Disciplining Foucault: Feminism, Power and the Body*. London: Routledge.

Scarry, E. (1985) *The Body in Pain: The Making and Unmaking of the World*. Oxford: Oxford University Press.

Scheper-Hughes, N. and Lock, M.M. (1987) 'The mindful body: a prolegomenon to future work in medical anthropology', *Medical Anthropolgy Quarterly*: 6–14.

Schiebinger, L. (1993) *Nature's Body: Sexual Politics and the Making of Modern Science*. Boston, MA: Beacon Press.

Schiebinger, L. (2000) 'Introduction', in L. Schiebinger (ed.), *Feminism and the Body*. Oxford: Oxford University Press.

Schilder, P. (1978) [1950] *The Image and Appearance of the Human Body: Studies in the Constructive Energies of the Psyche*. New York: International Universities Press, Inc.

Scott, J. (1992) 'Experience'. in J. Bulter and J. Scott (eds), *Feminists Theorize the Political*. New York and London: Routledge.

Scott, S. and Morgan, D. (1993) *Body Matters: Essays in Medical Sociology*. London: The Falmer Press.

Scully, D. and Bart, P. (1978) 'A funny thing happened on the way to the orifice', in J. Ehrenreich (ed.), *Cultural Crisis of Modern Medicine*. New York: Monthly Review Press.

Segal, L. (1990) *Slow Motion: Changing Masculinities, Changing Men*. London: Virago.

Seidman, S. (1994) *Contested Knowledge: Social Theory in the Postmodern Era*. Oxford: Blackwell.

Sheach-Leith, V. (2004) *Body Wholeness and the Infant: A Sociological Study of the Practice of Pathology*, unpublished PhD thesis, Department of Sociology, University of Aberdeen.

Shildrick, M. (1997) *Leaky Bodies and Boundaries*. London and New York: Routledge.

Shildrick, M. (2002) *Embodying the Monster: Encounters with the Vulnerable Self*. London: Sage.

Shildrick, M. and Price, J. (1994) 'Splitting the difference: adventures in the anatomy and embodiment of women', in G. Griffin, M. Hester, S. Rai and S. Roseneil (eds), *Stirring It: Challenges for Feminism*. London: Taylor & Francis.

Shilling, C. (1997) 'The undersocialised conception of the embodied agent in modern sociology', *Sociology*, 31: 737–54.

Shilling, C. (2001) 'Embodiment, experience and theory: in defence of the sociological tradition', *Sociological Review*, 49(3): 327–44.

Shilling, C. (2003) *The Body and Social Theory* (2nd edn). London: Sage.

Shilling, C. and Mellor, J.P. (1996) 'Embodiment, structuration theory and modernity: mind/body dualism and the repression of sensuality', *Body and Society*, 2: 1–16.

Shotter, J. and Gergen, K.J. (eds) (1989) *Texts of Identity*. London: Sage.

Showalter, E. (1985) 'Feminist criticism in the wilderness', in E. Showalter (ed.), *The New Feminist Criticism: Essays on Women, Literature, and Theory*. New York: Pantheon.

Simmel, G. (1969) 'Sociology of the senses: visual interaction', in A. Blaikie, M. Hepworth, M. Holmes, A. Howson, D. Inglis and S. Sartain (eds), *The Body: Critical Concepts in Sociology*. London: Routledge.

Singer, L. (1994) *Erotic Welfare*. London: Routledge.

Skeggs, B. (1997) *Formations of Class and Gender*. London: Sage.

Smart, C. (1990) 'Law's power, the sexed body and feminist discourse', *Journal of Law and Society*, 17: 194–210.

Smith, D.E. (1987) *The Everyday World as Problematic*. Boston, MA: Northeastern University Press.

Smith, D.E. (1990) *Texts, facts and femininity*. London: Routledge.

Sokal, A. and Bricmont, J. (1998) *Intellectual Impostures*. London: Profile Books.

Spelman, E. (1998) *Inessential Woman: Problems of Exclusion in Feminist Thought*. Boston, MA: Beacon Books.

Spivak, G.C. (1988) 'Can the Subaltern Speak?', in C. Nelson and L. Grossberg (eds), *Marxism and the Interpretation of Culture*. Urbana, IL: University of Illinois Press.

Spivak, G.C. (1990) *The Post-Colonial Critic*. London: Routledge.

Sprengnether, M. (1990) *The Spectral Mother: Freud, Feminism and Psychoanalysis*. Ithaca, NY: Cornell University Press.

Stabile, C. (1994) *Feminism and the Technological Fix*. Manchester: Manchester University Press.

Stacey, M. (1977) *Health and the Division of Labour*. London: Croom Helm.

Stacey, M. (1988) *The Sociology of Health and Healing*. London: Unwin Hyman.

Stafford, B. (1991) *Body Criticism: Imaging the Unseen in Enlightenment Art and Medicine*. Cambridge, MA: MIT Press.

Stanley, L. (1997) 'Introduction: on academic borders, territories, tribes and knowledges', in L. Stanley (ed.), *Knowing Feminisms*. London: Sage.

Stanley, L. (1999) 'Debating feminist theory: more questions than answers?', *Women's Studies Journal*, 15: 87–106.

Stanley, L. and Wise, S. (1993) *Breaking Out Again*. London: Routledge.

Stone, D.A. (1986) 'The resistible rise of preventive medicine', *Journal of Health Politics, Policy and Law*, 11(4): 671–96.

Strathern, A. (1994) 'Keeping the body in mind', *Social Anthropology*, 2: 43–54.

Sydie, R.A. (1987) *Natural Women/Cultured Men: A Feminist Perspective on Sociological Theory*. Milton Keynes: Open University Press.

Synott, A. (1993) *The Body Social: Symbolism, Self and Society*. London: Routledge.

Tallis, R.C. (1997) 'The shrink from hell', *Times Higher Education Supplement*, 31 October.

Taussig, M. (1993) *Mimesis and Alterity: A Particular History of the Senses*. New York: Routledge.

Thapan, M. (1995) 'Gender, body and everyday life', *Social Scientist*, 23: 32–58.

Thomas, H. and Ahmed, J. (2004) *Cultural Bodies: Ethnography and Theory*. Oxford : Blackwell.

Thorne, B. (1993) *Gender Play*. Buckingham: Open University Press.

Thurren, B. (1994) 'Opening doors and getting rid of shame', *Women's Studies International Forum*, 17: 217–27.

Thurschwell, P. (2000) *Sigmund Freud*. London: Routledge.

Tomm, (1992) 'Knowing ourselves as women', in D. Currie and V. Raoul (eds), *Anatomy of Gender: Women's Struggle for the Body*. Ottawa: Carleton University Press.

Tong, R. [1989] (1994) *Feminist Thought: a Comprehensive Introduction*. London: Westview Press/Routledge.

Treneman, A. (1988) 'Cashing in on the curse', in L. Gamman and M. Marshment (eds), *The Female Gaze: Women as Viewers of Popular Culture*. London: The Women's Press.

Turner, B.S. (1987) *Medical Power and Social Knowledge*. London: Sage.

Turner, B.S. (1996) [1984] *The Body and Society*. Oxford: Basil Blackwell.

Turner, B.S. (1992) *Regulating Bodies: Essays in Medical Sociology*. London: Routledge.

Turner, B.S. (1997) 'Foreward: from governmentality to risk, some reflections of Foucault's contribution to medical sociology', in A. Bunton and A. Petersen (eds), *Foucault, Health and Medicine*. London: Routledge.

Verbrugge, N. (1985) 'Gender and health: an update on hypothesis and evidence', *Journal of Health and Social Behaviour*, 26: 156–82.

Vice, S. (1998) 'Feminism and psychoanalysis', in S. Jackson and J. Jones (eds), *Contemporary Feminist Theories*. Edinburgh: Edinburgh University Press.

Vogler, C. (2000) 'Social identity and emotion: the meeting of psychoanalysis and sociology', *Sociological Review*, 48(1): 19–42.

Walby, S. (1995) 'Is citizenship gendered?', *Sociology*, 28(2): 379–95.

Walkowitz, J. (1980) *Prostitution and Victorian Society: Women, Class and the State*. Cambridge: CUP.

Waters, M. (1994) *Modern Sociological Theory*. London: Sage.

Watson, J. (2000) *Male Bodies: Health, Culture and Identity*. Milton Keynes: Open University Press.

Wear, A. (ed.) (1992) *Medicine in Society: Historical Essays*. Cambridge: Cambridge University Press.

Weber, M. (1978) *Economy and Society*. Berkeley, CA: University of California Press.

Whelehan, I. (1995) *Modern Feminist Thought*. Edinburgh: Edinburgh University Press.

Whitford, M. (1991) *Luce Irigaray: Philosophy in the Feminine*. London and New York: Routledge.

Williams, R. (1975) *Keywords: A Vocabulary of Culture and Society*. London: Fontana.

Williams, R. (1977) *Marxism and Literature*. London: Oxford University Press.

Williams, S. and Bendelow, G. (1998) *The Lived Body: Sociological Themes, Embodied Issues*. London: Routledge.

Williamson, J. (1978) *Decoding Advertisements: Ideology and Meaning in Advertising*. London: Boyars.

Wilson, E. (1977) *Women and the Welfare State*. London: Tavistock.

Winnicott, D.W. (1987) *The Child, Family and the Outside World*. Reading, MA: Addison-Wesley.

Witz, A. (2000) 'Whose body matters? Feminist sociology and the corporeal turn in sociology and feminism', *Body and Society*, 6: 1–24.

Witz, A. and Marshall, B.L. (2003) 'The quality of manhood: masculinity and embodiment in the sociological tradition', *Sociological Review*, 51(3): 339–56.

Wolff, J. (1990) *Feminine Sentences: Essays on Women and Culture.* Cambridge: Polity Press.

Wrong, D. (1961) 'The oversocialized conception of man in modern sociology', *American Sociological Review*, 26(2): 183–93.

Young, I.M. (1990) *Throwing Like a Girl and Other Essays in Feminist Philosophy and Social Theory.* Bloomington, IN: University of Indiana Press.

Young, K. (1989) 'Narrative embodiments: enclaves of the self in the realm of medicine', in J. Shotter and K.J. Gergen (eds), *Texts of Identity.* London: Sage.

Zola, I.K. (1972) 'Medicine as an instrument of social control', *Sociological Review*, 20: 487–504.

Zola, I.K. (1982) *Missing Pieces: a Chronicle of Living with a Disability.* Philadelphia, PA: Temple University Press.

Zola, I.K. (1991) 'Bringing our bodies and ourselves back in', *Journal of Health and Social Behaviour*, 32(1): 1–16.

Index